CONSULTANT SUPERVISION:
THEORY AND SKILL DEVELOPMENT

by

David W. Champagne
University of Pittsburgh

R. Craig Hogan
Wheaton College

Table of Contents

PREFACE

This book is meant to be *read* and *used* by you in doing your job of supervising and managing educational systems for students. It presents, explains and applies concepts and skills you need. For reasons not known to us, most of these ideas have not, in the past, been an important part of your preparation for the almost overwhelmingly difficult job of managing one of the most complicated institutions our society has bred. We believe that serious work with the ideas in this book will result in major improvement in your job performance. That arrogant goal we set for us as a challenge, for you as an expectation.

We must explain what we mean by "*read* and *used*" in order to give our goal substance. In each unit are questions and short activities which will allow you to discover whether you have mastered the ideas at a comprehension level.

We see this book being used by three sets of people:

a. It could be used by the individual manager who needs to become better than (s)he is. This book would probably be used by such a manager in the way we have described above. He would read it, perform the short activities included in each unit and make his own applications in his setting.

b. The book might also be used by the educational consultant interested in organizational development. This book would probably be used by her as a source book, or as a basis for training programs of varying lengths in educational systems. Each middle manager in training needs a copy of the book and materials. This consultant person organizing the training could be a senior member of the organization itself.

c. Finally, the book could be used by the college or university professor in charge of preparation and certification of middle managers for educational settings. This book represents a unique source of explanations and activities for competences at different levels of mastery. There are suggestions for using the activities as a total training program, but the professor may choose methods of particular interest to his and her program. Each activity is designed for that kind of choosing. Where there are suggested prerequisites or related units or activities we call attention to these suggestions.

All of these activities have been used in the field and in university graduate classes by real, practicing managers with well developed junk detectors on the alert. The activities have benefited from their feedback and we very much thank those who have contributed to them.

INTRODUCTION

The clear but friendly signs led us to the office. The secretary looked up, smiled, introduced herself and asked if she could help us. The pleasant experience of being attended to immediately and welcomed with a smile was followed by the eye-opening announcement that the principal was working with a teacher and the secretary wouldn't interrupt her unless it was an emergency or unless the principal was late for an appointment with us. She showed us to a lounge where the choice of soft drink or coffee and doughnut and walls filled with a student produced art exhibit kept us occupied for the 15 minutes until the principal and teacher she had been working with joined us.

"I'm sorry for keeping you waiting," she smiled, "but my work with the teachers is pre-scheduled, and as much as anything else, careful supervision of and assistance to my faculty is what I am paid for." We realized we hadn't called ahead, and had thus not allowed anyone to prepare for our visit. Our apologies were accepted graciously.

We explained that we were university-types interested in curriculum and supervision in schools, and asked if they would be willing to share some of their ideas and procedures with us. The teacher excused herself to get ready for her next class, but the principal said she would be happy to share some ideas with us in a few minutes before her next conference.

We walked around the building with the principal, pleased to see neither students nor teachers cringing when the principal neared. Most doors were open, and several times we had to stop, be ushered into a classroom, introduced to the students, and shown some students' products amid students' squeals of delight. The principal used us a part of the reinforcement system. We were also asked to be prepared to give the school our feedback as a price for the time they were sharing with us.

Just before her scheduled conference, the principal asked if we would be willing to come back some day and see how the school works. She was willing to check with some teachers to find out whether they would mind having outside persons sit in on the pre-conferences, observations and post-conferences which were a regular part of the supervisory procedures used there. She would also let us know when the curriculum teams were meeting and encouraged us to come back to sit in on one of their meetings if the teachers involved agreed to that. In our next visit she would also take time to explain the regular training program the district maintained for her and the other administrators: "It keeps my sense of priorities clear," she explained, "and besides, it's fun to be in contact with my peers. I like them and they have good ideas."

The previous story may not be your ideal school organization at all. It is part of ours, and we intend this set of materials to help you develop the skills to create as much of that in your own ideal setting as possible.

Establishing such an atmosphere in the school organization has never been easy. Educational organizations are among the most difficult human organizations to run well. Middle managers (the set of people below the top central administration and above the instructional level, such as principals, supervisors, team leaders, etc.) are increasingly required to serve many masters having conflicting sets of frequently changing and unclear expectations. These expectations are often translated into demands and blame. The expectations must be fulfilled in an atmosphere of total public visibility and rising criticism sometimes interspersed by chants of "accountability".

These forces place great burdens on the middle manager, who is trying to insure that, beyond or in spite of the criticisms, expectations and demands, favorable instructional changes occur. The difficulties are compounded by the fact that middle managers are, to a much greater extent than managers in many other organizations, limited in their functional powers by the semi-autonomy of the teachers, who actually carry out instruction. Middle managers in educational organizations can lead, but rarely can coerce program changes or improvements. The threat and anxiety created by managers who coerce tend to make them and their staffs functionally rigid, unresponsive, and defensive toward growth and experimentation. Teachers, fearful of the same outside forces prodding the middle manager to demand changes, and desirous as experts to remain autonomous, become reluctant to consider any alternative methods which originate outside of themselves. Consequently, they become resistant to having colleagues or others observe and criticize their classroom behavior. After months or years of demands and coercions, even less powerful supervisory personnel, who rarely order change, find it difficult to even suggest it. The unintended results of the efforts to require change or improvements have been: overt and covert resistance, failure of programs, unhappiness in the organization, epidemic paranoia, and phenomena such as increasingly conservative teacher unions. The deepening "us and them" trench lines leave the middle manager with terrible feelings of isolation, while not knowing how to break out of an escalating spiral of smoldering ill-feelings and ineffectual attempts to regain control and stability.

Introduction

There is a need for some method of supervision and development which can favorably effect changes in educational programs while at the same time avoid the unfavorable results of coercion and demands. The most effective methods of organizational development being used today are based on ideas advanced by Maslow, Argyris, McGregor and others. This group is generally grouped together under the label, Third Force Psychologists or Humanists. This program advocates this orientation, encouraging middle managers and their supervisees to work together to develop more effective instruction through cooperation and mutual respect. Douglas McGregor describes this type of supervision as being characterized by ". . . an environment which will encourage commitment to organizational objectives and which will provide opportunities for the maximum exercise of initiative, ingenuity, and self direction in achieving them" (McGregor, 1960, pp. 132-133).

The major purpose of this training program is to present training materials to help middle managers learn skills necessary to produce such supervision, and then to apply them appropriately to their individual settings.

David W. Champagne   R. Craig Hogan
University of Pittsburgh   Wheaton College

December, 1981

USING THIS BOOK

If you just skipped the table of contents, you might want to turn back to it and look at it again after we tell you how the book is organized.

We call the chapters in the book units, partly because we see them as units of work. Active reading, then applying the ideas in each unit to the short cases or exercises included with each unit, will give you immediate feedback on your need for the unit, and on your mastery of the content of the unit.

At any rate, the units are grouped in three sets:

A. INTRODUCTORY UNITS

The three introductory units are the bases for the remainder of the book. The perspectives contained in them are the window panes through which we will be looking at supervision—we want you to share them with us. Unit one presents a theoretical framework for our approach to supervision. The second unit focuses on the need for data-based supervision, then teaches you the higher level skill of being able to separate fact from inference in your supervision, a skill prerequisite to everything that follows in this book. Finally, Unit III provides a perspective on what is likely one of your major responsibilities, the evaluation of teaching, placing it into perspective so that you can use the remaining units in the book to enhance your ability to evaluate teaching effectively while maintaining a productive, congenial work relationship with supervisees.

B. PERSONAL INTERACTION SKILLS UNITS

Each of the units in this section teaches a set of interpersonal skills necessary for the middle manager in most supervisory roles. Within this set of units are ideas on helping, intervention style, values and behavior, and active listening. We recommend you work on some of these units while you are at the same time working on specific skills presented in the next sections. We assume minimal mastery of the interpersonal skills before you begin studying the technical skills of supervision.

C. INDIVIDUAL MANAGING AND SUPERVISING SKILLS UNITS

We have sorted out the specific important technical skills used by managers when working with individual staff members. These one-to-one skills include organizing and maintaining individual supervision, collecting data in observations, analyzing data, and using time. Not all of your time as supervisor-managers is spent in individual supervision, but this is an important dimension of your job. This one-to-one interaction deserves your highest skill level. In this section be sure what we mean by our titles before you select or eliminate units.

Now you may want to turn back to the table of contents and read the titles of the units listed there as a way of orienting yourself to those you expect to find most interesting.

Some of these units will be of little interest to you, either because you have previously mastered those skills, or because they are not required in your present role. Skip those units after making sure you really do have the skills, or that you really don't need them. We do suggest that you read the three introductory Units (I, II, III). We suggest also that you work in some of the Section II, Interpersonal Skills units and some of the skills units at the same time. Some of the interpersonal skills take a long time to achieve mastery, and you can continue to bring them up to mastery level while working on technical skills. Try very hard to complete any unit you seriously work in before you move on. Otherwise the lack of success may create avoidance of the book. Try, if you can, to develop some relatively formal mechanism for presenting evidence of your ability to use the skills taught in the unit to someone else. We are encouraging you to build in this last feedback a reinforcement mechanism to help you develop self-analysis skills. Using some other person you trust as a way of validating your own judgments is one means of improving your self-analysis skills. Besides, it's fun.

Unlike most books, you may want to spread your reading and use of this one over a fairly long time period. Developing and maintaining new behavior patterns and then using them correctly usually takes a long time.

Foundation Knowledge and Skills

Unit 1

A Framework of Theory and Concepts for this System of School Management and Development

Content Overview

This unit presents concepts embodied in the works of McGregor, Maslow, Argyris and others. It then integrates these concepts into a coherent system which will help you better understand the organization, management and development of your educational setting—especially the instructional program.

We have developed from this conceptual framework the specific sets of skills necessary for you to design (or redesign) and maintain the environment you desire in your setting. Each unit in this training program contains one or more sets of skills derived from the concepts.

Using the Unit

Most people who work through this unit report feeling overwhelmed by this whole set of ideas taken together. These same people report later that the ideas come together and form a useful base for action. This gestalt usually occurs somewhere in the third or fourth unit they complete. Take heart.

Competencies

Before you go on to the next unit you should demonstrate the ability to:

1. correctly apply concepts from McGregor and Maslow to explain most interactions in your organization,

2. suggest supervisory interactions consistent with Argyris' three criteria for effective interventions,
3. suggest supervisory interactions which are not consistent with Argyris' three criteria for effective interventions,
4. suggest ways to redesign your organization to make it more consistent with the ideas of Maslow, McGregor and Argyris.

We also hope you will begin to feel a commitment to using these ideas of McGregor, Maslow and Argyris as an important base for your supervisory activities.

Explanation and Rationale for These Competencies

Most of this training program is based on the ideas presented in this unit. This unit becomes an advance organizer for your entry into the total system. So that you can understand the rest of the program, we have tried to present the ideas in clear detail here, and have systematically organized all the instruction in the program to be consistent with these conceptual systems. We hope you see the connections.

Entry Skills Necessary

There are no special entry skills assumed for this unit. An open mind is useful—one per small group is required. Careful reading is expected. We have tried to reward a commitment to that kind of reading by sprinkling ideas throughout.

Douglas McGregor, Abraham Maslow and the Organization of Management.

Recently in a graduate class in supervision a colleague of ours collected some data analyzing the actual activities, interactions and sentiments of the group of educators taking the course. These educators reported what they actually did in their work settings as teachers or when they were teachers. The resulting data showed them:

1. feeling they do (or did) not have enough time to accomplish all of the many important tasks required of them,
2. feeling inadequately trained to perform many of the tasks,
3. having to perform many clerical and administrative duties they feel ought to be someone else's job,
4. feeling a frustration that they have little time to develop their skills,
5. feeling little active challenge from the organization to grow.

The organization, in other words, was not meeting many of their personal needs.

Is your organization meeting its members' needs? Is it meeting your own needs? Have you recognized the needs of your members and yourself? Have you deliberately planned the organization to meet these needs while achieving its own goals? The following explanation of two views of organizations may help you understand the forces molding your responses to these questions.

In 1960, Douglas McGregor (McGregor, 1960) summarized two antithetical sets of assumptions made about people. Each set of assumptions forms a philosophical base which dictates ways the management holding the set of assumptions organizes the institution they lead. Understanding these assumptions will lead to an understanding of organizations because, as McGregor asserts, "the theoretical assumptions management holds about controlling its human resources determine the whole character of the enterprise." (p.9ff.) He labelled these sets of assumptions Theory X assumptions and Theory Y assumptions. We shall do our best to present these assumptions as something other than the good guys' theory and the bad guys' theory, although we do feel one set of assumptions leads to less effective management than the other.

Theory X Assumptions

This older view of human beings leads to the traditional organization of management we all know, but don't necessarily love. Theory X assumptions are:

1. The average human being has an inherent dislike of work and will avoid it if he can.
2. Because most people dislike work, they must be coerced, controlled, directed and threatened with punishment to force them into putting forth adequate effort to achieve organizational objectives.
3. The average human being prefers to be directed, wishes to avoid responsibility, has relatively little ambition, and wants security above all (McGregor, pp. 33-34).

In this kind of organization, evaluations are made by managers about others. For example, in schools we create a personal file which contains the annual rating given by the manager to that teacher. Often our observation visits are unannounced—"to keep the person on her toes" some suggest—unless the teachers have fought for and won the right of prior notice. Most of the data in these files is not data at all but judgments. The actual behavior on which the judgments are based is rarely identified, and almost never recorded. There is an assumption in this whole series of monitoring behaviors that the faculty have been kept from slipping for another year. They haven't been able to make the beginning of the long slide to mediocrity. You may be kept on your toes by a similar rating process. Is the one you use on faculty as much a sham as the one used by others on you?

Many middle managers spend a large part of their days "supervising the halls or the cafeteria." What they are really doing is monitoring, checking and controlling students' and teachers' behavior. Their own behavior is perfectly consistent with the assumptions their organization is making about people, even if they have not identified these assumptions consciously.

How often have you been in a meeting where behaviors such as the following have occured?

1. The leader is reading a memo all have a copy of, to the followers.
   Assumption: Because they are lazy, if it isn't read to them they won't read it.
2. The leader is criticizing the lack of response to a form or a deadline set by the leader.
   Assumption: If I put up enough pressure, they will get the work out.
3. The leader announces a new, more efficient way to complete a task. He has planned it all himself with no consultation.
   Someone in the back row has some important data to demonstrate why the new plan will fail, but she withholds it.
   Assumption: 1. No one else is responsible for decisions. I'm the leader, I'll decide.
   2. He's made his decision, let him suffer the consequences.

In many subtle ways we act out our X assumptions about people. We punish wrong-doing and usually fail to reward right-doing. We make middle managers spend their days monitoring rather than helping, supporting or planning because these latter functions are invisible and therefore not rated highly by superiors.

Teachers have responded to these threats, punishments and checking in overt and increasingly effective ways. They form faculty associations or unions which fight for and win limitations on middle managers' prerogatives and practices. Teacher lobbies have been able to secure the protections of tenure laws for their members, and recently have acquired the right to strike or withhold services. However effective as a basis for management the Theory X assumptions were in the past, they are increasingly ineffective because managers have lost many of the real weapons they could once wield. Faculty members now must be lead rather than driven, since driving, through fear or threat of punishment, is not really possible any longer. It was never desirable, because of its transfer to the ways students were treated. Theory X assumptions are simply ineffective now as a basis for management in schools where the faculty view themselves as autonomous professionals with clear specialties of practice. Rarely is the manager able to convince either himself or the teacher that his expertise is on a level with his faculty members in any of the programatic or instructional goals that determine the outcomes of our schools. The manager lacks the power to coerce which is the basis of an X system

Almost all organizations, including schools, are presently organized using Theory X structures. Many current efficiency experts and "management-by-objectives"systems are only Theory X structures in new clothes. Some employees, intuitively realizing that the systems are only new ways to monitor, coerce, and control behavior, organize against them. The resulting union fights and contract wars between two relatively evenly matched opponents (the faculty organization and management team) often produce stresses within the system resulting in poor goal achievement by students and loss of public confidence in teachers and schools. Unfortunately, most of us, trained in Theory X by our society, accept Theory X and its accompanying maladies as the legitimate way for things to be.

Many of us meet most of our growth needs outside the organization, if we meet them at all. With recessions and declining enrollments in some schools, Theory X management may be effective again. Theory X will certainly be around for another generation and perhaps the best we can do is understand its strengths and weaknesses and try to use it as consistently and humanely as possible.

Theory Y Assumptions

There is another way to organize management, used not only in mythical places established by university professors whose businesses remain poor but happy, but in industries such as much of Japan's industry. Many private and semi-public research organizations made up of semi-autonomous professionals appear to be operated on Theory Y principles. Well managed universities seem generally to be Theory Y organizations although because of various accountability schemes, declining enrollments, and shrinking resources, Theory X assumptions and faculty unions are increasingly appearing. The corporate model is being imposed on a non-corporate type of organization whose products are ideas rather than swizzle sticks. The schools we work in are seldom managed in Theory Y ways.

McGregor's list of assumptions for Theory Y are the following:

1. The expenditure of physical and mental effort in work is as natural as play or rest. The average human being does not inherently dislike work. Depending on conditions established by management, work may be a source of satisfaction (and will be voluntarily performed) or a source of punishment (and will be avoided if possible).

2. External control and the threat of punishment are not the only means for bringing about effort toward organizational objectives. People will exercise self-direction and self-control in the service of objectives to which they are committed.

3. Commitment to objectives is a function of the rewards associated with their achievement. The most significant of such rewards, e.g., the satisfaction of ego and self-actualization needs, can be direct products of efforts directed toward organizational objectives.
4. The average human being learns, under proper conditions, not only to accept but to seek responsibility. Avoidance of responsibility, lack of ambition and emphasis on security, are generally consequences of experience, not inherent human characteristics.
5. The capacity to exercise a relatively high degree of imagination, ingenuity, and creativity in the solution of organizational problems is widely, not narrowly, distributed in the population.
6. Under the conditions of modern industrial life, the intellectual potentialities of the average human being are only partially utilized.

Of particular consequence is the fact that acceptance of the Theory Y assumptions means acceptance of the fact that the manager is both precipitator and inhibitor of employee satisfaction and productivity, as explains McGregor:

> If employees are lazy, indifferent, unwilling
> to take responsibility, intransigent, uncrea-
> tive, uncooperative, Theory Y implies that
> the cause lies in management's methods of
> organization and control (McGregor, p.48).

No organization can survive for long if it is not meeting its goals at some minimum level. We are not suggesting that the organization should be managed solely for the pleasure or fulfillment of its members. This fallacy will both bankrupt schools and not lead to a real sense of worth for its members. We are suggesting a real exploration of Theory Y assumptions to see if they have meaning for you in your setting and if the behaviors resulting from Theory Y assumptions are practicable for you.

Before we explore some of the meanings of these assumptions for middle managers, we have one final caveat from McGregor:

> The assumptions of Theory Y are not finally
> validated. Nevertheless, they are far more
> consistent with existing knowledge in the
> social sciences than are the assumptions of
> Theory X. (p. 49)

That mildly stated thought may indeed suggest many things if we take McGregor seriously. Both frightening and exhilirating possibilities emerge from Theory Y assumptions and implications: frightening because they suggest that we really can be responsible for what happens in the environments we manage, exhilirating because of the possibilities of working in an organization like that.

If the environment is not going well, generally it is because we are not sufficiently insightful or thoughtful or because we are not using the correct techniques. Frightening also because if we believe the Theory Y assumptions then we will have to learn to change our deeply ingrained habits of thought and action. Few of us face that prospect with confidence and security. This is especially true if we have never seen any really convincing demonstrations of other ways to behave.

What these assumptions mean to us is that members of the organization can and must see themselves as fulfilling their survival and personal growth needs within the context of the organization's structures and goals. Specifically, they must see not only that the goals of the organization are meaningful in a larger context, but that their own energy commitment toward these organizational goals will lead to the attainment of specific personal goals. Consultant supervision facilitates that.

Abraham Maslow

THE NEEDS HIERARCHY

We have made repeated references in this description of McGregor's ideas to the concept of "human needs". Underlying the whole of McGregor's assumptions is the Third Force Psychology of Abraham Maslow. Perhaps these two sets of McGregor's assumptions about how we organize management would become more intelligible if we develop a clear understanding of Maslow's ideas. We could then organize and operate management consistently with them. So, let us proceed to square two, and Abraham Maslow's Hierarchy of Human Needs.

First, we need some context and some sense of who Maslow is.

There have been two basic organizing ways to talk about people's minds and emotions—the psyche. One of these is the Freudian psychological set. The second is the behaviorist school of Watson, Skinner, et al.

Unlike most Freudian psychologists, Maslow did not use case studies or statistical research based on sick people for his inferences about why people behave as they do. Different from Skinner and other behaviorists, Maslow did not begin with pigeons or monkeys to then infer a theoretical set of assumptions on why people behave as they do. He began instead by studying those people around him who seemed most productive, most integrated, sane and developed in their personalities. Then when certain recurrent patterns of behaving seemed to be present he extended his data base to recorded information from past figures who were often described with similar adjectives. In his own terms, he developed his theories from the most fully human and not those with deep problems. Then he corroborated his ideas by looking at developing humans—babies and young children both normal and those who were institutionalized for one reason or another. He developed his theory of the hierarchy of human needs further by observing how people developed who had one or more of their needs frustrated through some naturally occurring events. The following set of ideas is the result of those observations and intuitions by Maslow (Goble, F. 1970, Maslow, 1970).

All human beings have a set of needs. All humans have the same set of needs. These needs in individual instances are easily frustrated; they are often twisted or obscured; but over and over again they reoccur. They form the basic motivators of all our actions in living. They occur and are satisfied in a hierarchy—i.e., an invariant sequence.

Basic Needs: Definition
A basic need meets the following conditions:
a. Its absence breeds illness.
b. Its presence prevents illness.
c. Its restoration cures illness.
d. Under certain, very complex, free choice situations, it is preferred by the deprived person over other satisfactions.
e. It is found to be inactive, at a low ebb, or functionally absent in the healthy person.

Until a basic need is satisfied the next higher needs are unimportant. As soon as one basic need is relatively fulfilled, it is no longer as strong a motivator for our actions. As human beings move up through this hierarchy of needs, they grow out of the category of basic or deficiency needs into those of growth and development. These growth needs are much less hierarchial and are truly never satisfied. They are, finally, the motivators for all our new learning.

The Hierarchy of Basic Human Needs
The basic human needs in Maslow's hierarchy are:

1. physiological needs
2. safety needs
3. belongingness, love and affection needs
4. esteem and self-respect needs

PHYSIOLOGICAL NEEDS
Physiological needs, the most basic and most powerful human needs, insure physical survival as individuals and as a species. They include the needs for food, liquid, shelter, sleep, sex and oxygen. Whatever else we are lacking we will demand that these basic needs be fulfilled; we ignore other needs until they are satisfied. The desparately hungry person thinks of little else than the securing of food. Of course, all needs are interrelated, and we sometimes try to satisfy some physiological need when it is actually a higher level need gnawing at us, seeking satiation.

Beyond a certain amount of food or sex we really don't want any more unless we are using that as a substitute for other needs. Once these basic physiological needs are fulfilled at adequate levels, other higher needs, such as the safety needs, emerge.

SAFETY NEEDS

Everyone has the basic need for a safe, predictable world with consistent rules, fair treatment and a certain amount of routine. When this need is not met the person becomes anxious and insecure, risking less and becoming defensive or neurotic. Attempts to satisfy this need are most easily observed in children, but are present in all of us. Inconsistent leadership or rules in an organization will cause members to stop risking and become negative, anxious and defensive. It is also true that clear limits are preferred to total freedom.

BELONGINGNESS AND LOVE NEEDS

When physiological and safety needs are being reasonably satisfied the needs for belongingness, love and affection begin to motivate needs-satisfying behavior. Maslow's definition of love, separate from sex, is to be understood and accepted by someone seen as significant (a significant other). We will all strive with great intensity for this sense of belongingness, acceptance and affection from some source in our daily lives. When satisfaction of this set of needs is thwarted in an organization we may cut off our commitment of energy to that organization, seeking fulfillment of our needs elsewhere. Everyone must be successful at giving and receiving love somewhere; if it occurs within the goal-directed processes of the organization, we will devote energies to those processes. If those processes actually cause feelings of being ostracized, not accepted, and disliked (the antithesis of what is necessary to satisfy these needs) we will withdraw from the circumstances (and people) causing the aversive feelings and seek to satisfy the needs elsewhere during the working day (cliques of friends, the faculty lounge, etc.).

Teachers whose belongingness and love needs are being met within the organization seem to be able to go on growing as people and as teachers for their lifetimes. We can help many more teachers meet some of these needs within the organization by encouraging and assisting in the process of helping them satisfy their personal needs in organizationally supportive ways.

THE ESTEEM NEEDS

All people have a basic need for self-respect. As part of that need we have the need for outside affirmation: respect from others. When self-esteem needs are being met, we feel a self-confidence, based on competence, mastery, and the ability to cope resulting from successive real achievements. One symbol of affirmation from others is the freedom to set our own tasks and directions. The others express their confidence that we are responsible. The need is also satisfied when we receive recognition of achievement, appreciation, and attention to our ideas. Finally, awards such as status and reputation fill this need.

The need may be unfulfilled within the organization when no mechanisms are available for recognizing achievements of individuals, students, teachers, middle managers, and upper managers. The organization becomes threatening of our needs when forces actually cause belittling of achievements, repeated evidence of lack of trust and confidence in the competence of individuals, and ignoring ideas or achievements of members.

THE GROWTH NEEDS

When the "deficiency needs" are satisfactorily fulfilled in our daily lives, we are able to act towards satisfying the higher, "growth needs". These are: 1. self-actualization needs, 2. know and understand needs, and 3. aesthetic needs.

SELF-ACTUALIZATION NEEDS

The motto of the State University of New York at Albany, "Let each be all he is capable of becoming", suggests the beginning of Maslow's definition of self-actualization needs. The motto is, however, much too passive to entirely embody Maslow's conception of self-actualization. It implies that we must be urged externally. Maslow feels that each of us has a need, an internal urge to grow, to become, to develop, and to fulfill ourselves. Because this need is relatively weak (easily frustrated, unfocused, or misdirected), when more basic needs are not being satisfied, psychic energy is immediately directed away from self-actualization to satisfying those stronger more demanding needs. Many lack the minimum fulfillment of the basic needs which would allow them to apply even minimal energies toward self-development. But, again and again we all return to a kind of yearning toward wanting to grow and develop. This nagging need never lets us stop striving to become. Probably much of the feminist movement can be more easily understood by relating it to the need for self-actualization; many women feel they have been socialized into repressing their own self-actualization needs so they may fill basic growth needs of lovers and children.

Satisfying the need for self-actualization, and avoiding having the satisfaction thwarted, is difficult because of the delicate nature of the requirements for satisfaction. The person must choose the direction of the thrust, and be committed to it. We who establish the structures (activities, interactions, sentiments, norms) of the organization cannot, therefore, mandate such growth. We must build organization structures that:

1. insure that basic needs are satisfied as much as possible
2. insure that directions for self-actualization can be explored and pursued freely, without restriction or duress.

A faculty in an organization fostering and encouraging self-actualization would be described as "involved, innovative, dedicated, inspiring"— all signs of growth toward self-actualization in members.

Unfortunately we generally lack the orientation to devise jobs and roles which meet even basic needs adequately. Beyond the basic needs, we fail to perceive that each job, if it is to inspire commitment and caring, must have built in self-development components. In schools and teaching we often give passing salutes to this area by scheduling two days of inservice per year. These often ill-planned experiences usually fail because the basic needs of individual members of the organization are not being attended to, or because members do not see how what is being presented relates in any clear way to their individually perceived directions of growth. The directions of self-actualization may be highly idiosyncratic. Members forced to participate in inservice programs centering around things other than their idiosyncratic interests may feel the inservice programs are irrelevant to their personal growth directions. Your managerial role is to help individual members relate their growth needs to organization goals.

However, one point should be emphasized. Because we have failed to consider a person's individual growth needs in the past, and therefore have failed in many ways to tap much of their potential for achieving organization goals, does not mean that we cannot change. We can accommodate to and benefit from persons striving toward their own goals. We can fit personal goal expectations into the stated goals of the organization. We can and must begin to individualize our planning of staff development efforts. We must develop directions and plans jointly with the members of the organization. This helping of individuals to fit their development into a framework of organizational accomplishment requires a different orientation to parts of your job. Certainly we know that merely giving higher wages and more fringe benefits is not effective in producing or motivating greater productivity, higher quality teaching, or more caring professionals.

THE NEED TO KNOW AND UNDERSTAND

Probably all of the growth needs are somehow related to the self-actualization needs. These growth needs are probably much more parallel sets of needs than they are hierarchial as the deficiency needs are. The need to know and understand can be characterized as a desire to systematize, to organize, to analyze, to look for relations and meanings, and to construct a system of values. Curiosity is an expression of this need. Some express this need by seeking out the mysterious, the unknown or the unexplained. Galileo, seeking new knowledge in spite of admonitions from his society and his church that he might be excommunicated, then pushing ahead in the face of danger to his soul because of his strong need to discover *why* and *how* things around him worked, is a famous example of the need to know and understand. We must believe that his basic needs were being minimally satisfied or we cannot understand his willingness to risk. We do know that when his basic needs were threatened, he stopped seeking answers.

Of course, different people in an organization will have their needs to know satisfied by different information, but an open organization will allow for these differences. Sharing long range goals or letting people in on enrollment projections or tax base figures might satisfy some members' needs to know. Recent federal laws like the Buckley Amendment and various sunshine laws about access to school records and files of all sorts seem to be an expression of this basic need to know. Often we inflict knowledge on people, like students, who do not agree with our definitions of their need to know. This is the result of a rather badly conceptualized idea of meeting others' needs.

Much of our choice of what we teach in schools is predicated on our belief, however unconscious, that our students have a need to know certain things — if not immediately, then in the future. All of these arguments are another justification for the need to individualize learning of our students. What they will be willing to learn is predicated on their individual need to know. Our job as educators is to help them broaden their perceived needs and relate those needs to broader human themes. This is a direct corollary of our managers' job, i.e., correlating staff members' goals with the organization's goals.

AESTHETIC NEEDS

We also have a need for beauty in our lives. We decorate our homes, our offices, our yards and our bodies; we enjoy the presence of art, sculpture, music, and drama and we insist that utilitarian objects are, as well, attractive and shiny. Each person defines this need in his own way. Cave dwellers in southern France who painted bison on the walls of their caves and places of worship, expressed this need. For many, the search for order or structure is closely related to the need for aesthetically pleasing adornments. Some speak of the beauty of an argument, of a basketball player executing a foul shot, or of an aesthetically pleasing solution to a political problem, which could conceivably be "beautiful but not valid".

Often, we alter the ugliness of schools by making the school secretary retype a report, not because it is illegible or badly written, but because it isn't typed neatly or spaced correctly to give it a pleasing appearance. Or we bring attractive living room furniture into a school reading room, or we have a school code of dress and days of "beautiful clothes" — for those who have the money to become beautiful. On beautiful days, or in beautiful rooms, students and teachers seem to act and interact differently.

Maslow concludes his sets of needs with a whole list of defining values or characteristics of people who are operating in these growth needs areas rather consistently. He says they value and live as though they value:

1. wholeness	6. goodness
2. completion	7. playfullness
3. aliveness	8. truth
4. simplicity	9. self-sufficiency
5. beauty	10. justice

How many of these values are consistently evident in the behavior of members of your organization? Does your answer suggest any need for changes in your organization?

Instructional Activity

Part I

1. Read the following essay about Crane High School.
2. After you finish reading the essay, you will be asked to characterize the organization using McGregor's Theory X and Theory Y vocabulary.
3. After you finish reading the essay, you will be asked to decide which of Maslow's needs the organization was seeking to satisfy, and which it failed to attend to.
4. In both cases, we will ask you to support your contentions with data from the essay.

Crane High School I

So many things here got in my way and bled off my energy from the focus I valued—teaching.

There was the following memo from the principal, delivered on 15 June:

"All teachers will be present for graduation on 21 June at 8:00 p.m. Standard professional dress will be worn. The final salary check will be individually given out in my office after the ceremony. I'm sure that you will all enjoy the exercise this year; we have reinstituted traditional music at the request of one of our school board members. This professional obligation to attend is one of our strongest duties. Anyone seeking to be excused should make an appointment with my secretary to discuss it with me. You will be allowed to sit with your families instead of in a special section. Please encourage them to come and show the flag."

Or the following dated 15 March:

"Your complete order for next year's supplies must be in the hands of your department chairman by 21 March so he may process these and decide which items you really need. All catalogue numbers and quantities should be clearly shown on the typed list you submit. Again next year, supplies will be delivered only on the first Monday of each month. Please be planned so you don't run out of things you need. Teachers leaving at the end of this year should still fill out a supplies request so that the incoming teacher will have some materials to work with. Be professional about this."

In January of that year, the whole faculty, acting out of concern for the students, had gotten together to draw up a program asking for help from the administrators and the board of education. We listed the following 6 areas of concern and asked for the help specified.

1. Many of us were new young teachers having some problems. We asked for an increased program of supervisory help to plan curricula better and to maintain clearer control of learning. Specifically, we desired clear programs of observation with feedback from the principal.
2. Many of the junior high school students seemed to need remedial help in reading and mathematics. We wished to stay after school and work intensively with them to give this help.
3. We needed an extension of route of the late bus which was run to take the athletic teams home after practice.
4. We wished for clearer sets of rules for student behaviors, for more organization of the homeroom period, for clear agreement on homework policies and for more effective use of the guidance resources of the school.
5. We asked for reorganization of the schedule of the junior high school students so that we could more effectively teach fewer members during any given block of time.
6. We asked for some input into the planning of faculty meetings so that we might get more benefit from them.

Five separate faculty committees carefully worked out the presentation we were to make at a special session of the board of education. We planned to make a brief, clear, positive, and conciliatory presentation, then have an informal discussion and await their decisions.

The board meeting began congenially, but after the presentation there was 15 minutes of increasingly icy and uncomfortable silence. When it became obvious that there was going to be no verbal reaction to our proposals, we raised in a body and retreated to lick our wounds. Two months later, when contracts were announced, 40% of the faculty were not rehired. All the young, committed, interested members were gone. I was invited back because the principal realized that a permanently certified science teacher in chemistry and physics is hard to find (and one of the board members had a brilliant son who was taking physics the next year—the kid liked me).

I left the following year because I would not volunteer my evenings during the winter to stand in the boy's room and be sure that none of the adults smoked there during basketball games. Again, I could have stayed if I chose; because the principal said to me one day, "If you'd only just put in an appearance at one basketball game, we'd forget about the whole thing". I chose to remember and left. The kids gave me a five minute ovation at the last assembly of the year when I announced I was leaving.

End of Essay

Part II

1. Is this organization generally following McGregor's Theory X assumptions or the Theory Y assumptions? _____
    List three specific activities or interactions from the essay which support your inference.

    1. _____

    _____

    2. _____

    _____

    3. _____

    _____

2. This essay reported only selected vignettes. It is, therefore, somewhat difficult to consider whether all needs in Maslow's needs hierarchy are being considered. We therefore respect the fact that your level of inference is going to be higher than you like when answering the following questions. Which of the Maslow needs is the organization probably satisfying? Give data from the essay for your responses:

    1. Need _____ Data to Support_____

    _____

    2. Need _____ Data to Support_____

    _____

    3. Need _____ Data to Support_____

    _____

4. Need _____ Data to Support_____

_____

5. Need _____ Data to Support_____

_____

6. Need _____ Data to Support_____

_____

3. Which of the needs was the organization failing to consider? Give data from the essay to support your inference.

1. Need _____ Data to Support_____

_____

2. Need _____ Data to Support_____

_____

3. Need _____ Data to Support_____

_____

4. Need _____ Data to Support_____

_____

5. Need _____ Data to Support_____

_____

6. Need _____ Data to Support_____

_____

4. What would you predict about the likely subsequent history of this High School over the next few years? Use the Maslow Hierarchy vocabulary in your answer.

_____

_____

_____

_____

_____

_____

_____

_____

5. Discuss your answers and the implications you derive from them in a group with people who have worked through this unit. In case you are working alone, talk to a friend who will listen to what you are learning and to your conclusions.

From our point of view, the organization just described is relatively unhealthy because it is thwarting the satisfaction of even the basic needs of its members. The sense of frustration, anxiety, and helplessness that members often felt was very real and at a high level of consciousness. Almost no one was able to concentrate on the teaching or on the kids' needs. Concommitantly the principal, the supervising principal and the board members also felt threatened and were more defensive and less effective than they could have been in another situation. The principal, also new to the system, felt truly in the middle and under pressure from both sides, since he was meeting no ones' expectations. As a result, he could formulate no clear educational priorities except survival in his job. In that pursuit he was successful since he chose to move with the power figures.

An axiom growing from the truth of the Maslow Needs Hierarchy is that the energy of group members trying to satisfy their own basic needs is so consumed by the struggle that there is little chance for them to also consider, accept and be concerned for others. When the others are in positions to actually thwart satisfaction of the needs, the sentiments go beyond neutrality or apathy to hostility.

The system and the kids were cheated. The morale and faculty interest in trying new ideas suffered for at least a decade after that year. The leadership remained the same and good new teachers didn't go there or didn't stay.

You may wish to apply these ideas directly to your own organization. We hope so.

Chris Argyris
Intervention in Social Institutions

Let us refocus where we believe we are before we present the ideas of Chris Argyris.

We have carefully developed a link between management and supervision because we believe that is an accurate picture. Supervision, the subset of management we are describing, is restricted to the following roles:

1. Supervision helps establish and maintain the social, psychological and emotional environment which encourages members of the organization to fulfill their personal needs within organizational goals.
2. Supervision assists in identifying those individual and group needs in attitude, skill and behavior which will assist members of the organization to become more fully functioning and thus more useful to the organization.
3. Supervision assists in planning and carrying out programs to help individuals and groups within the organization develop the attitudes and skills identified as being needed to meet organization goals.

There are not now, nor are there likely to ever be enough supervisors to effectively monitor very much of what is really happening in most instructional settings. No one will ever pay for that many staff. More and more instructional staff members are becoming highly educated specialists in instruction, learning and the management of learning environments. No matter how much we disparage the level of competence of individual staff members, the truth is that as middle managers, developing our own expertise in management, we can neither develop nor maintain the knowledge and special skills of all of the various areas of instruction for which we have responsibility. To pretend otherwise is to limit our effectiveness in the things we do well: organizing and managing the total environment. We must trust our staff because we have no real choice. But, we must also trust them because we are setting up the type of environment in which they are spending as much of their energy developing their competence as we are.

If we believe Maslow and McGregor, if we manage our environments so most members feel safe and cared about, believing in their own competence, believing the organization accords them this competence, then we have the best of all possible worlds. These same semi-autonomous professionals will respond with a commitment and energy that will result in high achievement of organization goals.

The ideas developed by Chris Argyris represent the conceptual cornerstone of the role we are building for supervisors.

The thinking of Chris Argyris makes an elegant souffle out of a starchy soup of separate unordered skills.

The solid strength of Argyris' ideas is the lath to which we can plaster elegant rooms of beautiful processes.

Whatever the image, we believe that supervision in educational organizations is, or should be, an intervention activity in Argyris' terms (Argyris, 1970, see also Argyris and Schon, 1978).

Argyris states that to intervene is to "enter into an ongoing system of relationships, to come between or among persons, groups, or objects for the purpose of helping them." He goes on to explain that such intervention "focuses on how to maintain or increase, the client system's autonomy." He explains that "An intervenor, in this view, assists a system to become more effective in problem solving, decision making, and decision implementation in such a way that the system can continue to be increasingly effective in these activities and have a decreasing need for the intervenor" and that "the intervenor must be concerned with the system as a whole even though his initial contact may be with only a few people. He therefore focuses on those intervention activities that eventually (not necessarily immediately) will provide *all* the members opportunities to enhance their own competence and effectiveness."

If individual instructional personnel in our system are considered as clients, this definition is completely congruent with our definition of supervision. If we consider teams, or grade levels, or departments, or buildings, or central office staff as clients, then this definition is completely congruent with the role of middle management explicated in this training program.

Argyris' definition demands that we believe our instructional and programatic staff are professionals, interested in growing in competence and actively participating in formulating and attaining organization goals.

We would like to argue the case for considering instructional staff as autonomous professionals from two points of view: (1) it is economically necessary, (2) it is the only system which can hope to use the creative energies of most of the staff.

Argyris suggests guidelines for intervening to establish such an organization. (You are an interventionist in your own setting, even though you are there every day.)

There are, Argyris states, three primary tasks for an interventionist:

1. An interventionist begins with the collection of valid information.
2. An interventionist helps the client make free informed choices.
3. The interventionist assists the client in developing internal commitment to the choices made (Argyris, 1970, p.17).

These three tasks are basic concerns for the interventionist-supervisor in all circumstances, regardless of the type of problem. Other ways of behaving, such as diagnosing the problem with little direct data or directing the client's choices and forcing the implementation of the imposed solution, violate the autonomy of the client, tend to make the client less able to function independently when next faced with a problem, and discourage the client's own contributions to the solution.

We will explain in some detail each of Argyris' tasks. We suggest ways of carrying them out in consultant supervision.

Valid Information

Argyris defines the information needed as, "that which describes the factors, plus their interrelationships, that create the problem for the client system". (Argyris, p.17)

He suggests that there are ways to check the validity of the information collected. He lists them in order of increasing power or validity.

The data are valid if:

1. they are publically verifiable,
   meaning that several independent sources suggest the same data,
2. they result in valid prediction,
   meaning that predictions from the data occur as predicted,
3. they have control over the phenomena,
   meaning that systematic manipulations of the situation result in effects predicted in the data.

There are several sources of data available to you as a middle manager. You should assess the validity of each source by checking the data using the three criteria listed above.

Other data less empirical than the data satisfying Argyris' criteria are nonetheless, important.

The clients' observations as well as your own independent observations are examples of these data. Still less empirical, but important, are others' impressions, conclusions or opinions. It is even conceivable that school directors' policy guidelines and organizational goal statements may be useful data in given situations.

The specific situation determines the relevence and validity of data. You and the client must, in addition to assessing relevence and validity, determine what data have meaning to the client. The data are not useful if, in the perception of the client, those data are without importance.

Free and Informed Choice

Does the client know the implications of his choice making? Do the choices indicate understanding of the objectives for which they are intended, and the possibility that the choices will or will not attain the objectives? Do the choices indicate an understanding and consideration of the data collected? Do the choices reflect an understanding of the economic, social, political constraints of the organization within which they are made? Was the choice made freely by the client based on this knowledge? If the answers to these questions are yes, then the choices are both free and informed.

Argyris suggests: "the requirement of free choice is especially important for those helping activities where the processes of help are as important as the actual help." He uses the example of a doctor. A client with a bullet wound may not choose to discuss the diagnosis or type of help required. However, a client with a chronic ailment would be consulted and permitted free and informed choices about treatment if there is a choice about treatments ranging from pills to surgery. If pills are chosen, the degree of follow-through is going to depend mostly on the patient and not on the doctor. We are more often called upon to give the second kind of help with a number of possible treatments, none of which can be claimed as certain solutions or directions. Many subsequent units in this training program discuss helping the client make free informed choices. We begin to make some suggestions here only as advance organizers.

Internal Commitment — "Ownership"

The client implements the choice because he believes it is a good choice with a good probability of success. It also meets his needs as well as helping attain the goals of organization. Making free and informed choices may be the most important part of developing an internal commitment to choices by clients. Internal commitment suggests an active reaching out: "Yes, I want to do that for these reasons", rather than a passive acquiescence: "Well, all right; I'll try that if you say so." This "allowing" and "accepting" means that the client has the right to say "no" without negative consequences resulting.

Future units include some explicit strategies likely to facilitate internal client commitment to changes. The most concise and simple guidelines are:

a. Offer a range of choices so the client has a sense, at least, of choosing the most acceptable alternative to her.
b. Help the client generate her own choices, explore the implications, and learn a choice-making procedure that works for her.
c. Attend to the client's needs levels so that he is more likely to be reaching out for growth experiences. These, in themselves, may carry a risk of failure.
d. Don't punish failures, but help the client learn from them. Reward the attempts at choice-making and the commitment to growth.

Instructional Activity Related to Argyris' Ideas

1. Read the following vignettes about Crane High School.
2. After you finish reading each vignette, you will be asked to make some choices and give some reasons for your choices about ways that a manager might have acted consistent with Argyris' intervention tasks in working with the staff at Crane High School.
3. In the last two vignettes you will be asked to generate a strategy you might have used which would be consistent with Argyris' tasks.

Our suggestions about possible strategies and our analysis will follow the place where yours are written. You can check our conclusions and analysis with yours.

Again we really do suggest your writing out your conclusions and suggestions so you will have to think through and make a commitment to your ideas. Looking back to the pages of description about Argyris is encouraged. We are not running a memory test. We are much more interested in your application of the ideas than your ability to correctly recite them.

Crane High School II

The following situations are extensions of real situations as remembered over time and distance. No actual intervention of the type we suggest ever took place. The only strategies known or followed by the managers at Crane were intimidation, repression and firing those who asked questions. As we have previously stated, that school, in the opinion of citizens we kept in contact with, continued to languish in a tide of repression for over a decade.

All of the teachers in vignette A were gone from Crane before they could get tenure. Their contracts were not renewed.

Crane High School II: A

In some ways the junior high school teachers here were among the most committed professionals I have known. Several of them, the science, social studies, math and English teachers who carried the bulk of the instruction of the seventh and eighth grade students volunteered to stay after school 3-4 days per week to help a group of students they agreed had major difficulties with basic skills in reading and computation. What they needed was a reordering of their schedules during the day so that they faced fewer kids each week. The 7th and 8th grade schedules were blocked in so that some of the teachers saw students either 2 or 3 days a week for the whole year. What they wanted to do was to see each student for 5 days per week for a term or for half a term. This would allow them to give more intensive help to fewer kids.

They also needed an extension of the Bus II run which took the athletes home. They wanted the remedial kids to be able to ride this bus home.

Of course both requests would have demanded a flexible schedule and joint teacher-principal planning to have worked effectively.

Intervention Strategy Questions: II A

1. Consistent with Argyris' intervention tasks, what would your first steps as manager be? Pick the strategy (a, b, c or d below) you view as most congruent with Argyris' intervention tasks.

_____a. You decide to go with the teachers' requests. You work out the scheduling, and institute the new procedures at the beginning of the next eight week marking period. You would of course inform the parents, the board of education, and finally you would tell the teachers of the results you had achieved in time for their planning.

_____b. You investigate the situation, decide that the data indicated that the teachers' analysis of the situation was incorrect, find out it would cost too much, and inform the teachers that they had not collected enough data, nor generated enough alternative solutions. Tell the teachers to rethink the situation and come back with other alternatives.

_____c. You tell the teachers they were interfering with management prerogatives and to go back to doing their jobs. It was nice of them to volunteer, but such thinking was your job not theirs. Give them a peptalk about trying harder within the present schedule. It would be too upsetting to change schedules in the middle of the year.

_____d. In response to the teachers' request, you sit down with them and decide what data were necessary to be sure that the problems they thought they saw were really what they appeared to be. After setting a time limit of two weeks for collecting this data, schedule a special faculty meeting of the junior high school faculty and anyone else interested. In preparing for this meeting both faculty and the manager would commit themselves to preparing and proposing at least three alternative ways of solving the problems the data identified.

Our Discussion of Crane High School II: A

Any intervention strategy following the three Argyris tasks must begin with the collection of valid data. Implied in this task is an adequate data collection process. Eliminate choice A immediately for this reason alone. Choice A also has other difficulties of arbitrary action, failure to develop alternatives, failure to explore implications and failure to build commitment to choices made.

Choice C also does not collect data. Eliminate it. But also, it does not show a commitment to developing the autonomy of the clients. It downright interferes with their autonomy and suggests further that they should not even pretend to autonomy.

Choice B does begin with data collection. The data are however limited to those deemed important by the manager. He has failed to collect perceptions of others. In the same way he did not generate solutions with the teachers nor pay much attention to their commitments. Last, the manager in this situation by his behavior failed to help the staff learn more adequate problem solving behaviors. This manager punished the staff for their risking rather than rewarding their efforts.

Choice D makes a commitment to Argyris tasks. It would take longer, require consensus decision making, and might end with a commitment of the parties considered to the decision reached. The process described here may not have broadened the decision processes to all affected by its implementation, (e.g. students and parents), but it does represent a beginning commitment.

Choice D is the best of the four alternatives listed if you are using the Argyris criteria for intervention.

Crane High School II: B

The cafeteria!, oh the cafeteria. There were three 22 minute lunch periods, A, B, C. Each fed one third of the school population. The whole academic schedule seemed to revolve around getting the kids fed. For some who ate first the food was hot and fresh. For some who ate last it was neither. For some who ate in the middle there was 22+ minutes of English, then lunch and then 22-plus minutes more of English. Before lunch, that group had rumbling stomachs and afterward heavy eyelids. For the ones who ate first, there was constant noise in the halls as others came and went to or from the cafeteria. They were trying to study math during these distractions.

And for everyone in or near the cafeteria there was the clamor, noise and more noise of 300 kids breaking loose from a morning of being quiet. The teachers on cafeteria duty tried to keep the lid on while the others ate in the same room with the kids. The Duty Roster rotated daily so that each teacher only had to patrol the cafeteria once every three weeks.

Intervention Strategy Questions: IIB

1. What would your first steps as manager be? (Consistent with the three Argyris tasks)

_____a. As manager you carefully observe the dimensions of the problem, you talk to kids. to teachers, to cafeteria workers and to the janitors. You consider several alternatives, select one, work out the details and announce the solution at the next faculty meeting. The faculty voted approval of your solution.

_____b. As manager, you hear complaints about lunch, you ask the teachers in faculty meeting to work with you in consulting kids, other teachers, the cafeteria workers and the janitorial staff. Together you and the teachers sift this data and bring several alternative solutions to the next faculty meeting. After discussion of the various alternatives, the faculty votes to accept one of the solutions.

_____c. You hear complaints from the janitors, the cafeteria workers, the teachers and the students about lunch time. You consider these, decide on a solution and bring in each group to see if they can raise any objections or see any problems with it. When they cannot, you announce its implementation.

_____d. You hear complaints about the lunch period from all sides. You decide that over the summer you will work out a new system and have it ready for the next fall school opening.

Our Discussion of Crane High School II: B

Choice B here most closely meets Argyris' three intervention criteria. It also begins to meet the spirit of a good intervention, it helps the clients learn the processes of good decision making so they are more likely to initiate in the future. In this last sense it incorporates McGregor's Theory Y and helps fulfill needs in Maslow's level 4, (desire for competence, respect and affirmation from others). This is the best choice of the four although it fails to build commitment among all sets of clients affected.

Choice D delays action and by its delay cuts off the very sources of data needed to make good choices. It is hard to consider alternatives when the cafeteria is closed.

Choice A cuts staff and others out of the choice making and therefore does not take advantage of their creativity.

Choice C fails to build commitment among the groups to be involved in the implementation of the solution. It does attempt to collect data from all concerned.

Crane High School II: C

Basketball—the king of the winter. Every other Friday evening from December through early March about 1000 people invade the school to watch 10 young men in revealing short-shorts and see through tank tops run up and down a hard wood floor throwing a large inflated leather ball through a round metal ring with macrame netting on the bottom. With smoking in the boys rooms and people wandering all over the school, the teachers refusing to play policeman for free, utter chaos is threatened.

Develop an intervention strategy that will follow Argyris' three tasks to manage the crowd, assure everyone's enjoyment and keep the school property secure. Write out your strategy below.

_____

_____

_____

_____

_____

_____

_____

_____

_____

Our Discussion of Crane High School II: C

Again using the three Argyris tasks for an intervention, did your strategy also help those who were to be involved in the implementation make free informed choices based on data, and then help them make a commitment to the solution of the problem? The actual solution is not one we are very interested in, it is the strategy for reaching it we are working at here. If you arrive singularly at an elegant solution without going through the processes then it may end being a very bad solution because only you were committed to its implementation.

Crane High School II: D

A large portion of the school faculty is young and inexperienced. Some of the older faculty though experienced have been resting on their laurels lately. You think there needs to be an extensive curriculum revision to meet modern needs.

Develop the outlines of an intervention strategy based on Argyris' three tasks that will assure a serious look at the curriculum in Crane High School. Try to make your strategy elegant enough to build Maslow level 3 and 4 fulfillment for many of the faculty members.

_____

_____

_____

_____

_____

_____

_____

_____

_____

_____

_____

_____

Our Discussion of Crane High School II: D

You know the arguments now about the three steps in an effective intervention. Here we would like to suggest some other data for you to consider.

The National Aeronautics and Space Administration (NASA) developed a simulated problem solving situation for their astronauts. National Training Laboratory and other training groups have used this problem situation for many training groups.

Research on the solutions generated by groups over several years showed the following conclusions:

Although an occasional individual could generate the most elegant acceptable solution, on the average, consensus group solutions were superior to individual solutions in spite of their taking longer to reach. The research conclusions about reasons for the superiority of the group solutions was that in addition to individuals bringing more total data to the group, the group generally considered more factors in making their decision. Rarely were group decisions as poor as the worst individual decisions.

This type of data constitutes another source of support for broadening the base of decision making by managers.

Now continue on to Unit II.

Unit 2

Fact and Inference

Content
This unit will help you increase your ability to separate facts and inferences when collecting and reporting data. It also is intended to increase your interest in making this separation, in knowing why this separation is important to your effectiveness as a supervisor, and in knowing when and how to make and report inferences with supervisees.

Competencies Taught in this Unit
When you finish this unit you will be able to:
1. identify facts, valid inferences, and judgments in statements made about interactions in education.
2. suggest facts that should be gathered to discover the validity of an inference.

Hopefully, you will also value the process taught in this unit enough to begin changing your supervisory behavior to include more separation of fact from inference and judgments.

Method of Demonstrating Attainment
1. The last pages of this unit contain lists of statements which might be made about a sample classroom observation included in this unit. You will demonstrate your competence by correctly identifying statements as facts (those things observable) or probable inferences (those with a high probability of being true) or as possible inferences (those with an unknown probability of being true). You will also be asked to correctly identify judgments (opinions based on experience and training).
2. In the last page, you will be asked to describe some facts you would collect to discover whether or not an inference is valid, i.e. whether it represents an accurate explanation of the facts you observed.

28

Entry Skills

Beyond reading, thinking and caring, there are no particular entry skills necessary for this unit.*

Explanation and Rationale for these Competencies

Much of your effectiveness as a middle manager is based on your ability to intervene in the ongoing parts of the system for which you have some responsibilities. The effectiveness of this interventionist role you must perform is based on your knowledge of the functioning of the system in which you operate. To gain this knowledge, you must gather and analyze data. As important, however, is your ability to separate data from inference and judgments. However much we may wish to have things occur in certain ways, we must develop the ability to see things as they are. Further we must learn to share this factual data, separate from inferences and judgments, with those whom we supervise. Sharing our data separate from our inferences and judgments allows others to hear the data and then to follow the reasoning to the inferences and judgments. Perhaps more importantly, this data collection and sharing assists those being supervised in learning to make their own analyses and plans. In effect it allows them to learn the processes of data collection inference and judgment making for themselves. That is real supervision in the sense we are developing here.

Teacher supervisors such as Dr. Morris L. Cogan (Cogan, 1974) emphasize the need for verifiable data to work with teachers to improve instruction. We extend his arguments to include *all* supervisees from superintendents to janitors in consultant supervision.

One way to begin to improve our supervision is to more often base it on careful data. This is the important message of both Argyris and Cogan. The new behaviors tried must be designed, implemented and evaluated using data. An extra benefit achieved from behaving this way is often a great reduction in hostility and anxiety in our supervisees. If they see that your supervision and recommendations are based on carefully collected, systematically shared data rather than guesses and judgments, they are more able to trust you.

Activity to Emphasize Need for Accurate Careful Data Taking

1. Read each of the situations that follow.
2. Indicate in the space provided what actions you would take, or what you would say.

---

* If you need these three skills, please send $.25 and a plain brown self-addressed envelope to Dr. R. Craig Hogan. He will send, by return mail, the unit titled *Faith, Hope and Charity*.

A. A teacher comes to you for advice. She states that the students in her class just before lunch are restless and inattentive. She suggests that the lunch period be changed for the rest of the year, a simple process in your school.

What do you do?

_____

_____

_____

_____

_____

Now examine your answers with the following additional information not available in the teacher's original request:

The behavior has only been observed by the teacher for a week.

During this week, a crew of workmen have been rebuilding the sidewalk outside the window. On further observation, it appears that the restlessness was only 5 students of 25 in the classroom. These 5 students sitting nearest the window occasionally half rose in their seats and looked out to see when a particularly loud bang erupted from the construction. Usually the students looked out the window during the teacher's lecture. All students earned about the same scores on tests and homework during that week as other weeks.

Questions about your original responses:
1. Before you made any recommendations or decisions did you elicit more data from the teacher?
2. Did you ask permission or otherwise decide to collect some direct observational data in the situation before making recommendations?

Do the same with these situations:

B. A teacher states that one student in his class is being disruptive and has a bad attitude toward the class. He plans to send a letter to the student's parents stating that the student should be referred to the school counselor because he is disruptive and unmanageable.

What do you say?

_____

_____

C. A teacher states that she is going to give up the new program she spent the summer writing because after three weeks of use, the students only increased their reading scores slightly.

What do you say?

Additional information on situations B and C which was not given or available in the teacher's original report of the situation to the supervisor:

For B: The student is a bright student who does outside work to prepare for the class. She stated she "loves" the subject. The teacher, in a later interview, stated that the child, "Picked information out of an encyclopedia to make me look bad and to delay the class". At one point, the teacher stated, "Keep it to yourself," when the student began giving more information than necessary for an answer. The child laid her head down on her desk and refused to participate for several minutes. The teacher reprimanded her.

For C: The teacher used the program for only seven actual teaching days because preparations for Veteran's Day pageants interfered with class. The slight gain in scores was larger than the increase students in previous years had shown in three months.

Although our examples and additional information lay responsibility much too heavily on the teacher, we suggest that they could be real examples. To the point of this exercise, however; if your suggestions were other than, "there is more data needed", or ideas to that effect, then you probably realize with the additional information how far off target any suggestions might have been if you had not elicited more data.

The programmed material in this unit will help you learn how to identify data and separate it from inference.

Fact - Inference - Judgment

Diagnostic Test

This short diagnostic test will give you an indication of where to begin the following materials.

Read the account of an observation which follows.

The teacher came to the supervisor with a concern because 25% of the students had failed a quiz and 50% had grades of D or D-. The supervisor asked whether the teacher had gone over the material in class. The teacher answered that he had gone over the material for three days prior to the quiz. The supervisor stated that she couldn't imagine how, after three days of instruction, the students couldn't pass the quiz. The teacher quickly answered, "They're dummies, that's why." The supervisor then said "Well, maybe so, but you've got to take some of the blame." "I will not," the teacher answered; "and you're not going to push me into it."

With each of the following statements, write in the blank, "F" if it is Fact, "Poss" if it is a possible inference, "Prob" if it is a probable inference, and "J" if it is a judgment.

1. _____The supervisor should have been a little more tactful.

2. _____The teacher was unhappy with the supervisor.

3. _____25% of the students had failed the quiz.

4. _____Telling the supervisor the students were "dummies" was wrong.

5. _____It sounded like the teacher was becoming angry.

6. _____The teacher stated that he had gone over the material for three days prior to the class.

7. _____Three days should be enough to study for a quiz.

8. _____The teacher did not review the same material used on the test.

9. _____The teacher is not willing to accept the responsibility in the situation for his students' learning.

10. _____The supervisor has "pushed" the teacher into things in the past.

11. _____The supervisor asked the teacher whether he had gone over the information prior to the quiz.

ANSWERS: 1. J; 2. Poss; 3. F; 4. J; 5. Poss; 6. F; 7. J; 8. Poss; 9. Prob; 10. Poss; 11. F.

FACT: If you did not identify one or more of the fact statements as facts, then you should probably begin below.

INFERENCE: If you found that you did identify the facts, but did not correctly identify the inferences with "Poss" or "Prob" in two or more instances, or marked another statement as an inference which was not, you should begin with page 36 Frame #6

JUDGMENT: If you did identify the facts and inferences, but did not correctly identify one or more of the judgments with "J", or if you marked two or more of the other items that were not judgments as judgments, begin with page 45. Frame #16

If you scored all the items correctly, then you probably don't need this unit.

Some suggestions are made on page 46 of other things you can do related to the ideas of the unit.

Fact, Inference, Judgment

The following pages are programmed. The answers for each of the blanks are in the box (frame) below the one in which the blank is found. Use an 8 x 10 card or other card to cover the frame below the frame you are reading. Proceed from frame to frame following the numbers in the upper left corner of each.

Special instructions:

1. Write out all of your answers in the blanks. It is important that you write the answers rather than think them so you can check yourself.
2. Immediately after writing a single answer, check the suggested answer to see if you had the right idea.
3. If your answer is not satisfactory, find out why before going on.

Frame #1

A *fact* is a statement whose content can be verified as true through the senses.

If the sky is dark, stating that "The sky is dark" is a fact because _____

_____

_____

> **Answer #1**
>
> it can be verified through the senses that the sky is dark

Frame #2
A non-fact is a statement whose content can be verified as false through senses.
If the sky is dark all day, stating that "It is a sunshiny day" is a non-fact

because _____

_____

> **Answer #2**
>
> it can be verified that it was not a sunshiny day

Frame #3
A statement is *unverifiable* if it cannot be demonstrated to be true or untrue through the senses.
Stating that the interior of Mars is inhabited by little green men is unver-

ifiable because _____

_____

> **Answer #3**
>
> it cannot be verified through the senses that it is either true or false

Frame #4
Read the following account of an observation. Assume this is all the observer's senses picked up.

> During the first three minutes of class, all 25 students read silently. Then the teacher asked students to respond to a question about the reading. Four students were not looking at the teacher. The teacher called on one student who was not watching. The student was not able to answer the question asked.

Write beside each of the following statements "F" for fact, "NF" for non-fact, and "NV" for non-verifiable.

a. _____ The teacher asked students to respond to a question.

b. _____ The teacher reprimanded the student who could not answer.

c. _____ All students were looking at the teacher.

Answer #4

a. __F__ because it is verifiable by using the senses.

b. __NV__ because data describing what happened after the student answered the question is not present. It is not "NF" because it cannot be verified, from this information, that the teacher did not reprimand the student.

c. __NF__ because four students were not looking at the teacher.

Frame #5

Often, the difference between a statement that is a fact and one that is not verifiable is very subtle. Using the observation in Frame #4, mark "F" for fact, and "NV" for not verifiable with the facts given. Remember that a fact must be verifiable with the account you have, which is what the observer's senses picked up.

a. _____ Most students were paying attention.

b. _____ Four students were not looking at the teacher.

c. _____ Four students were not paying attention.

d. _____ The student was not able to answer the question because she was not paying attention.

Answer #5

a. __NV__ It is not verifiable because there is no indication of what the other students were doing. Even if they were watching the teacher, however, they may not have been paying attention. They may have been daydreaming, or playing footsie with the students in the desks ahead of them.

b. __F__ That is a fact that can be verified.

c. __NV__ "Looking at" is not synonymous with "paying attention." In other words, the

> (Answer #5 continued)
>
> students may be paying attention even though their eyes are not riveted on the teacher's face. Eye-contact is not prerequisite to paying attention. What is important is that "paying attention" cannot be verified by the senses.
>
> d. __NV__   Again, it cannot be verified (1) that the student was not paying attention, and (2) that if the student was not paying attention, it would be the reason he did not answer the question.

This exercise may have been difficult for you. It is often difficult for people to begin to think objectively about occurrences. Many of us take for granted that the presence of one thing indicates that another thing is also occurring (a student is not looking at the teacher—the student must not be paying attention). Separating facts from non-facts is a set of skills that must be learned. The remainder of this programmed unit will help you begin to learn the skills.

This exercise may have been easy for you. If it was, you may want to go back to the diagnostic test and find out if you misread the original directions. You may also wish to continue as a review.

Frame #6
Read the following account of an observation and assume that it is all the observer received through the senses.

> The students were seated in four groups of six. The teacher walked from group to group spending about three minutes at each group without speaking. Students in one group were louder than the other students and students in other groups occasionally looked over at them.

Write "F" or "NV" beside each of the following statements as you did previously. After writing each answer, check it below before going to the next blank.

a. _____   There were six students in each group.

> (Check your answers before going on. Cover all the answers with a sheet of paper.) Move the sheet of paper from each answer after you have written your own answer.

b. _____   The teacher was not controlling the class enough.

c. _____   The teacher spent about three minutes at each group.

d. _____ The loudest group disturbed other students.

e. _____ One group of students was disruptive.

f. _____ The students were learning to become responsible for their own learning.

g. _____ Students not in the louder group wished they could be in the louder group.

Answers #6

a. __F__

b. __NV__ That is a judgment that cannot be supported by the facts available.

c. __F__

d. __NV__ It may seem that because one group was louder, and members of other groups looked at them that the louder group was disturbing the others. However, it could be that the louder group was spurring other groups to work harder in a competition; or the members of the other groups could be wishing they were in the louder group.

e. __NV__ It cannot be verified that the louder group "disrupted" the other groups. There are many possible reasons why the students in some groups were looking at the louder group.

f. __NV__ What the students were learning cannot be verified because there is no indication in the account of a verifiable action that indicates learning has taken place.

g. __NV__ For the same reason "e" is NV.

Frame #7

You may have the conviction that some of the statements in the previous frames were verifiable facts. They seem "mostly true" because they are inferences. Inferences are not facts. They are conclusions based on facts. They cannot be verified as absolutely true, but they may be true. One of the following statements cannot be verified as being true, but it is very possibly true. Circle the letter of that statement.

a. I hear sounds like thunder.

b. It is pretty dark out at 1:00 p.m.

c. I hear sounds like gusty winds.

d. It may rain.

> Answer #7
> d. The other statements are facts. "d" is a conclusion based on those facts. It cannot be verified as true because it cannot be verified through the senses.

Frame #8
In the previous frame, the conclusion in "d" is a(n) _____.

> Answer #8
> inference

Frame #9
You can determine whether a statement is fact or inference by judging whether it is verifiable through the senses or is a conclusion based on facts. Write "F" or "I" before each of the following statements to indicate whether the statement is a fact or inference. You have as data only the observation by the supervisor of a class he observed.

a. _____ Three students were not in class.

b. _____ Three students were absent because of sickness.

c. _____ The teacher wrote on the board for 15 seconds.

d. _____ Two students failed the test.

e. _____ Two students did not study for the test.

f. _____ The test was too hard.

> Answer #9
>
> a. ___F___ It can be verified by looking at the class.
>
> b. ___I___ While someone may say the students are sick, or it might be assumed that they are absent because of sickness, whether they are sick cannot be verified if they are not present.
>
> c. ___F___ It can be verified by looking at the teacher and timing her activity.

d.	F	It can be verified by checking the answers with the standard answers.
e.	I	It cannot be verified in the classroom; it could be verified if the students were watched for several days before the test, but that would be impractical. However it is an inference based on the fact that they failed the test.
f.	I	Again, this is an inference. There may be many reasons why students failed a test. The word "hard" is difficult to assess so the statement cannot be verified.

Frame #10

Separating fact from inference is difficult because all people have a tendency to view occurrences with inference. As human beings, we must infer to live. We infer that because we can obtain food from a supermarket today that we need not plant crops and raise livestock to feed ourselves tomorrow. There are even theories that we only see in two dimensions, and that we infer the third dimension (depth) so that without those inferences we could not judge depth.

While working with human beings, however, we must rely on the most valid inferences we can formulate. To obtain them, we need to gather facts, then make inferences based on a single set of facts. For instance, which one of the following inferences is valid?

Fact: 25% of the students in one class do not turn in homework.
Inference a: The homework may be too hard.
Inference b: All work may be done in class and homework is optional.
Inference c: The students may have forgotten to turn in homework. They had completed it.

> Answer #10
>
> All may be true. More information is needed.

Frame #11

The inference can be worded to indicate which of the several possible inferences is most probable and which are less probable. An inference should be stated with a qualification, such as "most," "may," "many," "possibly," or "might." No inference is definitely true—it would then be a fact. If the qualifier does not accurately state a conclusion that is based on the facts available, then it is an invalid inference. For the following statements, write "valid" or "invalid" to indicate whether the inference is valid based on the facts given.

Fact: Four students were not looking at the teacher.

Inference a: The four students were not paying attention.

   valid or invalid? _____

Inference b: It is possible that the four students were not paying attention.

   valid or invalid? _____

Answer #11

Inference a: *invalid* The statement is made as though it were a fact: they *were not* paying attention. Actually, the fact that they were not looking at the teacher does not indicate that they were not paying attention.

Inference b: *valid* The qualifier, "possible" limits the statement. Since one of the possibilities is that the students were also not paying attention, the statement is valid.

Frame #12

Read the following account of an observation of a supervisory conference:

> The supervisor began the meeting. First he greeted the teacher, then he listed three suggestions for the teacher to use in improving instruction. The teacher nodded his head after each suggestion and said nothing. When the supervisor stopped, there were 15 seconds of silence. The supervisor looked at the teacher. The teacher rolled a ball of paper between his palms looking at his hands. The teacher then said, "OK, I'll do them. I've got to get back to my study period." The two shook hands and the teacher left.

Mark the following statements as facts, "F", valid inferences, "VI", or invalid inferences, "IVI".

a. _____ The supervisor began the meeting.

b. _____ The teacher spoke only once during the conference.

c. _____ The teacher was not pleased with the conference.

d. _____ The teacher may not have been pleased with the conference.

e. _____ The teacher probably was not pleased with the conference.

f. _____ The teacher did not plan to carry out the suggestions.

g. _____ The supervisor may have felt that with this teacher giving concrete suggestions was the only way of conferencing.

Answer #12

a. ___F___

b. ___F___

c. ___IVI___ There is little factual evidence to indicate that the teacher was not pleased with the conference so that stating definitely that the teacher *was not pleased* is not valid.

d. ___VI___ Since there is some evidence that the teacher may not have been pleased with the conference, it is valid to say that he *may* not have been pleased.

e. ___IVI___ With this statement we come to the shaky difference between "possibly" and "probably." For an inference to be "probably" true, there must be solid supporting factual evidence; there is not much supporting evidence for saying that the teacher probably was displeased. The teacher, for instance, may have been tired, or anxious about a situation in the study hall. *Probable* claims too much here.

f. ___IVI___ There is no factual evidence for this statement.

g. ___VI___ There is little evidence to support this inference, but it is a possible inference that should be explored. This does not mean the statement is true, only that the way it is stated is a valid use of the inference process.

Frame #13

Those inferences which are invalid inferences do not have sufficient data to support them. Those that are only "possibly" true, likewise, have little data to support them. In the case of both, it is difficult to discuss the inferences because of their tentative nature. More data are needed.

The process of making an inference, realizing that it is invalid, or only "possibly" true, then seeking further data to see whether it is probably valid is the same as formulating a hypothesis and testing it—a scientific method of approaching human behavior. In your conferences with teachers, you will discuss the facts available, help the teacher make valid inferences based on the facts, and help the teachers suggest data needed to see whether possible inferences (hypotheses) are correct, highly probable, incorrect, or untestable.

We are suggesting a process for working with teachers as well as a way of separating factual data from categories of inferences.

Read the following account of an observation.

> The teacher stood behind his desk at the front of the room during the first five minutes. He asked questions about the day's assignments, calling upon students whose hands were not raised. At the beginning of the class, 10 of the 36 students raised their hands to answer the first question. After five minutes, only three students raised their hands to answer questions. When a student could not answer a question immediately, the teacher quickly asked another student. One student who could not answer a question closed her book quickly and looked at the girl next to her with a grimace. A boy who did not answer quickly enough shrugged his shoulders and leaned his elbow on the desk turning away from the teacher. After seven minutes of class time, four students began to make funny comments in low voices in answer to each question the teacher asked.

Mark the following statements about the observation as invalid, possibly valid, or probably valid by inserting, "not," "probably," or "possibly" in the blanks.

a.   It is _____ valid to say that students stopped raising their hands because the teacher did not call on them.

b.   It is _____ valid to say that the teacher was disliked by most of the students.

c.   It is _____ valid to say that the girl who grimaced was not happy about not being able to answer the question.

d.   It is _____ valid to say that the teacher intended to spur students not prepared for class to do more work.

e.   It is _____ valid to say that the boy who could not answer the question was unhappy about it.

Answer #13

a. <u>Not/</u>   either "Not" or "Possibly" fit here. If you
    Possibly   indicated that this is "probably" true
                 based on the facts available, we would

Answer #13 continued

    say that you need to be tentative about it and gather more facts before indicating that it is probably true.

b. __Not__

c. __Probably__ The non-verbal signals seem to indicate strongly that she was unhappy.

d. __Possibly__ This could be one reason for calling upon students who did not raise their hands. More data are needed.

e. __Probably__ for the same reason as "c" above.

We lean to the side of conservatism in making inferences since so often other answers seem to be the real causes.

Frame #14

It is difficult to interpret "possibly true" inferences because there may be many inferences in this category. For that reason, when you draw an inference which is "possibly true", you will wish to collect more facts to discover whether it is "probably true". For letters *a* and *d* in frame 13, suggest the kind of data or facts that need to be gathered to change "possibly" to "probably" true.

a. _____

_____

d. _____

_____

Answers #14

a.   You probably should have indicated that there is a need to discover whether the students would have stopped raising their hands even if the teacher called on them. Student interviews, or a control situation in which a control group is compared with an experimental group might supply the data needed.

d.   Ask the teacher before making this inference.

Frame #15

One other type of factual data is important enough to be presented here. You will use it quite often throughout the book. There is a difference between stating that "Student A dislikes Shakespeare" and "Student A stated she dislikes Shakespeare." The former is an inference; the latter is a fact. When a person states a feeling he has, it is probably true that his assessment of the emotion is accurate, but the listener cannot verify that with the senses. The observer in other words, can draw the inference that it is highly probable that "Alice is angry" when she states, "I am angry." Sometimes being careful with this subtle difference will earn you many points on the trust scale. At other times, some people will accuse you of being a plodding pedant.

Write "I" before each of the following statements which is an inference and "F" before each of the statements which is a fact.

a. _____ The student did not feel good.

b. _____ The student said she did not feel good.

c. _____ The supervisor became angry.

d. _____ The teacher was furious.

e. _____ The teacher frowned, shouted and slammed a book on the desk.

f. _____ The teacher stated, "I am furious."

Answers #15

a. __I__ There is no way of verifying this. It can be verified that the student has a high temperature, or that the student passed out, or that the student turned white, but it cannot be verified that she did not feel good.

b. __F__ It is verifiable through the auditory sense that she said she did not feel good. Whether she actually did or not is unimportant here.

c. __I__ Again, this cannot be verified. It is an internal state and others can only verify symptoms of it which might point to it as an inference.

d. __I__ It is an internal, unverifiable state.

e. __F__ These are overt, verifiable behaviors and therefore facts.

> Answers #15 continued
>
> f. ___F___ This is another overt, verifiable behavior that could lead one to infer that the teacher was furious.

Frame #16

The final category of statements we wish to teach you to discriminate contains judgments.

Judgmental statements are neither valid facts nor valid inferences. Their content cannot be verified because they are very subjective. For instance, saying, "The reaction of the students was favorable," could mean that the students did not protest, or that they jumped for joy and snake-danced down the halls. It is even more difficult to discover what is meant by "That class was good" (when peanut brittle, field goals, and chaste persons are also "good" in some people's judgments). Those judgmental statements can be identified by their use of "right", "wrong", "good", "bad", "should", "ought", "must", and all of the hundreds of judgmental words with little or no objective meaning (e.g., beautiful, awful, terrible, wonderful, fantastic, atrocious, ridiculous, nice*). Since they are neither facts nor valid inferences, we suggest that you avoid using judgmental statements in supervisory situations where you are attempting to report data and to draw inferences from that data.

In the following list of statements, identify facts (F), inferences (I), and judgments (J).

a. _____ You should have given a longer assignment.

b. _____ A longer assignment might have helped students become more successful in the test.

c. _____ 36% of the students failed the test.

d. _____ The test was bad.

e. _____ Ten of the 30 questions in the test were from an optional reading.

f. _____ The teacher should not have used items from an optional reading on the test.

g. _____ The items from the optional reading were too difficult because the students who averaged 95% or above on the test even failed them.

> Answers #16
>
> a. ___J___ The word "should" gives this away as a

*Current Ms. America winners may be viewed in some corners as merely facile laced possessors of excess adipose tissue judiciously placed.

judgment. It cannot be verified as fact, and there are no facts available to indicate that it is a valid inference.

b. ___I___   This is a conjecture which is actually an enthymeme* It is labeled as an inference because it is qualified by "might".

c. ___F___

d. ___J___   The use of a judgmental term also labels this statement.

e. ___F___

f. ___J___

g. ___J___   Although the data are mathematically correct, "too difficult" makes this a judgment.

This book is based on the need for objective facts upon which to base valid inferences in supervision. As you read the rest of the book you will become more able to use the information you have gathered in this unit to offer supervisory help to others, to help teachers deal with their classrooms and students, and to be critical of your own supervision. The ability to differentiate facts and inferences will be applied to gathering facts and making inferences in other units which lie ahead.

There are several ways you can now test your mastery of the specific skills we have been working at in this unit. You may wish to go back to pages 29-31, examples A, B and C to see if your behavior would now be different than it was at the time you answered those questions.

You may retake the diagnostic test to check your skill.

You may wish to get out an observation report you have written recently, and categorize the statements you made on it as facts, inferences (valid and invalid) and judgments.

---

*Our sincere apologies for this word. One of us has a classically religious background which we have not been able to exorcise. You are not expected to know this word and, hopefully, the spirit will never move us to use it again.

Unit 3

Supervision and Evaluation

Content Overview

This unit tries to bring the real world of many middle managers into focus. Most of you are expected to rate or evaluate others. At the same time you are expected to help them through supervision built on a trusting relationship. This thorny nettle can be grasped if you are clear. We try to help you toward clarity in this book.

Using The Unit

Read and Think!

Competencies

After completing this unit you will be able to:
1. Describe one set of behaviors which we suggest will help you carry both helping and evaluative roles with your staff.
2. Be willing to try to implement these behaviors with an open mind to their possible success.

Explanation and Rationale for the Competencies

Much has been written about the necessity of separating the supervisory role from the evaluative role. A good case may be made for the effectiveness of that separation. We no longer believe it. Although expensive, we could hire separate staffs of non-evaluative supervisors if we believed in that necessity. But we ask teachers every day to teach, to help their students, and then to grade i.e. evaluate them. If they are to learn to live with that conflict so must we, if we are to be of any real help to them. We have to learn to distinguish clearly between criticism of behavior and rejection of the person. Many teachers as well need to work through this apparent conflict to clarify their teaching role. Your model will greatly enhance their learning.

Supervision and Evaluation[1]   17 June

Dear Joe,

Supervision *and* evaluation? Supervision *or* evaluation? Supervision *as part of* evaluation? Supervision *vis-a-vis* evaluation? This issue won't go away, will it?

[1]The following is a letter written by Dave to a then special supervisor, now vice-principal in a school district where Dave was serving as a consultant. It responds to the question, "What is the relationship between supervision and evaluation when both these roles are performed by the same person?"

At our last in-service workshop with your district's administrators and supervisors, you asked for my reactions to your continuing question about how to cope with the schizophrenia imposed on you by these two conflicting and insatiable masters. At the close of our intense Saturday morning session which concluded three days of 26 people's determined efforts to deal with such issues, faced with the unreality I always feel in a motel conference setting, you still had this question. Your tired colleagues were also interested, but there was no way then to develop a serious, thoughtful response that would be satisfying to you, to me, or to anyone. Your question deserves an answer, however. This is my attempt to give you an answer. My answer. Perhaps it will help you to reach your own.

We should look at the recurrence of this question in the three two-day workshops on supervision we have just completed over the past eight months.

During our first workshop last fall, we, as outside consultants, tended to raise it more often than you did (out loud at least). At that time you were outwardly concerned with gaining control over a wide variety of new techniques and procedures; observation skills, inference-making, conferencing, setting goals, making commitments, establishing evaluation measures, and being worthy of trust. Because these techniques were real only in simulated settings, at least then, questions about whether they would work for you and whether you could use them acceptably were much more important to you than those related to the supervision-evaluation conflict.

By the time of the second workshop, in late winter, you had been practicing the techniques for several months and this supervision-evaluation conflict was reaching its highest intensity for many of you. The techniques themselves were beginning to work, and, as some teachers were beginning to risk trusting your real interest in helping them, you could see evaluation as destroying, or at least threatening, this fragile, developing relationship. The question about the boundaries between supervision and evaluation suddenly had much meaning for you. Our attempts to patch over these holes of anxiety only served to push the issue elsewhere to pop up again. What we were saying then that you could not hear, was that you were blowing the issue out of proportion. If you were each trustworthy, then the fact that you must wear two hats would become unimportant in the eyes of the teachers, and consequently in your own. Of course, what we failed to appreciate then, and have finally begun to understand now, is that our answers bore little relationship to your own experiences. We were dismissive of your concerns and thus left you to search for your own answers without much guidance about where to search. We apologize for our insensitivity.

During our just-concluded June workshop, we noticed that, although the question was raised, it had lost its intense immediacy for many of you. We heard several of the group expressing their personal resolutions as they have worked them out with their individual faculties. As many of your teachers observed the new attitudes and new skills you were exhibiting, they were responding in ways other than their past indifferences and hostility to your supervisory efforts. You sensed successful interventions on your part. Teaching behaviors were changing. They sensed new and fairer, more objective approaches in your discussion about their teaching. This beginning of a mutual trust provided enough light for some to see at least the possibility of an end to a long tunnel of mutual suspicion. These positive beginnings do not, however, negate the larger issue even though they remove much of its immediate pressure.

We must still think about, and try to clearly verbalize with each of our separate faculties, our personal answers. The clarity of our perceptions about this fundamental and inherent conflict is the base upon which trust is built. As we move toward discussing ever more important issues about teaching (i.e., human interactions and their relationship to important learning by students), there is implied, no, there is demanded, increasing basic trust between the supervisor and the supervisees. These two groups are the same ones which often drift into adversary relationships over issues of evaluation.

Thus, we come back again to your question: What is the relationship of supervision to evaluation when these two separate functions reside in the same person?

We'd better be clear that we both mean the same things when we use each of these words. Supervision is that set of procedures, skills, organizations and relationships used with instructional staff for the improvement of learning by students. We supervise in environments where we have some responsibility for the results of the teaching and instruction which takes place. Supervision is usually an open-ended process with techniques that are careful, but not prescribed.

Evaluation is the formal judging and rating process which results in specific records that are used to determine decisions about hiring, promotion, tenure, and similar concerns. Often it is based on law, or state or local school codes. There are often contractual negotiations which result in specific prescribed evaluation procedures. Whether negotiated or not, evaluation procedures are usually prescribed.

However much we as educators may wish to shed one of these roles, the fact remains that most of us have to do both at least some of the time. There should be some resources available in every educational setting which are only supervisory (i.e., helping), but there usually are not. In settings where these resources exist, they must be (and be seen by supervisees as being) powerful enough to maintain a confidential trusting relationship similar to that between a lawyer and client, doctor and patient or any other such professional example.

Unless or until we are able to make clear to our overseers (i.e., local community, state government) the conflict and real losses in ability to perform caused by these two roles residing in one relatively nonschizophrenic individual, we have no other choice than to operate as effectively as possible in the world where we live, and admit to our losses.

While awaiting that unhappily compromised end, I offer the following suggestions:

1. Discuss this inherent conflict openly and often with those you evaluate and supervise. These discussions should be both individual and group.

2. Share formally the various procedures to be used in these separate processes. As much as possible, let the procedures for both processes be jointly developed by faculty and administrative teams. In your district we have pointed out some of the subjective/objective conflicts we see in the evaluation instruments presently in use. Many of the categories and implied values on the rating scales seemed either vague or trivial to us. Of course, your district is hardly unique in this respect. But don't take any comfort from this fact. If you consider a category important enough to retain in your district, try to agree on exemplary behaviors representing these categories. "Displays behaviors consistent with those expected of a teacher in our district," is a category I have seen in some rating scales. I consider this kind of statement as rage-producing in addition to being undefinable. It is nonetheless frequently used on helpless teachers in punitive ways. You may be aware of recent court decisions which upheld the right of school districts to use rating scales as a major consideration in decisions where staff reductions became necessary as a result of changing student enrollment. Capricious categories like the above destroy trust and put too much power in the hands of the evaluator. Are you confident in your forms used in evaluation? What processes are you planning to produce better ones?

3. You remember the care with which we laid out the concepts of Maslow's hierarchy of human needs. If teachers feel their basic competence is being threatened, and if their security is under a rating gun, they are not often going to risk showing weaknesses or entering into serious self-development processes. Get your evaluative processes over with as quickly as possible. Share the results with the evaluatee and then get on to supervision. Where this is not completely possible, as when you are constrained to do two or three evaluative observations spread throughout the year, at least separate the two processes as much as possible. Indicate early what your evaluative rating will be if all continues as it appears when you make your earliest visit. (Of course, if this assessment begins to change, indicate this to the evaluatee at once.) No final poor rating should ever come as a surprise to the evaluatee. You must give up the tactic of using rating as a weapon to threaten teachers. Otherwise, they cannot risk honest self-disclosure and be open to supervision.

I might even wear a black suit (for piousness and purity) when I am evaluating, and more open clothes when I am supervising and helping because teachers need to know which I am doing and when.

4. Evaluation occurs on official forms. It occurs at times announced in advance. Issues to be evaluated are known to both parties. During supervision these forms are absent. The issues to be discussed are jointly negotiated with the person being helped.

If the person being helped does not feel some control over the intensity of the issues and the processes, it is not usually perceived as help. This, it seems to me, is a key point. The previous does not suggest that you be non-directive, or that you avoid sticky, difficult issues about someone's teaching. But, supervisees in supervision *must* have a choice as to whether or not they will work on these issues. The supervisee may make the choice *not* to work on these issues knowing that, as a consequence of that choice, at the time of evaluation, the rating form will show a low evaluation of that teaching area. In the event that this low-rated teaching behavior is considered central to effective teaching in the district, then failure to improve the quality of the performance would be considered grounds for dismissal. The teacher may refuse your help and decide to ignore the area, knowing the implications of that decision. Your obligation as supervisor is to make significant help available. Your obligation as evaluator is to make it clear what results you believe will follow that rating.

5. Finally, you have an obligation to base both your supervisory and your evaluative inferences on a data base as objective as possible. You should always carefully explain this data base and the inference chains you have constructed from the data. Hidden criteria and hidden processes are destructive to trust because they demean the person's competence. They also reinforce the very arbitrariness you are trying to get away from. Accompany your sharing of data with the sharing of all the written materials to be kept on a teacher anywhere in the district.

6. I guess the last point was not really the final one; I have one more lecturette. Raise real issues with supervisees. Your careful presentation of serious topics for discussion clears the air of the kind of trivial game-playing engaged in by both parties when supervision itself is an unreal pretense at help. If you really care, find the time to do supervision and respect your supervisees enough to discuss real things.

When you can discuss with your staff the real conflict between these two roles, the conflict becomes relatively less important. It is subjugated by the very real help teachers perceive themselves getting.

Enough! A reaction to this letter would help me to judge its usefulness. Share it with your colleagues and have some talk about the issues it addresses. As you can see, I've taken the liberty of sending a copy to your superintendent. You may wish to discuss it with him.

Sincerely,

Dave C.

cc: Superintendent of Schools

P.S. With your permission, I'd like to try to publish this; it is the cleanest thinking I've ever been able to verbalize about these two issues. Thanks for forcing me to deal with them.

D. W. C.

By November of the following school year, after some further training, continued support by his school system in developing supervisory skills, and transfer to a job as middle school vice-principal in the same system, Joe was asking and answering different questions. He was still in the helping-evaluation role in his new post.

He was also ready to serve with Dave as a training consultant. He was ready to teach others supervisory skills. After that session he wrote a letter describing his thinking about this issue and others related to supervision in his setting. We paraphrase the sense of it here. We think, while it is a personal resolution of the issue for him, that it also has applicability to the issue that bothers many of you.

When I heard the questions the people asked me at the workshop I did with you, I suddenly thought back to my own questions to you almost a year ago. They were asking the same question I had: "How do I do supervision when I am also an evaluator?" How can people trust me when I affect their job in my rating of them? And I'm sure my answers had little meaning to them in the place where they are now, intellectually and emotionally. What I really wanted to say was "Your questions are the wrong ones. They don't really matter. What matters is the clarity inside you about who are you and why you are doing what you are doing when you are doing it. What matters is the honesty you bring to the relationship and your caring about helping them improve. You demonstrate your concern in many ways — by being on time, by showing up, by being knowledgeable about their classes and their teaching, by listening, by discussing real issues, by collecting careful data and - - - - - -.

Yours is the wrong question; you should be asking yourself when you are going to develop the skills and the courage to work in this arena. It is rewarding and results do show.

I don't really know why I'm telling you all this; you told me the same thing a while back. I'm satisfied, now, that I can do both roles. That is true because I convey my clarity and concern in honest ways and I've decided what I'm about. Isn't there any way that others can learn this answer without having to live through it and find out for themselves?

Sincerely,

Joe

Besides thanking Joe, our answer to his last question is "generally no." Others, such as you, have to be convinced by their (your) own experience. The only help we can give you is to teach skills, encourage attempts to use them, tell you that others have succeeded in the struggle before. We also supply promises and visions of the future.

The technical discussion of the evaluation of teaching that follows is intended to serve as a basis for application of the techniques and concepts taught in the remainder of the book to evaluation of teaching. It does all we can do. The comfort with yourself will only grow with time and practice.

Measurement and Evaluation

There is a difference between measurement and evaluation that bears upon your efforts to evaluate teaching. Measurement is gaining some measure (inches, gallons, number of appearances, number correct on a test, etc.). There is no value placed on the number yet. For instance, what is the value of a pickle 7 inches long? No value can be placed upon it until the evaluators decide (1) Is length the right dimension to measure and to judge pickles and (2) Should a pickle be big or little to be most valuable?

In the evaluation of teaching, you must first decide what determines whether the teaching is acceptable or unacceptable. Is it clarity of speaking, number of students helped individually in one class period, number of inservice activities attended during the previous year? You then measure the dimensions you value. Finally, you must decide how many or much of them makes good (or acceptable or satisfactory or competent) teaching, and how little makes poor (or incompetent or unsatisfactory or unacceptable) teaching. With pickles individual taste is the only criterion which matters. With teaching we can look at the effects on students learning. That difference of an outside standard matters.

Together, both what will be measured and the expected amounts of them are referred to as the criteria for good teaching, although you will often hear only the first (what will be measured) described as the criteria. A measurement, then, is collecting data about what was to be measured; the evaluation is judging the worth of the teaching by comparing the specific measurement of a specific teacher's teaching in this area to some standards for satisfactory and unsatisfactory teaching. In the daily activities of your supervision, you will often help teachers measure aspects of their teaching. Usually, the teacher, and often you with the teacher, will evaluate the results to determine whether the teacher wishes to work on improving instruction in the area. At other times, the measurement will be turned over to a personnel committee or other body for the evaluation.

Purpose of the Evaluation of Teaching

The main purposes for any measurement of teaching attributes and evaluation based on the measurement must always be (1) to improve the quality of valued outcomes in students (learning, social growth, problem solving ability, self-confidence, etc.), and (2) to enable faculty to be successful and to feel fulfilled as professionals and as people. All other reasons for evaluating teaching must be means toward those ends. All designs for measurement and evaluation in teaching that hinder achieving either of those ends are superfluous and perhaps counterproductive of achieving those ends. It would be difficult to overemphasize this common sense notion since so few people seem to pay any attention to it.

The two most prominent means employed to achieve the ends of improving outcomes in students and enabling faculty to be successful and fulfilled are through (1) using measurement and evaluation along with rewards, incentives, and encouragement to encourage voluntary efforts by teachers to improve teaching, and (2) using measurement and evaluation to discover competence levels of teachers in order to make personnel decisions (hiring, promotion, tenure, training effects) that ultimately will result in improving the outcomes in students.

These different means, both important, could exist simultaneously in an educational system. Usually they do not, however. The measurement and evaluation designs of most systems focus on the personnel evaluative decisions to the detriment of encouraging voluntary and/or systematic efforts to improve instruction. Unfortunately, most teachers see the process of evaluation of teaching by administrators for personnel decisions as threatening and punitive, resulting only in negative criticisms and firings. They often see the criteria and judgments made as arbitrary, and based solely on the unsupported biases of the evaluator. The undercurrents generated are counterproductive to improving outcomes in students and to enabling teachers to feel successful and satisfied.

Much of the reason for this unfortunate state of affairs is in the fact that the measurement and evaluation of teaching is *done to* teachers by administrators or some quasi-administrative group (committee on promotion and tenure, faculty personnel committee, etc.). Teaching is an art built upon the discipline of education. Becoming a competent artist/teacher is a complicated, strenuous activity motivated more by growth level needs than the deficiency levels (although certainly a teacher fearful of not being promoted or given a renewal of contract will fight fires in her teaching to maintain the desired position). Threats and coercian may actually train the teachers' sights on lower level needs. When teachers focus on removing threats to safety and security, higher level growth towards teaching excellence is ignored. Achieving excellence in teaching cannot be forced or legislated; however, when the teacher is helped to focus on growth, and is successful, her outcomes with students will be enhanced. Her satisfaction and fulfillment will follow.

Questions to be Answered in the Evaluation of Teaching

Important questions in the evaluation of teaching, then, are:

1. Who is responsible for each step in the evaluation process: deciding on criteria, when and how to measure, and who collects and interprets the data used in the evaluation?

2. What criteria will be measured for the evaluation of teaching?

3. How will they be measured?

4. What levels of competence will be used in the evaluation?

5. What will be the consequences of the judgment?

1. Who is responsible for each step in the evaluation process?

Commitment to improving teaching, and satisfaction with the process, will result only from teacher involvement in the evaluation. At least, the teachers must be aware of the concrete, observable criteria to be used in the evaluation; at best, the teacher should be responsible for assisting in collecting the data, then using it herself often with help to improve teaching or submitting it to a personnel committee in her own way to make a case for promotion or continuation of contract. The chart that follows illustrates a continuum of teacher and administrator involvement in the evaluation process.

Graph Illustrating Control Over Evaluation*

May be characteristic of	Who decides what is measured?	Who decides how and when to measure?	Who sets evaluation criteria?	Who performs evaluation?	Who determines what will be done with the results?
Focus on Instructional Improvement, Growth, Theory Y Supervision	Instructor	Instructor	Instructor	Instructor	Instructor
	Instructor	Instructor	Instructor	Instructor	Administrator
	Administrator	Instructor	Instructor	Instructor	Instructor
Focus on Fitting Teachers Into Jobs, Weeding Out the Bad, Spurring Instructional Improvement Through Threats, Theory X Supervision	Instructor	Instructor	Instructor	Administrator	Instructor
	Administrator	Instructor	Instructor	Administrator	Administrator
	Administrator	Administrator	Instructor	Administrator	Administrator
	Administrator	Administrator	Administrator	Administrator	Administrator

*We like to put together charts like this to show the range of decision making possible. There are no absolutely correct positions for the supervision/teacher. We only know that the highest level of teacher involvement possible consistent with teacher/supervisor maturity, content knowledge and supervisory experience is the desirable process for maximum teacher growth.

The teacher should, as much as possible, perform or be part of performing, every step in the evaluation process. The two purposes of the evaluation of teaching are to improve the quality or amount of valued outcomes in students and to enable faculty to be successful and fulfilled. Both can be satisfied by involving the teachers; both may be thwarted when the evaluation is laid on teachers by an administrator or quasi-administrative group.

2. What criteria will be measured?

The criteria for the evaluation of teaching may be implicit or explicit. When explicit, they are written for all to see. EXAMPLE: From the faculty handbook, "One indication of teaching excellence is that the teacher attend at least 8 voluntary inservice programs on the improvement of teaching each year. A good teacher attends at least 6. A fair teacher attends at least 4. A poor teacher attends none or only one or two."

When implicit, the criteria are hidden in someone's mind. EXAMPLE: Supervisor Jean speaks, "I feel that your attendance at only 4 of the inservice programs this year shows a lack of interest in improving teaching, so in that area I would give you a poor rating." This evaluator has standards for making the evaluation, but the standards are vague and hidden, probably even from her. Because they are vague and subjective, they may change from person to person. EXAMPLE: Supervisor Jean speaks again, "Frank, you attended 4 of the inservice programs this year but I rated you as a good teacher because I know you really got involved in the ones you attended." When the supervisor makes the evaluation, and makes it using implicit criteria, the supervisee may see the evaluation as arbitrary and personal, resulting in a feeling of being unfairly treated. Animosity results. Energy used in animosity is not available for growth and development.

The decisions about criteria for an evaluation of teaching will be determined in part by the purposes for the evaluation. You may have reacted badly or well to our decision to use the inservice programs example to illustrate criteria for evaluating teaching. If your purpose in the evaluation is to measure interest in improving teaching, or to measure obedience to your commands, you may have reacted favorably to the inservice attendance criteria; if your purpose in evaluating teaching is to ensure that teachers are running a tight ship in the classroom, you may have had little interest in the number of inservice programs attended (but may have a considerable interest when the inservice program is about discipline in the classroom). All of these are implicit purposes. They must be discussed by the teachers and others involved in the evaluation so that they become explicit purposes that can be adopted, amended, or discarded. Again, we emphasize that the sole ultimate purpose of the evaluation of teaching must be to improve outcomes in students and aid the teacher to feel fulfilled and successful.

You will wish to use as criteria the actual outcomes in students when possible: learning of knowledge, skills, procedures, independence, self-direction, cooperative behavior, favorable attitudes, etc. All other measures commonly used are measures of teaching performance, which may not be clearly related to outcomes in students. They are akin to evaluating a sculptor by observing his sculpturing technique without ever looking at the resulting piece of art. He may have great technique, but produce wretched art objects; or, may have a sloppy, freewheeling technique that produces surprisingly valid art objects. Added to this problem is the fact that a rating of the sculptor or teacher's technique likely will be considerably biased by the preferences of the rater. Measuring the outcomes of the effort results in greater objectivity and focuses the energy available for evaluation on the right factors.

But as of yet, little satisfactory progress has been made in discovering efficient, economical ways of measuring outcomes in students for the evaluation of teaching; and there is always the danger of the Texarkana syndrome—teaching to the test. In the absence of satisfactory methods of measuring outcomes in students, we are left with measuring attributes of performance that possibly or likely will result in the desired outcomes.

A number of studies have been performed in an attempt to isolate the characteristics of the "ideal" teacher (Berliner and Tikunoff, 1976; Rosenshine, 1976; Rosenshine and Furst, 1976; and Ryans, 1960). Briefly, their findings can be summarized in the following categories:

1. INTERPERSONAL ATTRIBUTES (warmth, understanding, positive relationships, rapport, accepting student ideas, actively listening)

2. ORGANIZATION (planning, organization, structure, task orientation, explaining the purposes of instruction)

3. DISCIPLINE (maintaining control, following through with directions or threat)

4. INVOLVING STUDENTS (obtaining student involvement in learning, asking questions, acknowledging student ideas, encouraging students to answer questions)

5. SHOWING CONCERN FOR STUDENTS (accepting feelings, enhancing self-concept, praising students, dealing with student emotions)

6. BEING ENTERTAINING (being enthusiastic, interesting, stimulating)

Other attributes are less clearly classified with one another:

being clear when presenting instructional content
creating a favorable environment for learning
enjoying working with students
being creative and innovative
emphasizing teaching reading
engaging in professional growth activities
using a variety of instructional techniques

knowing the subject
being flexible
being consistent
being fair
providing opportunities for students to learn content
assigning seatwork
organizing students into small groups
giving students choices of activities
reinforcing student responses
asking new questions after a student has given a correct answer
giving a correct answer after a student has given the wrong answer

We suggest that certain general areas of teaching performance are more necessary to helping students learn than other general areas, using learning psychology as the source for our suggestions:

1. Instructions are sufficiently clear that students can successfully follow them.

2. Media (books, lectures, films, etc. as well as the teacher's speaking voice and nonverbal habits) are sufficiently clear that students can successfully learn from them.

3. Teaching is organized in some logical sequence that will result in learning; class sessions are planned and organized to result in learning.

4. The content of instruction is at temporal, qualitative, conceptual and complexity levels that students of this age level on the average can successfully learn in the allotted time.

5. Sufficient opportunities for practice and learning activities that will result in the desired learning are included in the instruction.

6. Sufficient opportunities for appropriate evaluation and feedback about the quality of learning are included in the instruction so that students can learn from the instruction.

7. The instruction prepares students for learning and motivates them to learn.

8. The learning environment is such that most students will be encouraged to learn.

This list of general areas, then, would have to be refined into a set of specific, observable criteria that could be measured. It omits such important considerations as whether the instruction is fostering favorable attitudes toward learning, independence, cooperation, self-direction, and so forth. These must be added by the teacher or district that values these outcomes in students.

The following are not clearly related to learning:

The teacher

    uses innovative techniques
    is on time for classes
    is well dressed
    conducts group discussions often
    is well liked by students (study findings are mixed)
    is entertaining (study findings are mixed)
    uses A.V. aids
    is published in the field
    attends inservice workshops

These lists of attributes of good teaching, it must be emphasized, are attributes of performance, and as such do not guarantee that students are learning. They are also so general that the teacher may have difficulty interpreting their meaning, measuring their presence, and improving instruction based upon the results. Evaluators similarly may have conceptions of such general statements that differ from the conceptions held by the teacher and other evaluators.

We emphasize the need to use descriptions of attributes that can be measured and whose meaning will be agreed upon by the teacher and evaluators. The sequence of statements below illustrates how differing interpretations may arise when evaluations are made using different levels of generality in supervision statements. As the specificity increases, the range of interpretation decreases.

General Statement	Alternative Interpretations
The teacher creates a learning environment that encourages learning	1. encourages students to speak 2. keeps students quiet 3. lets students be free and active 4. maintains order and discipline 5. presents clear lectures 6. makes use of group discussion 7. is informal and chatty 8. is formal and professional etc.

More Specific

The teacher encourages students to speak	1. calls on students in class 2. accepts student response 3. praises correct responses 4. redirects student questions to other students.

Measurable

The teacher calls on students in class	1. calls on students in class

If the criteria are very general, the teacher and evaluators will fill in their own implicit, more specific criteria and evaluate the teaching using them. As a result, they will not use the same criteria, and may not view the results in the same way. The teacher may have concentrated on improving the learning environment by keeping students quiet; the evaluator may believe that improving the learning environment means encouraging students to be active and free to speak; the resulting poor evaluation comes as a shock to the teacher, and animosity and decreasing interest in improving instruction results. Teachers in general will likely come to view the evaluation process as threatening, punitive and arbitrary.

The process of specifying the criteria for the evaluation of teaching so that evaluators and teachers agree on the meanings necessitates teacher involvement in the process. It also necessitates clarity of meaning and explicit criteria and processes for making judgments.

3. How will the criteria be measured?

This is perhaps the most controversial question in the evaluation of teaching, not because it is the most important consideration, but because this question has such strong affect attached to it by teachers who are being evaluated. Student rating forms and administrator "pop-observations" are widely used methods of measuring teaching performance. Each has severe limitations although both can provide some useful data.

Rating Forms

The forms used in the measurement of teaching attributes are usually "rating" forms, asking someone to make evaluative judgments about the teaching using *implicit* criteria. The following items are taken from actual evaluation forms:

How would you rate this teacher in comparison to others?
This teacher encouraged me to learn.
Strongly Agree   Agree   Disagree   Strongly Disagree

Because the items are vague and abstract, the rater must read into them his implicit criteria. The result is a "halo" effect on such forms. A teacher liked by a student or peer-evaluator will generally be rated high on any item, while a teacher not liked will be generally rated low. We would expect to see both strengths (higher scores for some items) and weaknesses (lower scores for some items) if the form were an objective assessment of teaching ability.

Such rating forms should be replaced by measurement of feedback forms that ask concrete questions not requiring or permitting such evaluations. The items should ask the rater for either:
1) Personal states and feelings, or
2) Objective observations
Each of these types of data should be clearly identified and separated

on the rating form used. The following items illustrate Category I: Personal states and feelings. Items like these if given to a range of students can provide a profile of student reactions to this teacher.

I was confused during classes.
Never   At Times   Often   Very Often
The instructor belittled me.
Never   At Times   Often   Very Often

You and the instructor, or a committee, can then use the resulting data to make an evaluation. The teacher's evaluation should always accompany the data. Of course the evaluation should then result in some decisions.

Each person asked to supply data about a teacher's teaching should be asked to supply data he is qualified to submit. It is inappropriate to ask students to judge the teacher's knowledge of the field; whether the teacher is knowledgeable in the field is an administrative problem. Judgments of content knowledge and appropriate selection should be made by peers or knowledgeable supervisors. Colleagues and administrators, who have a detailed resume before them and have discussed the field with the teacher can assess whether the teacher is qualified to teach the course.

Other Measures of Teaching

Certain of the attributes of teaching should be measured outside of the classroom:

1. Organization of the course (evident in plans and syllabi)

2. Appropriateness of evaluation methods (evident in tests given when compared to content emphasized in teaching setting)

3. Clarity of media other than those involved in interacting with students (such as films and books)

4. Content appropriateness for this level of student

5. Provision of opportunities for practice and feedback (evident in class activities planned, homework assignments, and so forth)

Gathering data in the classroom and providing some permanent record of it is difficult. Our data units suggest ways you can improve the reliability and range of data you know how to collect. Other data should be gathered from sources mentioned above. These other data may assist the evaluator in reaching judgments which are defensible and which isolate causative factors.

Again, teachers should be involved in determining how the attributes will be measured, and likely should have any forms used so that they can use them to improve their own instruction as the year progresses. Teachers should be systematically helped to become evaluators of their own teaching. In this way they become more able to control their own success in teaching.

Formats for Formulating Criteria

At least four formats for deriving criteria and using the criteria in the evaluation of teaching are being used in schools:

1. Teachers formulate their own lists of criteria of teaching, then enlist the help of the supervisor, district, or colleagues to measure proficiency and judge whether to improve the proficiency in any area.

2. Criteria of teaching performance valued by the district (or school) are listed for use by the teachers. The teachers arrange to have measurements of the attributes made in their own teaching, then work with the supervisor or colleagues to improve their instruction in areas they wish to work on or where deficiencies have been noted.

3. A small number of criteria of teaching with levels of proficiency are used as a basis for teaching evaluation at periodic intervals. Teachers and/or departments may add to the core any criteria they wish. Results of the data gathering for the core are voluntarily or by requirement submitted to the evaluators. Results of any added criteria are voluntarily or by requirement submitted as well.

4. A list of criteria of teaching is established for the district or school and all teachers are evaluated based upon it.

There are, of course, other designs used; the foremost of these is the common design in which the most general areas of teaching competence are listed on a rating form used by the supervisor or principal to evaluate teachers.

We favor #1 and #2 over the rest, but with the realities of most school districts assume that #3 will be the most optimal to ensure both a fair evaluation that involves teachers, and an evaluation that satisfies those wishing to hold educators accountable. However, none of these general procedures is even acceptable unless these criteria are based on the rapidly accumulating research base about what constitutes effective teaching for what purposes, under what conditions and with which types of students.

How the Data are Gathered

Any evaluation of teaching for personnel decisions should involve gathering data from as many sources as possible. A single administrator's observations used alone without supporting data from other sources is an inadequate evaluation.

In the ideal situation, the teacher is responsible for compiling and submitting data for the evaluation. The teacher arranges for having measurement forms distributed, arranges to have the materials given to those measuring attributes in them, arranges when administrators or colleagues will enter the classroom and what they will be looking for, summarizes and explains the resulting data, and submits all data and interpretations in a readable package to those responsible for the evaluation. In real settings a jointly managed evaluation is most likely to be useful and possible.

Timing for Gathering Data

New faculty or faculty being considered for promotion and tenure should be evaluated early in their careers so that they have the opportunity to use the resulting data to improve their teaching in preparation for the later, final evaluation. The early evaluation also encourages dialogue between the teacher and students. Students will value the evaluation and the school's interest in their learning if they see that the evaluation makes a difference. When evaluations are given at the end of the year, as is customary, students never see the results of their time and effort in submitting data about the teacher's teaching. The data collected then only makes a case. They are not helpful in improving instruction.

Organization of the course, tests to be used, books chosen, and other instructional decisions should be evaluated prior to the teaching so that changes can be made before students experience difficulties in these areas.

4. What levels of competence will be used in the evaluation?

An evaluation requires judgments that are never entirely objective. How good is good? The criteria must be made explicit, however, and remain consistent unless all involved agree to change them. Even the instructor working to improve his own teaching using a measurement and his own evaluation should learn that explicit, clear, measurable criteria are necessary to improve teaching and enjoy the resulting success. When you are helping an instructor to improve her teaching, you will similarly wish to ensure that you have agreed upon the level of proficiency expected during the improvement process.

Because the evaluation of teaching competence is so elusive and imprecise, it is recommended that you make only the grossest distinctions about teaching competence when evaluating for personnel decisions. The two designations "satisfactory" and "unsatisfactory" would be fine, although the addition of "unusual" or "meritorious" might give the exceptional teacher a necessary pat on the back.

We recommend strongly, however, that you avoid having a number of levels of competence, such as this design:

Level
1 Meritorous
2. Excellent
3. Very good

4. Good
5. Average
6. Below Average
7. Fair
8. Poor
9. Unsatisfactory

An evaluation of teaching design in which numbers are used to compare teachers results in similar or worse difficulties. An instructor with a score of 74 out of 100 is not better than an instructor with a score of 68. It may be equally true that an instructor with a composite score of 53 may be quite as effective in helping students learn as an instructor with a score of 76—we can't make judgments about these scores in the middle range.

However, when the average score is 50, and extreme scores are 89 and 16, we can make distinctions between the score of 89 and 16, and some other scores at either end of the scale. You are advised to make only these gross distinctions among teachers, placing the remainder in an average or satisfactory category.

5. What will be the consequences of the judgment?

The data gathered in the process should be used only for the purposes agreed upon by the teacher. In other words, if they are gathered so that the supervisor and teacher can use them to improve teaching, they should not be submitted for personnel decisions unless the teacher agrees to do so.

The ground rules decided upon prior to the evaluation must be carried through the evaluation, as though it were a contract. Altering them is unethical, and will likely result in hostility.

Scores resulting from an evaluation of teaching for personnel decisions should not be used to make fine distinctions among teachers. The tools are too imprecise to do so.

The resulting data should be seen by the teacher before being submitted to an evaluation committee. The evaluation should be available to the instructor soon after being made, and some appeal procedure should be in place. If the instructor is in danger of not receiving a continuation of contract, or not receiving promotion or tenure, some process should be in place by which the instructor can have a second evaluation, and even possibly a third. Hence, the need for an early evaluation when personnel decisions are made.

No evaluation of teaching for personnel decisions should occur without some provisions for helping the teacher improve his teaching competence. Otherwise, the evaluation becomes merely punitive.

UNITS IN THIS BOOK

The units in this book, designed to help you become a more competent supervisor, will aid you in this difficult process of combining instructional improvement with the evaluation of teaching. You have read Unit I, that gives you a framework for thinking about your relationship with the supervisee, and Unit II, that focuses on the need to work with facts and to be cautious about inferences. Their generalizations apply to the evaluation of teaching as well.

Units IV, V and VI will help you identify some of the biases you and the supervisees may hold that will affect the evaluation process and the judgments made about teaching. They will also suggest ways in which you can avoid the hostility and problems that arise from the values we hold that may bias our judgments about teaching competence.

Units VII, VIII, IX and X follow through with the previous consideration of values and biases by showing you how you can interact with supervisees to help them improve instruction while maintaining a productive, satisfying relationship. Those units are particularly important in preparing you for the evaluation of teaching because your interpersonal style will have a considerable effect upon whether the evaluation becomes aversive or whether it is a satisfying experience.

Finally, the remaining Units, in the "Individual Supervisory and Managing Skills" section, present specific, practical methods of working with teachers, holding conferences, gathering data, and analyzing the results of the data, all of which are necessary as you work with teachers to help them gain a perspective on their teaching through measurement and evaluation.

Interaction
Skills

Unit 4

The Me-ness of Supervision

Before reading this unit in detail, complete the following statements. Save the set of responses until we ask you to look at it. Just react to the statements without worrying about what we want. We want what you put.

Survey of Your Reactions

1. Teachers' dress should be _____

_____

_____

2. Students' dress should be _____

_____

_____

3. A good student is _____

_____

_____

4. A bad student is _____

_____

_____

5. The single most useful instructional technique is _____

_____

_____

6. Behavioral objectives_____

_____

_____

7. An effective principal _____

_____

_____

8. The school board's role is_____

_____

_____

Content of the Unit

This unit is designed to help you become more conscious of the values you and those you supervise hold. Your values most certainly are exerting an effect on the issues you raise, the ways you interact, and the data you collect. Probably you are unconscious of the effects of your values on your behavior and on the ways you are perceived. In one way this unit is a special way of looking at the data-inference questions we raised in Unit II. You may locate here some of the sources of your inferences.

Competencies in this Unit

When you have finished this unit you should be able to:

1. identify value statements you make while interacting with others,

2. identify ways you behave which imply values you hold,

3. correctly categorize the value statements you make,

4. list several specific values you hold of which you were not previously conscious.

Method of Demonstrating Attainment of the Competencies

You will demonstrate these competencies to yourself by logically extending and analyzing your own statements.

You will demonstrate the last competence to yourself by making a list of those values of which you were not aware but are now conscious.

Our Rationale for the Specific Competencies of This Unit

Each of us is a collection of deep-seated values embodying his conception of the world. The uniqueness of that collection of values makes the differences between individuals. Few of us realize the extent to which our conception of reality—the sum of our values—affects what we do. Values, however, are evident in preferences for particular clothes, food, sexual partners, religion, time for getting up in the day, side of a coat buttoned over the other side, choice of drink at breakfast, and the whole universe of other things we choose. Each choice represents a value.

Since every person's set of values differs from every other person's, there exists the necessity of value differences and potential value conflicts between supervisor and supervisee. These may be as unimportant as whether to place coasters under the water glasses at a conference, but they may be quite important, as in the following incident:

Act I Scene II: Teacher, Ed and supervisor, Marie

Ed: *I would like to give a lecture Tuesday on parts of the frog.*

Marie: *Well, don't you think a group activity examining a frog would be more interesting and effective?*

Ed: *No. It's better that they get the information correctly. It is easier to learn it right the first time than to catch mistakes and unlearn them. I'll lecture. Besides, there is too much information involved and I have only one period to give it to them before the dissection lab.*

Marie: *But, you are discussing what you want to do. The students' feelings about what they are learning are as important as the facts you are telling them.*

Ed: *The students will only get out of this class as much as I put into it. I'm the one who has studied biology for six years in college. I know the field, they don't. I'm the best person to decide how they should best learn the ideas in my field.*

If we characterized the set of values in the conversation above as a canopy of stained glass panes floating above each of the actors, the conversation might sound like the following:

Ed: *I would like to use my red pane Tuesday to teach parts of the frog.*

Marie: *Well, don't you think that my chartruese would be more interesting and effective?*

Ed: *No. It's better that they get the information correctly. It's easier to learn it right the first time than to catch mistakes and unlearn them. I'll use red.*

Marie: *But you are discussing what YOU want to do. If you would only open your eyes to the students' feelings, it is obvious that chartruese is the only really effective method.*

Ed: *My vision is perfectly good and red is the only real color; chartruese is obviously wrong.*

For various reasons, the value "red" has come to color Ed's view of the situation. He has looked through that pane of the canopy so long that he thinks that the situation is really "red." For him it is. The supervisor's view is also colored, only her pane is chartruese. The situation might be even worse if both looked through a pastel blue pane and never even discovered that there are other colors.

People, all of us, have a tendency to regard our views of the world, our canopy of colors, as "right." If another person says, "you shouldn't have done that! what you should have done is . . . ," they are asserting that what *they* value is more "correct" than what the other person valued. In a supervisory situation, where one person usually has more authority than the other, the stated value judgments of the person with the greater authority tend to become the way things are overtly done in this situation. If you value the supervisee's conceptualization and tasks, then it will help if you know and label your own values. Knowing and labelling your own values may also help you accept the different values of others and discuss values in terms other than right and wrong, should and shouldn't.

We also suggest that values are similar to inferences—sometimes based on fact, but sometimes not. Since this is true, there is a need to collect data to discover whether our values are probably true and should therefore influence our actions; possibly true and need to be checked out; or only true for us and therefore need to be advocated with care. We are thus suggesting that words more appropriate for supervisors than right and wrong are words such as "cause," "effect," "data" and "analysis." What can then follow is this statement to the supervisee: "If you value that action, then how will you behave? What will be the effect on your students if you behave that way?"

Act III Scene I (after enlightenment)

Ed: *I would like to use red Tuesday to teach parts of the frog.*

Marie: *My bias has always been that chartruese is better, but I have little data to support it. What do you have on red?*

Ed: *I have always used red, and I like it, but I don't have any real proof that it is better than chartruese.*

Marie: *Would you be willing to try both red and chartruese and we'll set up some ways of comparing to discover which seems to work better for whom? We could also see what problems we have in using either red or chartruese.*

Detecting, Defining and Categorizing
Your Value Statements and Behaviors

A. One way to detect your own value statements (or detect others') is to expose yourself to choices. You will choose an activity, color, teaching method that you value more than you value other choices. After choosing, examine the basis for the choice you make.

B. A second way to detect your own value choices is to listen to others' choices of actions or ways of doing things, then think about the choice you would have made in the same situation. If your choice is incompatible with theirs ("How could they consider doing *that?*") then you have a different value, just as your response to the possibility of buying a ranch-style home.

C. A third way to detect your value choices is to live in another culure for a period of months or years (This is the choice we recommend, but wait until you have finished the training program). This opportunity which comes to a few of us, lets us find that very basic values we hold are not the same elsewhere—things like a sense of time, the role of a teacher, purposes of education, the marks of an educated person, what supervision is, and what a curriculum is. All are things we tend to share as values in our culture, but, these basic agreements are not factual givens; they are cultural norms or values.

Some Categories and Definitions

The supervisee will probably more easily allow criticism of the inference than of the value. It may be possible, over a long period of time, with considerable presentation of data, to get a supervisee to reconsider a basic value, but the reconsideration will be the end of a long process of toe-dipping and mental restructuring to avoid cognitive dissonance. You would be well off not to wait dinner while the supervisee changes. Even that slow process will not result if: 1) the supervisee is backed into defending the value as part of himself by supervisor demands and coercion, 2) sufficient, valid data are not presented to help the supervisee make alterations of the value.

We suggest that in your professional supervision, values, like inferences, are most useful if they are based on available facts, data, or evidence, and if they are explicitly identified as values by the supervisor and supervisee. Any other strategy, such as trying to force acceptance of your value by using your authority, seems likely to run into heavy resistance and be ineffective.

Judgment

The use of judgments (which we identified in Unit II) is one way you express your values or criticize others' values. The following are judgmental statements:

"What you did was chartruese (right, beautiful, terrific, good)."

"What you did was day-glo-green (wrong, sinful, ugly, terrible)."

They can be reworked to identify them as value statements.

"Chartruese was or was not congruent with my own values."

"Day-glo-green is something I have always valued, but I don't really know its effectiveness."

Owning

Besides the fact that judgmental words convey little information other than, "I felt plus (or minus) about that," they disguise the personal nature of the value under the words "right" and "wrong." Our own prejudices become invested with some moral nature, especially if we have some form of authority, such as in the supervisory relationship.

One way out of this dilemma is to use the vocabulary of owning values:

"my bias about this is...."

"I value...."

"I have always had an intuitive preference for ...."

If you learn to value it, you can learn to use this and similar vocabulary, and can learn to hear yourself and others owning or not owning value statements.

The continuum on the following page may help you see where you and others are in some value statements.

Activity I Part I

Identify whether each of the following statements indicates that the value is viewed as (1) *personally owned* or *not owned*; (2) *tentative* or *right* by the person stating it. Also indicate, in the space to the right, whether you believe valid data is needed before the value statement can be the basis for action. Answers are on page 74.

Owned?		Tentative?			Data Needed?	
Yes	No	Yes	No		Yes	No
				1. I value the use of a tape recorder because of the indications in learning psychology that imitation has an effect on much learning.		
				2. Drill is the most effective way of teaching spelling.		
				3. I value the use of drill in teaching spelling		
				4. You should not reprimand a child in front of her/his peers.		

Vocabulary in Valuing: A Continuum

I Recognize This as a Value

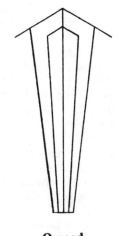

Owned

* Owning—giving specific conditions and data.

  I value frummaging because it is effective in the specific circumstances mentioned as indicated by the following three studies . . .

* Owning and giving data

  I have always valued frummaging because of the indications in studies in my own teaching.

* Owning only

  I value frummaging.

  Expressing as an emotion.

  I like frummaging.

Not Owned

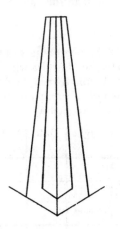

I Permit No Other Personal Values

I Regard This as a Fact or Moral Dictum

* No data, no owning

  Frummaging is an effective method.

* Qualified judgment

  You probably should frummage.

* Judgment

  Frummaging is right; you should frummage.

* Command

  You will frummage because it is right.

Our Categorization of Each of the Statements on Page 72

1. This is an owned statement of value viewed tentatively by the owner. Some general data are hinted at, but more specific data seem necessary to be convincing.

2. This is not owned and is regarded as right by the speaker. Certainly, data are needed to make this value more convincing to supervisees. This value statement should be regarded as personal and tentative without such evidence.

3. This is regarded by the speaker as personal and tentative. It is owned. It needs data to indicate whether it is valid enough to be acted upon.

4. This is regarded as not owned, right and factual by the speaker. While it may be true, it must be owned as a value and there must be data accompanying it to indicate whether it should be considered as the basis for actions.

If you didn't get all of these correct, discuss the categories and examples with a friend or trustworthy colleague. Then move on.

Enough examples for the moment. Once you see a couple of statements like these and know why they are judged by us as they are, you quickly and correctly begin to categorize them. Remember, we are neither denying nor affirming the truth of any one of these statements. They may all be true. However, as stated they are only unarguable dictums supported by little data.

Now we are going to raise the level of the bar and ask you to categorize the statements you made earlier before you read this unit or worked in it.

Activity I Part II

Turn back to the survey you filled out at the beginning of this unit. Examine your responses. Indicate, as you did in Part I, whether you stated each response as personally owned or not owned; tentative or right. Also decide whether data are needed to accompany the value statements. Categorize these statements in the chart below.

Statement Number	Personally Owned	Not Owned	Tentative	Right	Data Needed? Yes	No
1						
2						
3						
4						
5						
6						
7						
8						

Those statements represented the way you expressed yourself before you read the unit. How much better are you after the instruction?

Now we are going to ask you to sort out the actual values underlying the statements you made in the survey. For instance, if you wrote that teachers should dress the way they please, you are saying that you value teachers making their own decisions from their own taste on such questions, and that their dress is no one's business but their own, aren't you?

A. Write, in a paragraph below, the actual values you feel underlie the statements you made in that survey.
   (If you have time, complete part B of this activity).

B. Then have a colleague look at your survey and write out in his own paragraph (without seeing yours) what he sees as your values. Compare the two paragraphs. Are you seeing your values relatively accurately?—i.e., as another tended to see them.
   Your paragraph goes here.

_____

_____

_____

_____

How many of your value statements were owned? _____

How many of your value statements were tentative? _____

How many of your value statements had enough data attached? _____

_____

_____

_____

At this point what are you thinking should be changed in your supervisory behavior? _____

_____

_____

_____

If you can't think of any changes you might be planning for your behavior in your supervisory roles, are you sure this is the right training program for you?

Well, on to Activity II.

Activity II

This activity works at the same ideas we worried over in Activity I, but it goes at them differently. Don't take too much time with this activity since it introduces nothing new.

A. Write in about 100 words your description of the *behavior* of an

"ideal teacher."_____

_____

_____

_____

_____

_____

B. Identify below the values you hold that somehow have become a concept of ideal teaching.

1. _____

_____

2. _____

_____

3. _____

_____

4. _____

_____

5. _____

_____

C. On what factors are your good teacher characteristics, based?

Moral judgments? _____

Styles of dress? _____

Community standards?_____

Learning data from students? ____

The superintendent's values? ____

Similarity to your own values? __

Now that you are able to recognize some of your value statements, the time has come for you to do some serious introspection about some of your behaviors which imply value statements.

Your purpose as a supervisor is to make of yourself an instrument useful to others in their professional skill development. You become this instrument while fulfilling your own needs at the same time. Are there other reasons for being a supervisor?

Vocabulary and Relationship
See if you can identify values in the vocabulary of these interactions.

Episode 1:

Supervisor: Hi, Barb.

Supervisee: Good afternoon, Dr. Downes.

Episode 2:

Supervisor: Well, how did this conference go?

Supervisee: I certainly am glad we had this conference; you've pointed out all the things I've done wrong, and I now have your ideas on what I can do to correct those mistakes.

Episode 3:

Supervisee: Just everything is wrong, the kids refuse to do the work I suggest. They complain when I make them read the books over again. They score very low on tests I give them. They don't seem motivated with learning.

Supervisor: You've suggested several different issues here. Let's see if we can work on these one at a time. Now which of these is most important, and can we explore what you really mean by what you say. We have to carefully define what is happening in the situation and then decide what it really means before we move to solutions.

Episode 4:

Supervisee: *John*, I have run into something I don't understand with a couple of my students. They seem to be hostile to others and to me. I have talked to them, but I think it may be something happening in class. Can you come in and observe soon to give me some feedback?

Supervisor: Sure. When and what specifically would you like me to look for?

Episode 5 :

Supervisor: Here is the data I have collected on your class. The strongest pattern it shows is your questioning—85% of your questions in this class were either recognition or recall. The rest are at the application level.

Supervisee: Should I change that ratio?

Supervisor: Yes, in this type of class it should be at least 50% application or higher.

In each of the above episodes the supervisor and the supervisee chose to use certain words. Each made selected responses to the other. The choice of words is at least partially dependent on some of the following factors:

1. Perceived role of self.
2. Perceived role of the other.
3. The degree of autonomy and responsibility desired or perceived.
4. Reactions to the setting.

All four of these factors are related to some values position. Our episodes, because they are written, do not allow you to consider the elements of communication outside of the actual words spoken. While these non-verbal or para-language elements in the communications may be even more important than the actual dialogue, we cannot consider those elements here because we have no readily understandable code which will carry messages about tone of voice, inflection, affect, etc.

If you begin to take this process seriously, you may get into the insoluble maze of, "Does his perception of my perception of him include a perception that my behaving is intended to produce a perception exactly like his present perception?"* However, without going to excess, and as a way of illustrating our point, we are going to take each of the episodes with which we began this section and spin some of the analysis suggested to us** by the dialogue. We repeat each episode so you can avoid shuffling back and forth in this unit.

* If you really want to get deeply involved in thinking about relationships, read R.D. Laing's *Knots*. We practically guarantee blowing your mind away.

** In no way are we implying that these are the only possible interpretations of these episodes. They merely seem likely to us.

Episode 1:

Supervisor: Hi, Barb.

Supervisee: Good afternoon, Dr. Downes.

Analysis: Supervisor uses first name and informal greeting.
Supervisee uses formal greeting and surname with title.

Possible Inferences and Relationships:

The supervisee perceives the supervisor as higher in status and the relationship as formal The supervisor is either trying to be friendly to reduce perceived status differences, or is using the power of his office to use the first name and to reinforce his dominance in the role of supervisor.

Supervisor may be perceived in a different age grouping, or may wear a different style of clothing than the supervisee. These physical factors may tend to reinforce either's perception of the relationship.

Episode 2:

Supervisor: Well, how did this conference go?

Supervisee: I certainly am glad we had this conference; you've pointed out all the things I've done wrong, and I now have your ideas on what I can do to correct those mistakes.

Analysis: Supervisor asks supervisee's perceptions.
Supervisee states perceptions in an extended fashion and suggests comfortableness with the results and relationship.

Possible Inferences and Relationships:

One inference we see is that the supervisor is interested in the supervisee's perceptions of the conference. The depth of interest is not clear, but the supervisee apparently takes the question seriously enough to give an extended and specific answer. The supervisee also appears to accept the supervisor as one who identifies weaknesses or errors, and who subsequently suggests ways to correct these errors. The supervisee appears to accept his role, and to be reinforcing the supervisor for carrying it out in this episode. The supervisee may have learned this perception of their roles from present interactions or past interactions with other supervisors. This shared role perception appears to be reinforced by the joint behaviors of the two people involved. In many ways this relationship may be comfortable for both parties in it. The supervisor's feelings of being useful, of coming up with answers, of power, of competence and of respect from others can all be reinforced in this relationship. The supervisee's lack of responsibility for identifying or changing his own behavior is supported. There can be a real comfort in knowing someone else is going to solve the problems and be responsible if they are not solved.

Episode 3:

Supervisee: Just everything is wrong, the kids refuse to do the work I suggest. They complain when I make them read the books over again. They score very low on tests I give them. They don't seem motivated with learning.

Supervisor: You've suggested several different issues here. Let's see if we can work on these one at a time. Now which of these is most important, and can we explore what you really mean by what you say. We have to carefully define what is happening in the situation and then decide what it really means before we move to solutions.

Analysis: The supervisee is (1) suggesting a strong affect, (2) identifying several problems, and (3) locating the blame outside his own responsibility. The supervisor appears to be trying to separate the problems, get the supervisee to accept some responsibility by choosing what is most important, and finally, establish a strategy for dealing with the situations. She also appears to be trying to elicit data about behavior rather than inferences drawn from unrelated data.

Possible Inferences and Relationships:

Some of our statements contain inferences. We both recognize this. The supervisee appears to have shifted responsibility for the situation to the students, divesting himself of the responsibility for doing something about this situation by unloading it on the supervisor. Consider what would happen to the relationship and the setting if the supervisor's response to the supervisee had been, "You poor man; can I help by getting some of the worst troublemakers out of there?" At this point, the supervisor would have been accepting the supervisee's interpretation of causes without any other data, and would then have begun to give sympathy and support for this non-responsibility of the supervisee in the situation. The supervisor's action was a middle ground between attacking the supervisee and accepting his perception of the world. She asked the supervisee to accept some responsibility for what is happening by picking out his most important problem, and by asking for data which clearly defines the situation. This position does not offer personal support, but does promise a strategy for beginning to seek solutions. The perception of the supervisor about her role seems to differ from the expectations of the supervisee. These differences must eventually be resolved if the relationship is to become a helping one.

Episode 4

Supervisee: *John.* I have run into something I don't understand with a couple of my students. They seem to be hostile to others and to me. I have talked to them, but I think it may be something happening in class. Can you come in and observe soon to give me some feedback?

Supervisor: Sure. When and what specifically would you like me to look for?

Analysis: This supervisee defines a problem, suggests how she feels about it, describes what she has tried, and asks for specific help in solving a problem which she presently cannot handle by herself.

The supervisor responds to the supervisee in the terms asked for and moves immediately to specifics and begins to negotiate times and foci.

Possible Inferences and Relationships: This supervisee asked for help; she saw the supervisor as a source of data she could use to generate her own solutions. She sees her supervisor as a person capable of providing the quality and quantity of help desired. This suggests a perception of self-responsibility for solutions and a degree of autonomy and status equivalent to the supervisor's.

The supervisor accepts this role and reinforces it by committing himself to acting on the request and moving in at the earliest time desired by the supervisee. He is using a conceptual frame congruent with Argyris' three intervention tasks by preserving and enhancing the client's sense of autonomy and control.

There is an apparent shared value of autonomy and supervisee initiative.

Episode 5:

Supervisor: Here is the data I have collected on your class. The strongest pattern it shows is your questioning—85% of your questions in this class were either recognition or recall. The rest are at the application level.

Supervisee: Should I change that ratio?

Supervisor: Yes, in this type of class it should be at least 50% application or higher.

Analysis — Possible Inferences and Relationships:

Write or think about your own analysis and inferences about relationships and values if this pattern of interaction continues. Then decide whether it is useful or growth-encouraging for either party in the relationship.

Other Me-nesses

The three dimensions of personality we discuss here seem to be valuing complexes which energize each of us to act as we do.

Dimension one: Task Orientation.

Some people are very much interested in accomplishing their tasks. If this factor predominates in your behavior, we would call you a task-oriented person. Task-oriented people often say things such as, "Let's quit wasting time,and get down to business" or "enough of this digression, let's get back to work," or "why are we wasting all this time talking about how we feel; let's just keep personalities out of this and get the job done." You would probably like your administrative assistant or executive secretary to be task-oriented. This person might not be fun to be with, but he would get jobs done, on time and completely. There must be a bit of compulsiveness associated with this type of person.

While you might like your secretary to be task-oriented, your receptionist needs other dominant characteristics to facilitate greeting the public. If you find that accomplishing the task is more important to you than either maintaining satisfactory relationships with others, or acquiring and exercising power, then you may need to understand that the task-oriented values you hold are very personal and idiosyncratic. Imposing task-oriented behavior demands on others who are less task-oriented may be counter-productive as they rebel. Understanding your task-oriented values may help you be more tolerant of others.

Dimension two: Affiliation.

Some people are very much interested in establishing relationships that may not have any special purposes except mutual enjoyment. They talk a lot about their feelings, and it is important for them to like the persons with whom they work. Relationship-dominant people tend to live in a world where their actions and reactions are dominated by their feelings about the persons around them.

"I will do something for someone if I like them and not do something else because I don't like the person who will benefit from completion of that task."

While not totally conscious of this reasoning, many relationship-dominant people act very consistently with it. Deadlines for tasks may not be very important to this person if those deadlines interfere with the relationships he values.

In no way are we putting this person down. Our society does not monetarily reward this kind of person very often, but you often want to be in their company in social situations. They are the glue that holds social situations together. A counselor, therapist or friend you seek out may be relationship-dominant. If you find that interpersonal relationships are more important than power or task-oriented behaviors, you will have an intricate value system made up of affiliating values. Understand that you may need to be tolerant of task-oriented people who seem to be more concerned with things and production, and of power-oriented people, who place the organization and position above people.

Dimension three: Power

Some people are dominated by power values. They seek power for themselves, or seek the reflected glory of being near those they perceive as having it. This power-dominant person may need clear lines of authority and accountability to be a productive member of a group. When in a position of authority, this power-dominant person has few hangups in giving orders, establishing directions, making decisions or setting expectations for others. In a low status position, this kind of person has few conflicts taking directions, doing what is expected and following rules. He works best in situations where power is clearly visible and unambiguously used. Many executives are clearly power-dominant. Organization lines and charts with clear role definitions and accountability expectations evolve out of power orientation. Probably most of our presidential aspirants are power-dominant. They have learned how to get and maintain their power, but they often lack the personality balance to lead others to task solutions. The ruthless power drive necessary to achieve the top job often disqualifies the person for effectively coping with relationship problems. Did you ever wonder why so little attention was paid to interpersonal relationships and to instructional programs in your organization when these goals are the purpose for the organization in the first place? Do you see some possible implications of power-dominance here which might begin to explain this phenomenon? If you believe yourself to be power-dominated, our suggestion is that you temper it with concern for organization members and their personal needs.

Again, however, these are not bad or good orientations of people; they are orientations which have something to do with effectiveness in certain tasks or settings. Power-dominant types, while often having difficulty being with or understanding relationship-dominant types, fit well with task-dominant types. One reason may be that the task-dominant person is willing to subjugate his power or relationship needs and let the power-dominant person decide on the procedures as long as the task is accomplished.

Of course, each of us is a unique combination of portions of all three of these characteristics, with one factor more or less dominating. Some researchers have concluded that "helping people," such as supervisors and middle managers with supervisory responsibilities, are most effective if they have no extreme dominance of the three characteristics. Perhaps what we really judge as effective supervisory behavior in these three dimensions is the degree of flexibility of the person to be one or the other, or a mix of the three at a given time (Kolb and Boyatis 1970) depending on the needs and dominating characteristic of the person with whom the supervisor is interacting.

Ideally then, the effective supervisor may be a person who can tolerate some lack of power domination and has a developed motivation to complete tasks but within the structure of caring relationships.

The relative balance of our orientations toward the task, power achievement and maintaining relationships will in part determine our effectiveness in interacting with kinds of people.

We need all three types of people in our organization. Preserve us and our children from school teachers and counselors who are power-dominated to the virtual exclusion of task and relationship development. You may know some of these types in your organization—perhaps the cranky old teacher who runs his classroom like a company in the Prussian army. All the students are at the recruit level and he is general. One of those is enough in one lifetime in any organization.

Yet as you know, all our organizations need people who can confidently give directions without major conflict and guilt feelings. We hope they do it with compassion, but happily there is someone interested in getting things done and telling us relationship types when to go and when to stop.

And, most of us want somewhere in our lives a person who makes no demands, solves no problems, has no need to dominate—who is just there relating. We may only want ten minutes a week of this kind of relationship but that ten minutes is still important. Isn't there a secretary or a janitor or someone in your organization who fills this function? They may not do much, but they always seem available to listen. They never rush or seem busy.

Conceptual Levels

All of us, to be able to act, must make decisions. The ways we categorize information and the number of categories of information we actively use in making these decisions is characterized by Harvey, Hunt and Schroder (1980) as the conceptual level on which we operate. We shall concentrate here on applying these ideas to the supervisor although they apply equally to the supervisee.

Some individuals base their behavior on a few variables which seem to be related to or integrated with one another. These individuals are characterized as using "low complexity" in their deciding. Others consider many dimensions and integrate these dimensions into a Gestalt overview. These individuals are characterized as "high complexity" in making decisions.

The system developed by Harvey, Hunt and Schroder defines four major stages in a continuum of conceptual thinking.

Stage	Behavorial Characteristics Of Individuals In This Stage	Reactions To The Environment
	Low Complexity:	
Stage I	This stage is characterized by extremely fixed patterns of response, categorical, black-white thinking. The person tends to see things evaluatively—in terms of rights and wrongs, and tends to categorize the world stereotypically. He prefers social relationships which are hierarchical, in which some people are on top and some on the bottom. He tends to reject information which does not fit with his present belief system, or to distort the information in order	This person tends to be rigid and inflexible and becomes even more so in an open social system where the rules allow many choices. He needs structure, clear rules, support, and specific expectations. He has great difficulty viewing the world as others see it. When in a position of authority, he tends to be dogmatic and demanding. Reasons for actions, if given, are usually based on authority and are not situational.

to store it in his existing categories. Stimuli either fit into a category or are excluded from consideration. This exclusion of considerations that do not fit pre-existing stereotypic categories reduces the individual's ability to consider "gray areas" or "degrees." This person has no conceptual apparatus that can generate alternatives; the result is fast 'closure' in choice or conflict situations.

Stage	Behavioral Characteristics Of Individuals In This Stage	Reactions To The Environment
	Moderate Complexity:	
Stage II	The individual in this stage is beginning to break away from the rigid rules and beliefs of Stage I. A person here tends to resist authority and control from any source. Although still tending to stereotype things in the environment, this person is considering more than the stereotypic points of view. This person still has difficulty seeing or understanding the points of view of others or of maintaining a balance between task and relationship orientations.	This individual tends to be negative and sometimes hostile to rules or to people seen as representing authority. He is in a stage of breaking away from old modes and may seem somewhat inconsistent or inconsiderate of others' points of view at times. However, combinations of points of view are beginning to be used. He needs structure but needs to be able to negotiate some rules for personal conduct.
Stage III	Moderately High Complexity:	
	Someone at Stage III has easy relationships with others, takes on or considers others' points of view, tends to view relationships as more important and gets side-tracked from task completion. Is cognitively balancing alternative views and is integrating even some apparently conflicting ideas. Can understand others' points of view.	This person is comfortable with less structure in the environment, can observe the effects of his own behavior from several points of view and can tolerate and understand others' ways of operating.

Stage IV   highly complex relationships. Can balance task and interpersonal relationships. As new conditions or information become known, this person adapts belief or cognitive structure to accommodate these. Can negotiate with others' rules for operating in given settings.

This person is adaptable, but operates best in more open systems built from conditions in the system. He is effective in complex environments.

This conceptual levels schema has many implications. We do not intend to exhaustively catalogue them to discuss each in detail. We present this schema as one more set of human behavior variables you may wish to consider in your assessment of ways you behave, of your values positions and their origins, of strategies which might be effective in your supervisory behavior, and of the flexibility of behavior which may be necessary on your part for you to be effective with the wide range of individuals you may find in your organization.

Answering the following questions will help you conceptualize the levels. You might share your answers with someone else, or discuss them in a group.

1. If you think about our descriptions in terms of supervisory behavior, would a Stage I conceptual level supervisor be effective? With whom? What kind of structure would this kind of thinker need to be maximally effective?

2. With whom would conceptual level IV supervisors be effective? What kinds of roles and work environments would encourage this person to be most productive?

3. Should conceptual level III supervisors adopt different strategies for supervisees who appear to be at different conceptual levels? Some managers pride themselves on treating all their supervisees alike. Does this seem to be an effective way to function if the supervisees are functioning in different ways?

4. If strategies, expectations and rules were changed by supervisory persons to be congruent with the conceptual levels of their supervisees, would the supervisors be perceived as weak, inconsistent, lacking in clarity or competency by supervisees?

5. Are you adaptable enough to relate effectively to supervisees of varying conceptual levels? Can you tolerate the ambiguity and openness required to accommodate supervisees who are functioning at a higher conceptual level than you? Can you operate in the rigid category-system of a conceptual level I thinker well enough to give him guidance?

6. What kinds of facts, inferences and judgments would be most meaningful to each of these conceptual level thinkers?

Think through some of these issues and come back to them as you work with the following activity. It would help if you wrote responses to each of the questions so you can perform an analysis of your answers after completing this activity.

Activity III

PURPOSES

Why do you react the way you do in supervisory situations? What are possible effects of these reactions? Do you wish to react in other ways? Use the simulated situations presented in this activity to draw some conclusions about your values and needs and your reactions in supervisory situations. Especially, react to your own responses in terms of the dimensions we have just presented.

There are no right or wrong answers in this activity. You should be looking at the depth of your analysis and of your reasons for your responses.

DIRECTIONS

1. Read each of the following situations. Answer the questions listed after each situation.

a. You are a supervisory specialist in your setting. The person in charge of a task group calls you on the phone and says, "I need help. One of the members of my group is a very ineffective instructor. His students constantly complain to me that he doesn't follow the rules all the other instructors use. Can you come over and straighten this guy out? After all, I'm responsible for his work."

1. What are the first three questions you ask?

a. _____

_____

b. _____

_____

c. _____

_____

2. What alternative questions did you consider and reject?

a. _____

b. _____

_____

c. _____

_____

3. Identify the probable conceptual level of the caller. _____

Give supporting data. _____

_____

_____

4. Identify the conceptual level of your questions. _____

Give supporting data. _____

_____

_____

5. Which dimensions of the Task-Power-Relationship triad seem dominant in the caller? _____ In your responses? _____

Give supporting data. _____

_____

_____

b. As the newly appointed leader of an instructional team planning objectives and instructional strategies for the next school year, you wish to have a first meeting to explore the issues before settling on instructional strategies. As this meeting gets underway, one of the members of the group says, "We are all agreed on the objectives; can we get busy right away on the task at hand? Maybe each of us could write one unit?"

1. As the leader, what is your reply? _____

_____

_____

2. What alternative responses did you consider and reject? _____

_____

_____

3. Based on the speaker's words, would you say his question is Task,

Power or Relationship oriented? _____ Why?_____

_____

_____

4. Was your next statement Task, Power or Relationship oriented?

_____ Why? _____

_____

_____

5. What probable conceptual level were your responses?_____

Why? _____

_____

c. One of your colleagues has the same role as you in your setting. Her supervisees have been coming to you to complain about the way she is treating them. So far you have listened, but been very non-committal. Your colleague comes to you explaining that she has seen you talking to her supervisees and is wondering what they want since they have been the ones who have been giving her some trouble with getting their jobs done on time.

1. What is your response to your colleague? _____

_____

_____

2. What alternate response did you consider and reject? _____

_____

_____

3. What conceptual level is your response? _____ Why? _____

_____

_____

4. Was your response Task, Power, or Relationship oriented? _____

Why? _____

_____

5. What are the possible reactions of your colleague? _____

_____

_____

2. Answer the following general questions relating to the situations you have just worked through.

   a. Is this pattern of responses representative of how you will react in

"real" situations similar to these? _____

Why? _____

_____

   b. What implications do you see for yourself, as a supervisor, resulting from this pattern of responses? _____

_____

_____

   c. What other learnings resulted from this activity? _____

_____

_____

LEADERSHIP STYLE

A final dimension of your supervisory effectiveness which we would like to consider in this unit is your leadership style in task groups. This style springs from your experience, the alternatives you know, your values, and who you believe you are.

Most of us have some expectations through verbal and non-verbal acts. When we are leaders we act out our expectations. We structure situations in specific ways. We set certain limits and expectations for other members of the group. Our behaviors tend to repeat themselves in clearly identifiable patterns, congruent with the expectations. These patterns are what we mean when we speak of leadership style. This leadership style may change slowly over time as new skills or behaviors are added to the leader's repertoire. This style may also change as the person changes the internal conception of what a leader is and does. Generally, however, for most persons this style is a relatively unvarying trademark.

Often the formally appointed leader is not the real leader of a group. The leadership of a group may change as the topic, process or time change. Nevertheless, leadership behaviors exhibited, tend to be consistent.

In the following pages we list some common "leader" behaviors used in task groups. We define these behaviors both directly and by examples. We list most of the common leader behaviors, but there will be specific classes of behaviors omitted from the list. Our omissions represent value choices within our attempt to keep the number of categories rememberable.

Common Leader Behaviors in Task Groups

Behavior	Definition And/Or Examples
1. Direct Structuring	Telling others what they should or must do (e.g., "This is where we should start." "John, you begin."). Sometimes the language is less direct but the meaning is the same (e.g., "Janet, will you report first?" Janet has the right to refuse, but is expected to comply. "I think we've had enough of that topic; let's move on to the next item on the agenda").
2. Open Structuring	Asking the members how they wish to proceed, what they want to discuss, what is important to them, etc. Here the leader is asking the group to set its own directions. He is eliciting a direct structuring response from other members of the group.
3. Clarifying	Paraphrasing, restating, checking others' perceptions of her own statements. The leader is trying by this process to be sure she and other members got the same message as the one sent.

Behavior	Definition And/Or Examples
4. Reinforcing	Leader approves of member contribution or gives group member reassurance about membership within the group. This reinforcing can take the form of verbal or non-verbal praise, recommending the group follow a member's suggestion, writing down a member's statement, listening carefully and asking a member to repeat a statement because it is important, etc. There are many ways of demonstrating approval or agreement to group members.
5. Confronting	Challenging other group members' opinions, facts, values, memory, interpretations or behavior is confronting leadership. This behavior might use phrases such as, "Yesterday you said . . . and today you are saying . . . Can you explain the apparent discrepancy between these statements?" or "You say you value others' views, but right now I perceive you as attacking John because he disagrees with you." The supervisor is trying to hold up a mirror here to reflect what he sees as inadequacies or inconsistencies in behavior. He may also be exhibiting his power.
6. Attacking	This behavior differs from confronting because it is usually a direct assault on the member's opinion, values, etc. in an attempt to change that person's opinions, values, etc. Attack carries a judgmental quality which is absent from the confrontating behaviors.
7. Silence	The leader gives no overt verbal response to members' initiation or noninitiation of activities, ideas or processes. Usually there is an expectation that someone else will fill the gap with some contribution.
8. Reporting member's or own feelings or inferences about feelings	"I feel very good right now about the process we are using." "You seem to be feeling defensive about this issue." "The group seems to be feeling boredom with this issue." Often this behavior is used in connection with reinforcing. Sometimes

Behavior	**Definition And/Or Examples**
	there is the expectation that this leader is modelling a behavior he would like others to use. The purpose here is to verbalize feelings which may be inhibiting or facilitating the groups' processes.
9. Relating Examples	The leader states examples of perceived similar situations from her own or from others experiences. Sometimes the leader draws inferences and conclusions from the experience she has related.
10. Being Humorous	Telling a joke, pointing out some funny process, making fun of self, playing with words. The intended purpose of this behavior is to ease tension, change the pace, wake people, get a fresh start on a problem, and change the focus of attention in the group.

11.* _____

_____

_____

_____

Which of these behaviors would you use in your leadership of a task group? What are the values you see expressed in each of these leadership behaviors?

Summarize your perceived values as expressed by your choices of behaviors you would use? _____

_____

_____

Which of these values were you *not* conscious of before doing this unit? _____

_____

_____

*If you think of other categories of leader behavior important to you add your own categories.

What overall implications of all these ideas do you see for your supervisory behavior? _____

_____

_____

The intention of this unit has been to help you realize how the me-ness of you as supervisor could get in the way of creating a theory Y organization in which your supervisees seek you out as a trustworthy helper. We suggest that you fill in the following chart as an indication of the understanding you now have of your me-ness.

List here several values you hold that you now understand.	**List here supervisee values which might (or have) conflicted with the values you listed.**
1.	1.
2.	2.
3.	3.
4.	4.

Explain below how owning your values as values, not carved-in-stone "rights," may affect supervisees. Use Maslow and McGregor in the explanation.

_____

_____

_____

Explain below how helping the supervisee understand and own her values and understand your values will affect the supervisory relationship. Use Maslow and McGregor in the explanation._____

_____

_____

Summary of Some of Your Me-nesses

Rate your own orientation using your own estimation by assigning a rating of one to five for the dominance of each of the following orientations in you.

Explain here the orientations of people who do or may have conflicts with your behavior because of your orientation.

1. Task   score

2. Power   score

3. Relationship   score

Explain how you might use this knowledge to improve the supervisory relationship. _____

_____

_____

Identify what you believe to be your own conceptual level.

Identify conceptual levels you may have or do have problems with.

Explain how you might most effectively alter your characteristic behavior to more effectively work with supervisees of other conceptual levels. _____

_____

_____

This summary provides a profile of you—your values, orientations, and conceptual level.

How might that profile affect your supervision, or how has it affected your supervision? _____

_____

_____

How will the knowledge of your profile affect your future supervisory behavior? _____

_____

_____

We have tried to apply the categories to your actual functioning in a task group. This total unit in several specific dimensions has tried to increase your sensitivity to yourself as an instrument of supervision. We have not tried to make you a better person, a better lover, or a therapist. You may be even a little worse at the latter; however, we do hope you have made some deeper analyses of how what you do is connected to what you believe and how everything you do creates impressions others read.

Unit 5

Personality Style

**The Clash of Opposites; the Harmony of Congruence;
the Agony and Ecstasy of Being What You Seem to be—
Or How to Get Along by Really Trying, Understanding
and Accepting Yourself and Others**

Content

The title of this unit is not really meant to be funny. It is intended to signify the complexity of trying to know more about ourselves in order to better cope with the effects we have on others, with the effects our individual perceptions of the world have on our interpretations of reality, and with our recognition that others see the world differently, having themselves to cope as they try to cope with us.

We try in this unit to help you understand how your perceptions and judgments usually operate. These aspects of your personality have an immense effect on your behavior.

We explain these ideas by presenting Carl Jung's typology of decision making. His ideas, while complicated, are understandable. We will be guilty of oversimplifying them. They are, however, useful tools to help us understand the world. You may understand, as you discover your own typology, why you have trouble relating to a unit like this, or why you relate easily to this unit.

Activity I

Our own survey of 32 choice-making questions follows. This survey is intended to be used by you to help you determine your personality typology in the dimensions defined by Carl Jung. There are no good and bad types.

This survey is similar to a profile which might be used to help you decide whether you prefer apples or oranges; science or literature; carpentry or painting. Fill it out before you read the explanation which follows. Jung himself would probably be appalled at the whole idea of a scale being used to measure these dimensions. We think that such a reaction has something to do with his personality type.

CH Preference Survey

Just as every person has differently shaped feet and toes from every other person, we all have differently shaped personalities. As no person's foot-shape is right or wrong, no person's personality shape is right or wrong.

The purpose of this survey is to give you a view of the shape of your personality preferences, but that shape, while different from the shapes of others' personaltiy preferences, has nothing to do with right or wrong, or with mental health.

When you have finished the survey on the next three pages, score it using the score sheet on page 101.

Then write the letters of your typology in the four blanks below.

_____	_____	_____	_____
I or E	N or S	T or F	P or J

The following items are arranged in pairs; each member of the pair represents a preference you may or may not hold. Rate your preference for each by giving it a score of 0 to 5 (0 meaning you really feel negative about it, 5 meaning you strongly prefer it, or do not prefer the other member of the pair). The scores for a and b MUST ADD UP TO 5 (0 and 5, 1 and 4, 2 and 3, etc.)

Write a number in each blank to reflect the way you are, not the way you wish you were.

Do not use fractions, such as 2½.

I MOST OFTEN

1a _____ am quietly friendly and reserved

1b _____ attract others to me by being outgoing

2a _____ allow commitments to be made if others make them	2b _____ push for definite commitments to insure that they're made
3a _____ try to think of new methods even if old ones are available	3b _____ use methods I know well that are effective
4a _____ draw conclusions based on unemotional logic and careful analysis	4b _____ draw conclusions based on what I feel about life and people
5a _____ set a schedule, stick to it	5b _____ don't set deadlines
6a _____ consider every possible angle a long time before making a decision	6b _____ get the information I need, then make a decision as soon as possible so I can go on
7a _____ speak out in discussions after carefully thinking out my idea	7b _____ speak out in discussions as something pops into my mind
8a _____ use beliefs and convictions to make decisions	8b _____ use evidence and reason to make decisions
9a _____ plan ahead based on projections	9b _____ plan as necessities arise just before doing things
10a _____ have my life ordered and planned	10b _____ have my life flexible, open

I PREFER OR LIKE

11a _____ being called factual and accurate	11b _____ being called imaginative or intuitive
12a _____ making decisions about people based on empathy, feelings, their needs	12b _____ making decisions about people based on evidence, knowing the facts, and logic
13a _____ active energetic time with several people	13b _____ quiet, thoughtful time alone or with a single friend
14a _____ being thought of highly for my thoughts, ideas	14b _____ being the center of attention because I'm outgoing

15a _____ finding possibilities

15b _____ examining details of things

16a _____ being thought of as a thinking person

16b _____ being thought of as a feeling person

17a _____ activities and occurrences others are joining in on

17b _____ inner thoughts and feelings

18a _____ abstract or theoretical

18b _____ concrete or real

19a _____ helping others express their feelings

19b _____ helping others make logical decisions

20a _____ change and keeping options open

20b _____ knowing and planning in advance

21a _____ possible views of the whole

21b _____ the factual details

22a _____ meeting new people, introducing myself

22b _____ watching people or being with one person I know well

23a _____ ideas and theories

23b _____ facts and the real

24a _____ convictions

24b _____ verifiable conclusions

25a _____ discussing a new issue at length in a group

25b _____ puzzling out issues in my mind, then sharing them

26a _____ carrying out carefully laid details precisely

26b _____ designing plans and new things without necessarily doing the detailed work

27a _____ logical people

27b _____ people who express feeling

28a _____ being free to do things on the spur of the moment

28b _____ anticipating what will need to be done and doing it ahead of time

29a _____ being the center of attention

29b _____ being a watcher

30a _____ imagining the new and different

30b _____ examining details of the real

31a _____ experiencing emotional situations or experiences with people

31b _____ discussing or writing down a logical analysis of an issue

32a _____ starting at a prearranged time

32b _____ starting when all are comfortable or ready

The following is a scoring summary sheet with abbreviations for aspects of the personality profile. Write beside each item number and letter the score you gave for the item. If you answered 1a with a 3, put 3 in that space, 1b with a 2, put 2 in that space.

Transfer all your scores to this sheet. Check the scores.

Then add all the scores for each of the eight columns.

At the bottom of the page are summary boxes. Place the sum for each column in the summary box containing the same letter as the letter at the top of the column.

Now that you have your eight total scores, go ahead and read the explanations.

Number	Question Score	Number	Question Score
I	E	N	S
1a. _____	1b. _____	3a. _____	3b. _____
7a. _____	7b. _____	11b. _____	11a. _____
13b. _____	13a. _____	15a. _____	15b. _____
14a. _____	14b. _____	18a. _____	18b. _____
17b. _____	17a. _____	21a. _____	21b. _____
22b. _____	22a. _____	23a. _____	23b. _____
25b. _____	25a. _____	26b. _____	26a. _____
29b. _____	29a. _____	30a. _____	30b. _____

Total I_____   Total E _____   Total N _____   Total S _____

Number	Question Score	Number	Question Score
T	F	P	J
4a. _____	4b. _____	2a. _____	2b. _____
8b. _____	8a. _____	5b. _____	5a. _____
12b. _____	12a. _____	6a. _____	6b. _____
16a. _____	16b. _____	9b. _____	9a. _____
19b. _____	19a. _____	10b. _____	10a. _____
24b. _____	24a. _____	20a. _____	20b. _____
27a. _____	27b. _____	28a. _____	28b. _____
31b. _____	31a. _____	32b. _____	32a. _____

Total T _____   Total F _____   Total P _____   Total J_____

I =	N =	T =	P =
E =	S =	F =	J =

Explanation of the four pairs of dimensions

Four pairs of personality dimensions emerged from Jung's clinical work with people who came to him for therapy. He found that each person has characteristic perceptions of reality and judgments or appraisals of those perceptions. Jung carefully explains these characteristic orientations and judgments in his book, *Psychological Types*. The types have since been reexamined, described and often redefined by various writers and researchers. We are reporting our interpretations from Jung's *Psychological Types* (1929), from a series of lectures by Marie-Louise von Franz (1961), from an explanation of Jung's analytic psychology by Jolande Jacobi (1970), from a review by Mogar (1969), from the widely researched work of Isabel Myers-Briggs (1960), and most recently from Kiersey and Bates (1978). We urge you to consult at least one of these sources to check our interpretation of these ideas.

Attitude Types

(1) Introvert or internal

If your score for I (introversion) was higher than your score for E (extroversion) your orientation to the world is more inner-determined than outer-determined. You are energized by going into yourself. You are usually cautious in relating to objects and people. You usually don't communicate your feelings freely, especially in groups, and you may resist external forces and demands unless you can redefine them in your own terms. Your inside world is so interesting to you that the outer world rarely holds your attention for long. In new situations you usually step back and decide what they mean to you rather than moving forward to let the situations define themselves. Often you do not explain yourself to others and sometimes your independent decision making leaves others confused or wary because you haven't explained yourself. But, it is more important to you to know why you are doing something than it is for you to explain yourself to others. You are generally more comfortable with some one person you know well than you are with any group in which you are expected to interact with many people at the same time. Probably if you play games or sports they are individual rather than team. If you play team sports, you want others to follow your strategies without your having to explain them in detail.

(E) Extrovert

If your E (extroversion) score was higher, you have a positive orientation to the world, freely relating to and responding to external objects and forces. Group norms and demands probably determine or affect much of your behavior and decisions. Many of your pleasures or activities occur in the context of a group. You may worry about acceptance from others and thus try to "fit in," to dress, eat, talk and have opinions like those around you. It is hard for you to strike out in, or maintain, new directions not sanctioned by some group you value. You rarely are censored for holding and expressing opinions that are seen as "far out" since you are sensitive to and value others' opinions and approval. Sometimes you worry about what other people think of you, and in situations where group expectations are not clear, you tend to become anxious.

The Four Functions

Independent of the previous pair of attitude types are the four functions:

    a. two ways of collecting data about and perceiving reality.

    b. two ways of appraising or judging the reality you perceive.

Reality Perception

(N) Intuition

If your score was higher for (N) Intuition than for (S) Sensory you are more comfortable exploring and discussing possibilities, conceptual schemes, ideas, theories, hypothesized structure, and future orientations than with discussing only what is concrete, factual and verifiable here and now. You may begin with the factual, but quickly move to speculating beyond it to "what if" questions. You eagerly try to fit new data into some conceptual scheme or gestalt you already know. You often come away from external objects or occurrences with impressions and understandings rather than accurate recall of concrete details. Isolated details or the sifting of endless data seem stupifying unless you can fit them into some pattern. When you read a report you begin to look for implications of its ideas before it is even completed. If the report ends with little or no analysis, you will do your own analysis.

(S) Sensory

If your score for (S) Sensory was higher than that for (N) Intuition, then you are probably more concerned with facts and details than with theory or abstractions. You may even regard the theory as superfluous, or may use someone else's theory if you are pushed to relating your facts to some conceptual scheme.

When directions are given, you are concerned with hearing and understanding the specific details rather than with spending much time seeing how everything fits together. You carry out directions by completing each detail in order as directed. In group situations you may be uncomfortable if the participants are discussing the interrelationships of global ideas without being concerned with specific facts or details they seem to ignore. You remember these facts and details accurately. You may be a much better observer of what is than the (N) Intuitive person. You see what is there. If you are charged with writing a report, you are likely to fill it with factual information and then stop. Analysis or implications of that information are not for you. That task remains for others.

Judging What Has Been Perceived

There are two dichotomous ways of making judgments based on the perceived realities: These are, (T) Thinking or (F) Feeling.

(T) Thinking

If your score was higher for (T) Thinking than for (F) Feeling then you prefer to make judgments of your perceptions using logical thought processes—the rational mode of judging. You order, rank and weigh factors logically, using *if*, *then* statements with careful cause-effect considerations. You want to keep emotions out of decisions. Some people may consider you cold or unfeeling. You are comfortable with orderly rules and see little reason to go outside these logical processes unless you are convinced by superior logic. You move from step 1 to the end of a process. You may bring feelings into your decision making, but only as one factor, and then you do it in a logical fashion. You may quantify the feelings to be added to the rest of the equation which ends in a decision. You relate most easily to people who think in ways similar to you and are probably suspicious that people who make feeling-type decisions are not very dependable and may not be very bright.

(F) Feeling

If your score was higher for (F) Feeling than (T) Thinking then you prefer to judge the perceptions you received by relying on your convictions and impressions. Your decisions may contain judgmental words, such as like-dislike, right-wrong, good-bad. You are often less able or willing to give reasons for your decisions. You may be somewhat impatient with people who "plod" through logical processes, and while intimidated by their ability to explain themselves you still feel you took the more important things into consideration. You have a clear value system that you feel is *better* than logic. Your explanations are often filled with personal orientations about your feelings. You consider these personal feelings to be important parts of your decision-making process. If you have this dominant judging mode then you may not be very successful with the logical processes many bureaucratic organizations demand. You may, on the other hand, inspire loyalty because of your ability to "feel" out decisions. You may also seek out people who decide using the same mode you use, but you may have strong conflicts when their feeling judgment conflicts with yours: they are wrong, and you are right.

Mode of Approach to Making Judgments

(P) Perceiving

Some people approach the act of judging gingerly, if at all. They examine an issue from all sides, back away, wish to consult other sources, wait, delay, procrastinate, reconsider and then, having been forced by some factor into deciding, are hopeful that they might be able to go back and reopen the question. If score for (P) Perceiver was higher than that for (J) Judger you may be somewhat like this person. Dominant perceivers often decide at the last minute, having put off, until then, an unpleasant process. Pinning these persons down is often difficult. They prefer to let things happen rather than to choose. An appointment schedule is an abomination tolerated under pressure but not to be confining. The appearance of an old friend is likely to delay or change a previous decision to be at a certain place at a prescribed time.

This person may eventually make a better decision by having considered many factors, but the delay may have caused a lost opportunity, and may have frustrated to distraction those waiting to spring into action.

If you are a P, you may also have been uncomfortable with deciding the relative weights you wished to give to the questions on our survey. You wanted more time to decide. You wanted to consider more data.

(J) Judgmental

If your score for (J) Judger was higher than that of (P) Perceiver then you make decisions easily and quickly with little conflict. Sometimes your judging process operated too quickly with too little data or consideration. You get into trouble because you lept before you were sure of a landing place. Whether you decide to buy on the basis of logic or feeling, you decide quickly. Perhaps later you regret not having asked about the warantee or whether the price included additional benefits, but you rarely worry about actually deciding. Usually, you have little anxiety after decisions are made. You consider them finished, and act on them without worrying whether they are the right or wrong ones. You only reconsider decisions when evidence piles up that the first decision is not working. Then you change easily, again making a firm, quick decision. Judgmental people have little difficulty keeping appointments or meeting schedule deadlines. Yoke a perceiver to a judgmental person and expect sparks to fly, especially when each has relatively equal status. Joint decisions by these two may be of higher quality, if each can occasionally escape the other to let his piled up frustrations vent and dissipate. Both perceiver and judgmental person must value each other if this combination is to work to its potential.

Your Profile

Jung suggests that it is likely that one attitude type, one perceiving function, one judging function and one way of approaching decisions has been more developed than the others in each person. The result is the personality profile represented by your survey scores. Having gotten success with this mode early, you have come to feel comfortable in using it, and you have developed it more. This profile tends to remain stable over long periods of time. However, you may have found that your scores were relatively balanced between I and E, or N and S, or T and F, or P and J. The balance may be a result of error in our survey, or of the fact that you actually are relatively well balanced in that area.

That function (N, S, T, or F) with the highest score is your dominant function. Conversely, the function with the lowest score is your inferior function. The other pair is your set of auxiliary functions.

The attitude dimensions (I or E, J or P) will affect your behaviors and your working relationships. If you were more strongly I than E, you may have a tendency to act on internal reasoning without consulting others. That may cause problems in the supervisory relationship because, as you learned in Unit I, the supervisor and supervisee must share, honestly and equally, the decision-making and responsibilities in the relationship. You may need to learn consciously to communicate more of your inner reasoning as you supervise, encourage the supervisee to participate in making even the smallest decision and accept those decisions not congruent with the inner decisions you would have made. You will also have to be wary that the E supervisee (especially an ESFJ supervisee) does not push you out of the decision-making process entirely through sheer energy and extroverted forcefulness.

Both the E and I supervisors will have to be tolerant and patient with the I teacher who is accustomed to working on her own and making decisions without communicating the mental processes generating her decisions. When you are involved in helping the I teacher clarify values, you may find incongruencies and ambiguities in her belief and action systems. It has been suggested that the inner working of an I are communicated with more difficulty than the inner workings of an E because the I spends more time with them. The E, only visiting the inner world occasionally, views a clear expanse of mind uncluttered by the musings, convulutions and introspections of the I.

The E, however, may be less willing to explore those inner workings and may balk in values clarification exercises. The defenses may come in the form of joking.

The other two attitude-types, P and J, are indications of the amount of structure you require in your world. If you are charactereistically a P, you prefer less structure, and are overly cautious about making decisions. You may find your supervisees or others in the organization uncomfortable with that aspect of your personality. They may demand decisions and structure of you, imposing them on you, if necessary (much to your dismay). With other P-types, you may find making decisions an impossible task. A pair of P-types, asked to make a series of decisions, may have an impotent relationship.

If you are a J, you may need to be tolerant of your more P supervisees and colleagues you cannot seem to pin down. Help them find a structure, or force them to be structured in their dealings, with you at least, by gaining definite commitments from them ("When do you think you will have that done?", "Can we make an appointment now to get together and discuss it when it is done?"). The J may also need to learn to relinquish much of his automatic decision-making to the supervisees if the supervisees are to become autonomous professionals in the relationship. The J type supervisor may need help in learning this skill.

The Typology Combinations

With the four pairs of personality characteristics there are sixteen possible combinations forming sixteen typologies:

ISFP	ISFJ	ESFP	ESFJ
INFP	INFJ	ENFP	ENFJ
ISTP	ISTJ	ESTP	ESTJ
INTP	INTJ	ENTP	ENTJ

Jung himself probably considered the I-E attitudes as most important. Most subsequent researchers after Jung focus most attention on the N-S and T-F functions. Consequently, they are most fully explained here. The remaining "attitudes" are considered as they affect the four functions.

You are aware of your superior function. You also have a superior *pair* of functions that will include the superior single function plus the strongest of the auxiliary functions (highest score on the survey). Your superior combination will be SF, ST, NF, or NT.

You also have an inferior combination made up of the pair of functions that is opposite your superior pair of functions. The remaining two combinations are your auxiliary pairs of functions. Write beside each combination below whether it is your superior, inferior, or auxiliary:

SF _____

ST _____

NF _____

NT _____

Typologies In Relationships

Last year in one of our classes an S superior function, F dominant auxiliary function (SF combination) friend came to see what was happening. The class was a curriculum analysis class heavily into an NT discussion. This guest became so bored, anxious, hostile and uncomfortable that the class instructor called an early break so his friend could escape. He ran out and was not seen again in that setting. The friendship was never quite the same after that. In order to maintain the relationship at all we had to operate almost completely in the SF mode. This auxiliary F function for the NT class instructor was the only mode in which both could operate at all comfortably. That friendship could not stand the stress and the SF dominant function member soon withdrew from what he perceived as a discomforting relationship.

Jung suggests that when we interact with a co-worker, supervisee, boss or other person whose superior function is our inferior function and vice versa, there is likely to be a clash which ends in each blaming the other for the problems in communication. He also suggested that this clash is "the real basis of marital problems, of difficulties between parents and children, of friction among friends and business associates, and even of social and political differences." (Jacobi, 1970, p.20)

NF teacheres are almost totally uninterested in an ST supervisor's data and thinking. Both the type of data presented and the logical way the supervisor tries to get NF's to change their interaction patterns with kids are the wrong strategy. On the other hand, NT teachers will take ST supervisor's data and put it into their conceptual frameworks as they impose their understanding on the supervisor's sensory, logical reality. The ST supervisor may not know why this kind of teacher needs to be so abstract, but is willing to accept this type since at least the teachers are willing to go through some logical processes once they are finished with the foolishness of all that theorizing.

We conclude our unit with a short discussion unlike most of the discussions in this book. It is relatively straightforward, NT discussion of each of the four combinations. We include some S data but very little. There is no (or very little) F (feeling) mode in the writing. We are both strong NT's. Many university types are. Look carefully at the writing in the remainder of this unit. It is highly NT. Compare it with the rest of the unit and program. You may see some implications for you in your need to vary your modes of interacting—if you are an NT or NF.

The Combinations: Their Effect on Supervising and Teaching

Combination 1: (ST) Sensory-Thinking

Sensory-thinking persons work well with logical processes using concrete facts. They might be described as down-to-earth, practical, pragmatic, efficient, realistic or logical. They may gravitate towards professions demanding these talents, such as accounting, engineering, building or finances. Combined with extroversion and judging this person would have the capacities for making an excellent business manager.

The sensory-thinking person may have considerable difficulty understanding and accepting the views of an intuitive-feeling (NF) person (such as an artist, writer, or architect). That may be part of the reason for some of the animosity between business and English composition departments, made up of intuitive-feeling (NF) persons. The sensory-thinking business faculty demands ST expository writing while the NF English people often teach creative writing.

Students who are ST may learn best in structured modes, such as programmed learning, or in carefully laid out and explained step-by-step procedures. They readily learn concrete facts. The structure and attention to concrete facts in most of today's classrooms are ideally suited to the ST. Schools, in others words, are largely ST institutions, reflecting the ST nature of American society.

ST students may be unhappy with unstructured, "touchy-feely" or "brainstorming" discussion groups involving intuitive or feeling discussions of abstract ideas. They may say, "Let's get down to business," or

"But what are the facts?" Teachers anxious to teach conceptual schemes rather than facts may clash with the ST student. Teachers anxious to teach values clarification may find little response from the ST student if they present these processes in feeling ways.

Combination 2: (SF) Sensory-Feeling

The SF person perceives reality in concrete occurrences, here and now, judging or appraising using feelings, beliefs and convictions. The SF person is social (especially if extroverted) and needs the personal contact provided in positions such as counseling, sales, or public relations. SF's may be the ones to give of themselves and sacrifice for others because of their capacity to empathize. The SF person may, however, be regarded as flighty and mindless, "great for parties, but not long on serious discussion."

The SF person may have problems working with the NT person, who dismisses the SF person's concerns with feelings or interactions of people while emphasizing the possible causes, effects and methods of structuring life so the occurrences do or do not occur again. The SF may have difficulty with logical thought processes and may adopt hollow stock phrases such as, "what will be will be," or "the only real answer to life's problems is love" when discussing things with the NT person. SF persons may avoid discussions with NT persons when the discussion falls into deeper considerations such as cold impersonal analysis of philosophical issues.

An SF student learns best in a social classroom where knowledge and facts are presented with interpersonal interaction. The directions must be clear and detailed because SF students attend carefully to details. The NT classroom, where global, intuitive issues and possibilities are being presented in logical ways may leave the social, fact-oriented SF student unhappy and restless.

Combination 3: (NT) Intuition-Thinking

It happens that we are both NT's. The NT's enjoy exploring hypothetical structures, possiblities and the future, making logical, thinking assertations about the ideas created through intuition. They are found in college teaching, research, and management where foresight and thought are necessary. Their approach is characterized by creative, intuitive, impersonal, logical analysis.

To the NT person, the SF person may appear to be interested in only the mundane and trivial. While the NT person is trying to discuss a proposed alteration of the entire curriculum she is proposing, the SF person frequently stops her to clarify details the NT regards as trivial, and to discuss isolated examples of personal experiences in similar curricula which the NT regards as too isolated and personal to really be germane to the discussion of an overall scheme. The SF person may later lighten the NT's serious discussion with some humor or a gregarious suggestion the NT finds disruptive. Ths SF person, in other words, concerned with concrete details and isolated social incidents, may have an unnerving effect on the NT who wishes to impersonally analyze larger, Gestalt effects and structures as they generally affect most people.

The NT student learns best in an atmosphere of creative analysis of abstract ideas. He may, in other words, be ingenious in literary criticism, scientific theory, mathematical principles, and conceptual frameworks in all fields. The NT student may not be rewarded for creativity and ingenuity in the normal ST classroom, and probably will be uncomfortable and anxious for some "meat" in SF discussions of concrete interpersonal incidents. The SF teacher, wishing to have a free discussion of how the ideas in a science lesson two weeks ago have influenced specific interpersonal dealings in each student's life may find the NT student quickly wishing to end the discussion and get to her independent class project, or to the book on Freud or McGregor hidden in the desk.

Combination 4: (NF) Intuitive-Feeling

The NF person is generally sensitive, committed, and creative. NF's are involved in the arts, and may (one of us has observed) be English instructors. They are ingenious, as the NT's are, but emphasize social relationships and people more than the NT. While the NT is logically, impersonally analyzing an overall scheme in a field, the NF is envisioning the overall scheme as it affects the participants, and may be developing such an overall scheme into a short story or novel with real, interpersonal characters. Mogar suggests also that such people are found in psychology and psychiatry—gestalt rather than Freudian, however.

An NF teacher, wishing to have a creative class in which ideas, processes, and social interaction are more important than facts, may find the ST supervisor, who suggests that structure and concrete facts are the province of the classroom, abhorrent. Conflict may be apparent in such areas as history and English where current disagreement over the importance of content and processes is fermenting. Especially in writing instruction, which is traditionally the ward of English (made up of NF's) but which is crucial for success in such professional fields as business (an ST field) disagreement is occurring. The English writing classroom, designed by the NF English teacher to foster personal development, creativity, and free flow of ideas, may appall the ST business department who plead with the English instructors to help students communicate facts logically, clearly and concisely without the NF sensitivity and passion for language use.

Little is being said here of the entire typology (both attitude-types and both functions together) because that would require another unit of explanation. You will, however, be able to piece the implications together. For instance, what would be the result of an ESTJ supervising an INFP? How could the probable conflicts be resolved? Or, for instance, when choosing a curriculum team, would it be more effective to have a variety of typologies to give depth to the decisions, or would it be more effective to have typologies with superior and auxiliary functions and attitudes in congruence to encourage cooperation and compromise?

Thus far you have confronted views of interactions explained by McGregor, Argyris, Maslow and Harvey. The concepts of all will begin to form a Gestalt in your mind as you think about and apply them in your organization. As an NF or NT you may be interested in our speculations. As an ST or SF you may not be. You might be wishing for some answers, not more questions. You can see how differing typologies will affect the relationships occurring in the interactions, activities, sentiments and norms. You can also see the implications for helping supervisees collect data and make free, informed choices as autonomous professionls. What typologies would most easily and quickly be able to do those things? Which not? Is your typology conducive to helping them do those things? What can you do to alter your supervision, if necessary?

Maslow's hierarchy also has implications for the typologies. It has been suggested that persons working on their deficiency level needs may be able to function only in situations congruent with their typologies. They may become quite frustrated in other situations. On the other hand, persons working on their growth needs may be able to develop their auxiliary and inferior functions more fully.

Finally, you can imagine which typologies most need relationship-oriented, affiliative supervision, which may be most task-oriented, and which may be power-oriented to the exclusion of the other two dimensions.

While this is an explanation (and there may of course be many others) of some of your conflicts, your increased understanding of yourself now does not allow you to continue blaming others if you have a responsibility for managing an environment. You can attempt to people your organization with those who are like you. This may result in harmony among the working staff but will make the organization blind to the needs of clients who have other personality typologies. And of course your organization may at the same time be rendered incapable of making decisions or of considering other factors in its attempts to decide. It may end in failure.

Danger:
The typology can become a lethal weapon if used by a supervisor to shift blame to the shoulders of the supervisee. If the supervisor suggests in any way, overtly or covertly, that the supervisee should change his typology, then it is being used as a weapon, piercing the self-worth and self-esteem of the supervisee in the name of supervision. The supervisor can help the supervisee understand his type and participate in finding ways to alter behavior if the superviser agrees he wants to.

Since most educational organizations serve a wide range of clients, you have little real choice in the end, if you are to provide an environment which nurtures all clients. You must become more flexible, or at least more considerate, of other modes of deciding. Since you are the manager, it is you who must change. Yours is the ecstasy of understanding, and the agony of developing tolerances for difference—you must succeed by really trying.

Final Note:

   We conclude with these questions. Can you supervise SF's if you are an NT? What kinds of data will help ST's make decisions about teaching methods? What data will be interesting to SF's to get them to initiate a different method for NT students suffering in their classes. Are these adjustments possible in an ST organization? Can we allow NF teachers breathing room for their own creativity, or must we continue to drive them out of teaching? Can we, at the same time, help them find structure?

   And what of the future NT's and NF's? We desperately need to conceptualize and solve our society's problems. How do we allow their development in an ST bureaucratic organization called a school?

Unit 6

The "Thou-ness of Supervision

Content Overview

This unit cuts little new ground. However, it shifts your attention. No longer do we ask you to look into a mirror. Here we ask you to stand, unnoticed in shadow, looking at others. Observe what they say or do. Then infer meaning from their behavior. As you gain experience in this role, you will be able to consciously make and use these inferences without interrupting your own behavior. You will be letting this feedback shape the strategies you use to inform, persuade, direct or emphasize.

Entry Skills

We assume you have completed Unit IV and are able to correctly identify your own value statements.

Explanation and rationale for this set of competencies and this focus on others with whom you work or supervise.

Values and biases are not right or wrong—only different. We can, instead of bickering over the "best" method of frummaging (teaching, grouping students, handling discipline, choosing content, sequencing learning activities) discuss our data which indicate the effects of various methods. Without such data we are limited to owning our values as supervisors or teachers and presenting them as tentative and possible but not valid. One of our roles as supervisors is to help the supervisee recognize and own his values and understand them as being "different" from ours but no more or less right—until we can check them with corroborating data. If you, as supervisor, make most decisions in your relationship with a specific supervisee, and the supervisee expresses satisfaction in the relationship (i.e., feels positive), it is probable that the supervisee values your being a decision maker in the relationship. It may be that this is a basic and important observation on your part. You can check to see whether the supervisee demonstrates this value in

114

relationships where he is the authority figure in the classroom with students or as secretary behind the counter with parents. In this instance, does the supervisee as authority figure make all decisions? You may be satisfied and even reinforced when the supervisee defers to your judgment, but you may be much more in favor of the teacher sharing decision-making with students. Or, you may favor the secretary deferring almost all decisions with parents to you. On the other hand, your supervisees may not be satisfied with (value) your making decisions in your relationship. Then there may exist a value conflict which is getting in the way of effective supervision. These are not trivial or entirely obvious implications of the differing values of two people in a relationship.

You know that:

1. external control and threat (which might silence attempts by others to verbalize or act out their values) are not the only methods of bringing about growth and attainment of organizational objectives (McGregor);

2. every person has needs for feelings of self-esteem, self-respect, confidence, competence, adequacy, independence and freedom, which may be threatened by your imposing your values or not soliciting theirs (Maslow);

3. supervisees should increase their autonomy and commitment to choices made which probably means acting out their own values (Argyris).

Understanding and accepting the values of others (and, hence, them) can allow you to help satisfy these needs. Challenging, overriding, attacking, ridiculing, or refusing to understand the values of the supervisees, and asserting that our values are right while theirs are wrong, will frustrate those needs. We need to be wary of:

"We have got to do what is right (my values) for the kids."

"I have got a responsibility to make sure there is good teaching (those things I value) going on in the classroom."

All these things may result in defensiveness, conflict, loss of self-esteem, loss of independence and freedom, and loss of autonomy and commitment to growth.

We are not suggesting that we as supervisors be valueless like bean bag chairs passively waiting to be punched into whatever shape fits the contour of the sitter. It does mean that we need to make an honest, thorough effort to understand and work with the values supervisees hold. When supervisees know that we understand their values, and still accept them as persons, though different from us, we are beginning to create for them the safe environment necessary for us to collect data together on teaching-learning interactions.

By accepting and understanding supervisee values, then making instructional decisions based on data, you minimize external control and threat (McGregor), enhance the supervisee's feelings of self-esteem, competence, adequacy, self-respect, independence and freedom (Maslow), and develop and maintain supervisee autonomy and commitment (Argyris). The purpose of this unit is to help you begin to identify supervisee values so that you will be able to indicate to the supervisee your understanding and acceptance of these values using the verbal skills in the next unit.

Vignette I

Bob worked as a biology teacher in my school. Young, dynamic, and extraordinarily knowledgeable in his field, he was incredibly popular with the kids. They ran *to* class, not *away from* it. They were prepared because they knew he would challenge them. Of course, he had the most able students and they were almost all children of professional people, but the projects they turned out—gosh, were they good. The kinds of questions they asked showed deeply developed understanding of the issues behind the facts. It was a joy to be there. Bob wanted to be able to have real discussions in his classes. He defined these as long interchanges in which he merely moderated or was quiet while the kids pursued an argument with order, logic and passion. Among his other skills, Bob was a behaviorist. He knew in detail how to shape behavior, even that as complex as the sharing and initiating behavior required for a lively interesting discussion.

I observed the "normal" verbal communications patterns in Bob's classroom:

Question and Answer Pattern I

BOB: *What is the relationship of the Framis to the Obbertauff?*
      (10-15 hands would go up.)

STUDENT: *The relationship can be looked at in two ways: First . . .*
      (and would give an extended answer)

BOB: *That's a really great answer, here is some more information on that . . .*

STUDENT II: *I read in my father's physiology journal that, . . .*

BOB: *I didn't know that, can you bring in the information for me to read?*

STUDENT III: *Last summer when we were on vacation, we visited the research labs in Rochester, and we saw Dr. Filbut; he told us . . .*

BOB: *Some recent work related to this but at variance with his conclusions is . . .*

This recurring pattern of extended answers with Bob adding more information or commenting on each student's contribution was observable throughout the period. It was exciting to hear students so interested, involved and informed.

But Bob felt the interaction would be better if students reacted to other students instead of just to him. He was very clear. He wanted to change the pattern to:

Question and Answer Pattern II

   A. Teacher question

   B. Student I response

   C. Student II reaction to Student I

   D. Student III adding information

   E. Student IV drawing a conclusion

   F. Student V asking a question

   G. Student I, II, III, IV beginning to turn to answer of question

   H. Student VI correlating this information with today's lesson from the book

   I. Student VI wondering if the information and ideas could be applied to a problem she has read about in the newspaper that morning.

Teacher: Reinforcing the students' interest and asking related questions

This Nirvana of students freely discussing the material and relating it to their own world seemed possible with Bob's classes. He would have to be very conscious of his own behavior, and non-verbally encourage and reinforce, sometimes as a switchboard staying out of the center. "I'll try to let the kids be in control—move into the shadow."

We planned questions and teacher behaviors.

We planned non-verbal reinforcement strategies and cueing techniques.

We planned for everything but Bob's hidden values.

In the next classes, I observed the following question-answer patterns:

Pattern III

Teacher:	Question
Student A:	Answer
Teacher:	Response
Student B:	Answer
Teacher:	Adds information
Student C:	Initiates more information
Teacher:	Relates new research
Student D:	Applies this information to topic

Teacher:	Asks related question
Student E:	Answers related question and asks new question
Teacher:	Answers question even though five other hands are raised.

Any difference between this pattern III and pattern I is accidental. At every opportunity where students could have carried on the discussion without the teacher, he stepped in and brought the control and focus back to him. This occurred even when the students demonstrated willingness to carry on without him.

We tried several times to change this pattern, and he continued to say he wished to change, but made little progress. Finally we agreed to postpone working on this pattern until Bob decided to raise the issue again. He never did.

END OF VIGNETTE

Supervisors are not psychologists or therapists. Bob's behavior was different from his expressed values. Because his behavior proved difficult to change, and because he was already an extraordinarily effective teacher, as supervisor, I decided to honor his values and autonomy by not trying to change his practice against his wishes. He apparently valued the teacher role of being in the center, of keeping the kids dependent on him. Beyond clarifying this value with him, I could not go unless I wished to violate my own values of encouraging his autonomy. His value was helping the students in some ways, and holding them back in others. On balance, my value-laden judgment is that he was more positive than negative. I left that issue and we went on to other things.

You may or may not agree with this decision. That is your value.

It is probably important, however, to realize that any strategy you follow is coming from your values. Just as important to realize is that your strategy is impinging on another's values. Our understanding of other's values will always be incomplete. The extent to which we can understand the value structure of even one other person is limited. Accepting and *trying* to understand how others view the world may be the best we can be.

Activity I

The following short activity gives you practice in two skills:

1. Identifying and categorizing value statements of others.

2. Analyzing possible implications of these value statements of others.

Read the short description of a subcommittee of the administrative council of Frisilee School District (15,000 pupils). Those in attendance are doing the final shaping of a proposal to be made to the school board at the next regular meeting. We have some questions for you after you complete your reading.

Those in attendance and speaking are

1. Superintendent: Bill or Dr. Reeves
2. Assistant Superintendent for Curriculum and Instruction:
3. Principal of Adams High School: Jeff of Mr. Brown
4. Principal of Wilson Junior High School: Jean or Ms. Solinski
5. Teacher from Oak Street Elementary School: Frank or Mr. Hibbard

Vignette II

Bill sat at the bottom end of the rectangular table in the board room. He worked on stroking his pipe as he opened the meeting. Sometimes the pipe and its accountrements seemed a way of helping him remain aloof—with, but apart—from the group. He sat, seemingly comfortable behind his wall of smoke.

Bill: *"Alice, would you summarize where we concluded our last session; tell us what you have done since that meeting, and lay out the purposes of today's final meeting before we present these recommendations at Wednesday's board meeting?"*

The question's form was really a directive to Alice who was sitting at the top end of the table. The rest of the group was scattered in those relatively less powerful positions along the sides.

Alice glanced at Jeff Brown, the high school principal. He seemed most independent of the three—perhaps he could be counted on to raise some good questions. Then she plunged in; getting started well is always difficult.

Alice: *"Thanks, Bill, I'll be glad to. We have decided in this proposal to lay out the assumptions to be used as the basis for all the curricular decisions we will be making over the next five years. Then, after we get the Board's approval of them, we will use these assumptions to estabish specific policies for each level of our school program. Since your summary ending last meeting, I have written out, in a sequenced way, the assumptions list you developed. All of you have copies in front of you. We will go over these today to put them in final shape for the Board meeting. How do you want to handle this, Bill?"*

Bill: *"You just go right ahead Alice, I will sit and listen to the discussions."*

Alice: *Thinking (Nuts, when does he ever get out in front? This isn't my program—it's his. Why doesn't he publicly own it? Oh, well).*

Jeff: *"Dr. Moreno!"*

Bill: *"Yes, Jeff, go right ahead."*

Jeff: *"Dr. Moreno, I don't believe number two on this list. 'We assume that if an individual child is not learning at an acceptable rate, the staff is not succeeding in designing an appropriate program.' There are some children who will never make it. Their background, their intelligence, their families, or their behavior limit them. Nothing we can do will make much difference. Attempts on our part to assume responsibility for lack of learning with children like these is unrealistic and just dooms us to failure."*

Bill: *Thinking. (Now why did he pick on that one? It is the main idea and the one most difficult to realize. We just have to begin to start with the assumption that every student can learn and try to insure it. I thought he would understand the need for that.)*

Bill: *"Mr. Brown, I believe that any other posture than the one stated is unprofessional. We are educators who should know how to work with each child. If we set lower expectations, even for one student, we cheat that person of his potential."*

Jeff: *"Well as principal of Adams High School, I just don't think it is realistic, and furthermore, I don't think teachers will support that radical a statement."*

Bill: *Thinking. (Did he think I was going to back down on this issue? Did he really think I could be challenged that way? Not one word of that assumption is going to be changed. Some of the others yes, but this one, NO.)*

Frank: *"Dr. Reeves."*

Bill: *"Yes, Frank. I am glad you are willing to share your thoughts with us. We need input from the trenches."*

Frank: *"Perhaps, I should keep quiet in the presence of my betters, but that number two assumption is my ideal also. However, there will have to be a whole different way—uuh—what I mean is that we will need lots of support in resources if we are to make that assumption anything more than words on a paper."*

Bill: *Thinking. (At least someone understands what we are trying to do.)*

Bill: *"I believe in it, and we are going to try. Thank you for your understanding and support, Frank."*

Frank: *"Thank you, Dr. Reeves."*

Bill: *"Now, are there any further questions?"*

Jean: *"Dr. Moreno!"*

Bill: *"Yes, Ms. Solinski."*

Jean: *"I just wanted to say to the group that I think Dr. Reeves' program is very clear, and even if we don't all agree 100%, I think we all ought to pull together and present a united front at the Board meeting on Wednesday. After all, the public will be there, and we will have enough trouble with the lunatic fringes without bickering among ourselves in front of others."*

Bill: *Thinking. (Nuts, I wanted their support, but I did want an honest discussion to work out the bugs. I wonder if I said anything too harsh to Jeff. It looks like I might as well close up the meeting; we aren't going to get any real discussion now after Jean's speeches.)*

Jeff: *"Dr. Reeves."*

Bill: *"Yes, Jeff, go right ahead."*

Jeff: *"Well I was just trying to raise questions that I think will come up on Wednesday. Of course I will support you and Dr. Reeves and the team in public."*

Bill: *Thinking. (Now Jeff wants to get back in; apparently he doesn't sense any real opposition so he is going to support it. Maybe someday we will really deal with issues instead of shadow boxing.)*

Bill: *"Thanks folks, I know I have your support. Alice, you have done a really good job getting this all together in such a neat form. If there are no further issues to be raised, I think I would like you to present this to the Board on Wednesday. I would like to be free to moderate and to read reaction."*

Alice: *Thinking. (I wonder if in his last life he ate a lot of chestnuts by open fires, and he had someone else bring them out of the pan to see if they were cool enough to eat?)*

Bill: *"Now that we are agreed on that, Alice, I think I will run the next section of the meeting. Let's try to anticipate questions and plan our answers to them. Alice will you write down these questions?"*

Alice: *"Yes, Bill."*

END OF VIGNETTE

Activity II

Fill in the following chart with some examples from the vignette of the value categories and statements asked for.

1. In column one, indicate the *name* of a specific person who made a value statement.

2. In column two categorize the first response in the transcript to each value statement as *supportive, opposing* or *not responding* to the value statement.

3. In column three suggest whether you think the first response to the value statement made the person expressing the value feel valued *positively* or *negatively* by the responder.

Column I	Column II			Column III	
Person who made value statement	1st response, supportive, opposing or not responding to the expressed value			Your inference about the way the person felt	
	supp.	oppos.	not resp.	+Valued	-Valued
a.					
b.					
c.					
d.					
e.					
f.					
g.					
h.					

Our analysis follows:

What we include in our analysis is and probably must be inferential. We try to own these judgments and use words such as *may* or *possibly* to identify them.

Our first point is that we believe all the statements made in this meeting were value statements. They emerge out of complex personalities that carry their value canopies around with them. No small slice of behavior is conclusive, but if the same patterns were observed over a long period of time, then you could increasingly rely on your judgments about the values inside the canopy of the personality. .

Bill's first statement may express the value that he sees himself as in charge, but somewhat removed from owning the actual content of the proposal. Finally he sees others as doing the actual work of getting the proposal ready.

Alice's first statement expresses among other values, the value that the professionals do the work, the board approves the policy so the professionals can then get on with their work. She also apparently values having things written out for others to react to. She is not publicly owning the assumptions; they belong to the superindendent. The assistant superintendent probably feels (+) valued by the superintendent.

The superintendent's second response supports his value of watching from the sidelines—a coaching stance, calling the signals but keeping his uniform clean.

The High School Principal doesn't want to accept responsibility for all students learning or not learning. He doesn't really value this active a role for educators. He also values questioning the statements of his organizational bosses, but not too much or too long.

The response by the Superintendent to this initiation suggests a strong values conflict. It also suggests that the Superintendent believes that his values define the profession. He is not owning his position as a value, but as a given.

The High School Principal's reaction to the Superintendent suggests that he feels (—) valued or not valued, and he reacts with some hostility. He uses an electric word like *radical* to respond.

The teacher's initiation suggests his value that somehow he should be quiet in the presence of his supervisors; he also supports the ideas of the power figure.

The principal of the Junior High School values a united front and the appearance of consensus in front of others. She also seems to view the community as the enemy. Finally she sees a disagreement as bickering.

The High School Principal publicy expresses the value that he believes he should support the team and the superintendent in public. Probably he feels (—) valued by the group. Even the lowest status member can imply criticism of his views.

Finally, the superintendent, by his statement, tacitly supports this value of personal support. He also reinforces the lack of any real discussion of the issues with the group. He maintains his value of being in control, without committing himself to the product.

As a summary to this unit, we would like you to consider the following way of operating as an organization.

Everyone in the group is required to write out their ten most important values and wear these on a sign in every meeting they attend.

Why not? Wouldn't that be honest, certainly easier to deal with, and save a lot of trouble trying to find out other's secret cards while keeping yours covered?

Wouldn't "owning" your values have a similar effect to wearing such a sign? Can you stand that degree of exposure? If you can infer other's values from their behavior, aren't you already exposed?

The next unit contains specific techniques you can use to listen, to clarify, to confront and to understand other's values. Enjoy!

Unit 7

Clarifying, Listening and Understanding

Content

This unit is designed to help you develop some verbal skills that will be useful to you as you talk with your bosses, colleagues, and supervisees. Using these skills will help you to :

1. establish a safe accepting environment,
2. reinforce openness, and
3. raise the likelihood that your communication is clear and accurate.

Using these verbal skills will allow you to practice giving and receiving feedback while understanding and accepting the values of others. The last two units helped you understand the importance of this acceptance; this one shows you how to demonstrate your acceptance.

Competencies

When you have finished this unit you will be able to comfortably, accurately, skillfully and appropriately use paraphrasing, perception checking, values clarification, and last-resort-honesty verbal techniques. (The two of us had a verbal fight about what we should call last-resort-honesty. One of us opted for confrontation; the other opted for last-resort-reflection. We settled on last-resort-honesty. No one wins all the time!)

Method of Demonstration of the Competencies

"He really cares. He listens—you just know he understands. He can help you know how you feel. It is not always easy or comfortable, but that's who I go talk with if I want to sort out what I am thinking. There are no half understandings or fuzzy sliding over of difficult truths: he won't waste your time—or his. And yet, I feel that I am OK, I never feel judged."

Are these statements about the new you? That is the goal we are seeking in this unit.

124

Rationale and Explanation of the Competencies

You are aware of the need for considering supervisee feelings of self worth and self-esteem, of the need for real data in the supervisory process and of the need to accept your supervisees as persons. This acceptance includes a non-judgmental attitude toward their values. There are specific verbal skills that you can learn through practice that will help you accomplish these goals. Each helps you insure that both of you agree on the content of the communications you are exchanging. You are also communicating your interest in the supervisee and his ideas. In addition, your ability to reflect this interest in your supervisees allows your supervisees to hear how they themselves sound to at least one other person.

They are techniques, and as such may be too often or too little used. Overused these techniques become wearisome and trivial. Underused, the success of the communication is endangered by the impenetrable bush of impreciseness, the dark, confusing wilderness of generality or the suffocating flood of redundancy.

All artists in any field practice techniques as a continuing part of their professional growth. This practice is an intense and necessary training for becoming a creative interpreter of human experience. Only when all these techniques and skills are highly polished parts of the total performance does the artist become truly creative.

> To be really listened to, what a joy. To be honored with attention, to be caressed with understanding, to be heard with no judgment— I would tell all and trust with such a person. I have only known two people like that. One I climbed a mountain with, the other helped me become.[1]

The other night while I[2] was writing this and thinking about it, I went with my family to the opening night of the New York City Ballet's performance of the Nutcracker Suite at the performing arts center near our farm. I got so interested in reading the program notes that I missed the first few minutes of the program. There was an article about the relation of technique to performance which sent me back mentally to my writing. Edward Villela, principal dancer and one of the world's best, speaks to the point:[3]

> ...to have all this technique, to have worked years and years—and it's a very rigid disciplined technique, to have gained an extraordinary control of my body, and then through that control, to be able finally to be free. For as a dancer you're free—totally. The only

1. Champagne, D.W., *The Making of a Monster: The Story of a University Associate Professor* (in process), 1977, p. 50.

2. The next few pages are written in the first person. They are reporting some of Dave's experiences. We did not wish to blur the writing by attempting to homogenize it. We hope you understand this shift.

3. *The New York City Ballet* by John Unterecker in Saratoga Performing Arts Center, 1974, Onstage Magazine/Program, Volume 1, Book 1, by Publishers Enterprises Corporation, Bethesda, Maryland, c. 1974, p. 15.

thing you need is the confidence that all of that training gives you. Then you're free to do anything you like on stage. You first expose yourself. Naked. Not literally, of course, but spiritually. It's a great feeling. And it leads through into being completely yourself.

Villela is no more free than you or I, but he is able to be free of concentration on technique because he continually develops greater mastery of it.

While supervisors have neither a canvas on which to freeze their creations nor an audience to cheer their performance, they are creative artists in every sense of the word—unappreciated perhaps—but artists. Their art is more difficult than many in at least one important way; they must create spontaneously and repeatedly in new situations. Theirs is not a product observed after many hours of private practice. The quality of their art even more than other artists is the creative interweaving of technique as they respond to subtle verbal and non-verbal cues. Often the true genius of intuitive leaps is born and goes unnoticed except in the creative inner soul of the virtuoso supervisor—for if the technique is obvious or even noticed by the client, then the performance is flawed by that much. The technique must be chosen for the thought, rhythm or feeling being expressed or responded to and must be totally unobtrusive. If the client goes away humming the technique, the interaction was a failure.

We will try, and fail, to teach you when a skill or technique is appropriate. Only you can learn, and this learning will be painfully built from experience and practice—simulated and real. My hands ache with the cramps of learning where my pudgy fingers go on guitar frets to make chords, but until I gain mastery of the technique there will be no music. Your verbal skill may be as hard to come by as my dexterity with guitar strings, but practice will help both of us.

This introduction closes with two stories from the author's past. Not having confidence in his storytelling ability, he draws the *correct* moral of each story for you.

Both of these stories come from the same setting. The incidents happened within a couple days of each other.

Setting: Once upon a time a long time ago in a small and beautiful college town in Southern Utah, I was a participant, with several colleagues, in a two-week leadership training workshop which focused on sensitivity training.[1]

In the kooky, mixed euphoria-despondency, inner-directed self-examination atmosphere induced by our sensitivity trainers, we were all sitting in our group talking, when suddenly our two leaders, with some secret signal for technique 102a, stood up, rushed toward each other, embraced and started crying. As a performance, it rated at least three stars on a five star scale; and when they had originally done that in

---

[1]This was really a valuable experience. It was made available for a young doctoral student through the understanding of his program director.

response to some feeling in some other group in some context where it was spontaneous and real, it must have been a development point for the group. In our group at that time and place it was only unreal, staged and ineffective *for me*. It simply did not apply to where we were in our group at that time.

Because of the appearance of phony staging of technique in this instance by the leaders of our group, I began to be conscious of their technique to the extent that my learning from the experience and from myself was interfered witĥ.

Moral: The use of techniques you learn must be natural, real and appropriate to the setting and to the moment.

Story 2

The head trainer, or dean of the workshop, called an open planning session of the leadership group. We, as participants in the workshop, were allowed to listen. The dean made the following statement during the planning: "If you've done one of these workshops, you've done them all . . ." He went on to qualify his statement, but I didn't really hear the rest. He was not listening to us individually; he was responding mechanically and technically to noises he heard representing growth stages of types of individuals. This dean of trainers could perhaps be alibied for by saying that he was coming off a hard and long summer of workshop training and was tired. He cannot be excused, however, since he was incompetent at that time to practice on us no matter his usual technical skill. He was unable to concentrate on us as individuals. It was also a fact that this trainer and the group with whom he was working were having great trouble relating to and learning from one another.

Moral: Having gained your technical skill, you must use it with care and compassion. You must attend to the person with whom you are using it. If you are not capable of this kind of focused attention, declare youself incompetent and reschedule your supervision.

Organization

Each specific skill introduced here is first explained and then exemplified in simulated situations. Finally, you are asked to practice your use of the skill. So far, it has been our observation that most people only use a new technique when they must display it in real situations. This amount of practice does not produce acceptable levels of mastery.

Paraphrasing

Often we are not sure we understand completely what is being said to us, or that the persons with whom we are talking understand their own meanings and feelings about what they are saying. Sometimes we need to restate what is being said. Paraphrasing the content of a statement heard may help to insure that both agree on the meaning of the content.

Paraphrasing means stating out loud the sense of what has been said to you. Your restatement tries to capture both the cognitive and the affective components of the message you are paraphrasing, re-expressing the total message you heard with original emphases of the speaker.

This essentially simple technique somehow comes out sounding difficult and abstract in written form.

The following example of the use of paraphrasing will clarify the explanation. The paraphrases are italicized:

T: I know why they didn't complete the assignment in the correct way. They just didn't listen carefully and write down the directions; then they try to get me mad by asking over and over again for the same directions I have already given.

S: I understand. You're saying that *they didn't fulfill the requirements of the assignment because they didn't listen carefully to you and write them down as you gave them. Then they asked you to repeat, over and over again, the same directions you gave.*

T: Yes, exactly.

S: I get the feeling that gives you some frustration. Is that true?

T: You bet it does. If they would just take the effort to listen closely the whole problem could be avoided. The directions are complete, and they can understand them when I say the same thing over again two or three times.

S: O.K. So *you feel the directions are complete when you give them, and the students seem to catch on when you follow the first statement with a repetition of the instruction two or three times.*

T: No. I never repeat right after giving the instructions once. It is usually at the end of the period, sometimes as they are leaving, so there is no opportunity to repeat. I mean that when I repeat them at a later time, after they ask questions about them, they seem to catch on.

The supervisor in this situation is using only paraphrasing because we are pulling the strings. In real circumstances he would use other verbal techniques as well. You can see, however, that the paraphrasing insured that both of them understood the conversation, and then it led to a point from which the supervisor and supervisee might be able to explore the forces causing the disturbing effect. It also, we might conjecture with confidence, let the supervisee know that the supervisor is listening, regarding the supervisee's statements as important, and accepting those statements without the harsh criticism that threatens feelings of self-worth and self-esteem.

Some examples of other lead-ins to paraphrases follow:

1. Did I hear you right? What you said was . . . .
2. Let me run that out again . . . .
3. Here is what I heard you say . . . .
4. Is this what you meant? . . . .

5. The sense of that for me was . . . .
6. I hear you saying . . . .
7. What I got from that was . . . . Was that the whole idea?
8. You seem to be feeling . . . . when you say . . . .
9. You are feeling . . . . and you don't like . . . . right now.
10. My feeling right now is that we are not understanding each other; here is what I think you are saying, ...
11. My attention wandered on that last—can I try and see if I got all you were saying? . . . .
12. What you are saying is this . . . .; but your face and body are saying . . . . Can you clarify the apparent differences for me?

13. What you are saying is . . . . and what you were saying five minutes ago was . . . . Can you clarify the apparent differences in those two statements for me?

14. What you are saying now is . . . . and what you were saying five minutes ago was . . . . Can you tell me, do these mean the same thing, or have you changed your point of view?

(Notice that in 7, 12, 13 and 14 two techniques are interwoven: paraphrasing and direct questioning.)

We would like to suggest here that reading about this technique is relatively useless to you unless you actually try it out. You have to experience how you feel actually paraphrasing. You need some feedback on whether you were easy and natural, or phony and pretentious. We suggest you turn to the appendix under this unit and actually do the first few activities. The ability to use and not overuse this technique will develop through practice with feedback.

Final Comment

Well used, this technique can serve to:
1. focus a discussion,
2. teach client responsibility,
3. develop your own and client listening skills, and
4. serve as a check on moving too fast before things are clear.

Used as a space filler, or as a phony attempt to be non-directive, the paraphrase can be used as a great put-down.

We recommend you use paraphrasing when you are talking with:
a. someone who uses long, involved bursts of communication containing many issues, to slow that person down and encourage him to focus his own communication,
b. someone who seems shy and reticent, to slow you down and allow the other to bring out needed detail and affect without being steamrollered,

   c. someone who seems not to be listening to himself, who seems to
      be just filling space with sound, to help him stop, introspect and
      focus,
   d. someone it is ordinarily very difficult for you to pay attention to,
      forcing you to pay attention closely enough to find meaning in
      what you usually regard as unworthwhile verbiage.

As described thus far, the paraphrasing is simply a method of checking the surface, obvious meaning of statements. Whether the statements
mean what the speaker meant may not be discovered through paraphrasing. For that reason, a more probing method of paraphrasing
might be advantageous in some circumstances. In this form, the hearer
rephrases his understanding of the speaker's statement by placing it into
the context of what has been said previously, or by making a logical
extension of it by asking whether a hypothetical example, as in this
example taken from the dialogue on page 128.

   T: I know why they didn't complete the assignment in the correct
      way. They just didn't listen carefully and write down the direc-
      tions; then they try to get me mad by asking over and over again
      for the same directions I already gave.

   S: I understand. You're saying that they didn't fulfill the require-
      ments of the assignment because they didn't listen carefully to
      them and write them down as you gave them. Then they asked you
      to repeat, over and over again, the same directions you gave.

   T: Yes, exactly.

   S: So all the students are sitting there, quietly, looking blankly at you
      while the directions are being given, not asking questions.

   T: Not really. They don't sit quietly. They're busy talking to some-
      one, getting ready for class to end, or writing a letter, or reading a
      comic.

The example, which explains for the speaker the picture the hearer
has gotten, has served to bring out other understandings of the situation
that were in the speaker's head but were not conveyed to the listener.
Such paraphrases might begin with
   I could imagine that . . .
   So what really happened was . . .
   Then here is the total sequence as you describe it . . .

Perception Checking
   Perception checking is the other end of the telescope from paraphrasing. Here you are asking others to paraphrase what you have been saying. You want to know if your communications are clear, if all of your
message has been received, or if the person with whom you are talking
has been able to absorb all that you are trying to communicate.

Often we are not communicating with others because we are not listening to them. We merely wait for silence so we can begin talking, not trying to hear and understand. This situation may be as true of your supervisees as it is true of you. This technique and the previous one are attempts to improve listening in supervisory interactions. A sample of a supervisory exchange which uses a perception check follows (the perception check is starred).

S: Then that's agreed?

T: Yes.

S: Let's check our notes on the procedure. I'd like to suggest we check my understanding, then yours. O.K.?

T: Fine.

S: Here's what I have. You'll first plan; then we'll go over the plans, then you give these new directions with these materials; and on Friday, when the workshop participants come back for the afternoon session, we'll check—with me sitting in the back, I'll arrive about 10 minutes before the participants, and our expectations are that at least two-thirds of them will have been able to complete the process. Does that sound right?

T: Yes, that's right.

*S: O.K. Let's review what you've got in your notes to be sure we're agreeing on the same thing.

T: Well, first I am to plan by myself; then I give the participants. . .

S: Sounds like we're talking about the same thing. I'll see you there 10 minutes before.

This example of one perception check was fairly straightforward. The supervisor and the coordinating teacher had just worked out a fairly complicated sequence of steps which were going to be followed. The supervisor wanted to be sure that the coordinating teacher knew the total sequence, and, further, is really committing herself to it. So she asked for a perception check.

The use of perception checking can be threatening if used poorly. The supervisee may regard it as an indication the supervisor doesn't believe him intelligent enough to understand and remember. For that reason, it is probably important that the supervisee value perception checking as much as the supervisor. At some early conference, you might explain, using the term "perception check," your concern that both members of the conference agree on the perception of the ideas. In future conferences, your request for a perception check at critical points may be understood and easily accepted, even valued. You also need to be prepared for the delightful circumstance in which the supervisee, growing in autonomy and responsibility, asks you for a perception check.

Other possible ways of asking for perception checks follow:

1. I'm not sure that I was very clear; can you read that back to me?
2. Your last statement indicated your idea of what I've been saying isn't quite the same as mine. Can you restate for me the whole idea as you see it?
3. Where are we?
4. This is a key point. I need a check to see that we are both hearing the same thing. Would you summarize our agreement to this point?
5. Hey, you look (happy, puzzled, confused, excited, overwhelmed) all of a sudden, what did I just say?
6. Can you summarize our agreement (or my proposal) before you state your reactions to it?

Some situations in which this technique may be useful are:

a. Any negotiations between two individuals or groups where it is absolutely necessary to ensure understanding of what is being discussed.
b. When you get a clue that you are being misunderstood or some subtlety is escaping the person with whom you are talking.
c. When you feel that somehow you may have mistated or misrepresented a position and you need to check out what has been received.
d. When you feel that things have moved too rapidly and some of the details are not registering with your supervisee.
e. As a way to summarize a conference or major issue in a meeting before moving on.

Again we strongly recommend practice of this technique. The first practice should probably be with a friend who knows you well and who agrees to your strange behavior. He should know what you are doing so he can give honest feedback on your mastery of the technique. Only after you have gotten some facility with your friend should you try this with a person who is only a colleague or a supervisee.

Non-Directive Reflection

Sometimes supervisors begin to get the feeling that they should become replicas of Carl R. Rogers,[1] the non-directive therapist. We all seem to have these feelings at one time or another. Trying to affect behavior alone without at the same time realizing that we are having some effects on personality is an exercise in selective perception. It is

[1]Among the many books Carl R. Rogers has written, we would recommend *On Becoming a Person, Client Centered Therapy* and *Freedom to Learn* as basic teaching for any field where human beings interact.

bound to at least partially cripple our effectiveness in intervention activities.

However, we are not therapists. We are not directly treating the psyche of our clients. We are trying to help them focus on, or change, attitudes or behaviors which appear to directly affect their instructional behavior. We specifically delimit our practice as supervisors to those professional areas concerned with instruction. We leave the directly therapeutic to the therapists. One verbal technique that borders on therapy is the use of non-directive reflection—the supervisor paraphrasing content and affect from the supervisee's statements: "You are saying you are angry about that, and you are saying your anger may be affecting some of your reactions."

A person using non-directive reflection has a self-image resembling a plane mirror, neither sending the ideas and feelings that he perceives out in all directions and only reflecting back a small part to the source (a convex mirror), nor focusing all the ideas and feelings down so they are more concentrated (a concave mirror), but simply reflecting them back in the same direction from which they came with the original intensity and meaning. Essentially, the non-directive technique provides a delayed echo for the person so he can hear himself and interpret or understand his own meaning. The interventionist has no directions in which she is trying to lead or push the client. It is not as though you, the interventionist, hold no values; but in using this technique you are deliberately withholding your values from the client. You are essentially a transmitter of the client's thoughts, adding as little of yourself as possible.

We are not saying this technique is easy to learn or use. It is not. It requires a very high concentration on what is being said, how it is being said, and what is being felt by the person saying it.

The use of the paraphrase is one of the basic skills in this technique. A person who is good at this technique goes beyond paraphrase by often making inferences about something they perceive is being thought or felt by the supervisee but is not being expressed out loud or in complete language. These inferences are sometimes injected into the reflection, but are always identified for what they are. A final skill we have identified in the non-directive reflection is that the interventionist occasionally also reports his feelings or reactions to what is being said or expressed by the client. This category of response seems to exist in most of the scripts Rogers reports. While it seems a part of the technique, it may be simply a deviation from it. An example of this kind of utterance is, "I'm very puzzled by what you are saying. It sounds as though you have reached a conclusion, but you don't want to express it out loud because you don't think I'll approve of what you say." Here the interventionist is reporting his own feeling while making an inference for which he probably has little evidence. Sometimes, if well used and the feeling or thought expressed is real, this last skill will help the client make a break-through in his thinking about an issue. Sometimes, even if wrong, this kind of statement will get the client to rethink an issue and get out of a rut.

To summarize, non-directive reflection is probably 75% paraphrasing, 24% inference making and intuiting the client's thought or feeling, 1% reporting your own feelings or thoughts, and 150% hard, careful listening and observing.[1]

Rogers' use of this technique has effectively resulted in the personal growth of many of his clients. His interventions occur usually in one-to-one interactions over long sequences of interviews, but he does use the same technique in small group psycho-therapy. He reports some sequences of 70 or more interviews with different clients with very few effective sequences of but one or a few interviews. As supervisors we do not have the luxury of that kind of time or that small a case load. However, since our clients are adequately functioning people, they generally need less intervention from us and need it at more behavioral than psychic levels. We may still be able to show some effectiveness with this technique in our necessarily shorter interventions as supervisors because of this adequate, or better, level of functioning of our clients.

Considering Argyris' three conditions for effective intervention (review these if they are not vividly etched in your memory - Unit I), the following seem to be some possible kinds of situations in which non-directive reflection may be appropriate:

1. When a client is trying to decide which of two instructional techniques is right for him to use in a given situation and the decision is his to make.

2. When a client has had a strong personal reaction to a situation in an instructional setting and wants help in determining its meaning to him; (e.g., he lost his temper with a student or a class group for no reason he understands; really felt turned on to certain students as persons and doesn't know why; or has created a group highly dependent on his direction and doesn't like the results).

3. When a client is reaching for a clearer definition of her instructional role as she begins to believe that she is giving the students mixed signals about their expected behavior.

4. When a client feels that students are not making sufficient progress in learning, has yet to identify the cause, and feels it is important to him to work it out himself.

The following simulated dialogue may help make this technique somewhat clearer. Be forewarned that it is made up of words carefully chosen to make the technique as clear as possible. The whole dialogue is an attempt at non-directive reflection on the part of the supervisor.

The authors harbor a strong prejudice that use of this technique is most appropriate when the client is well aware of your value not to provide certain kinds of answers on certain issues. Also, the client should understand that you believe he should make up his own mind, and that on issues like this you, as interventionist, will likely become as non-directive as you are able. In other words, a solid, trusting, long-standing working relationship may be necessary for the use of this verbal tool.

T: I've got a problem. In my fifth period class, things somehow seem sour. One or two students seem to be harboring some kind of anger or resentment and they are letting it out by sabotaging the class morale. They make fun of any student who gets serious and begins to think about the meaning of an issue.

S. O.K. Let me see if I've got this straight. You've got two students who are presently appearing to sabotage the class by making fun of others who are serious? You seem very angry at them.

T: You're darn right I'm angry. Those two little snots have left me livid every day for a week. Just when I get the class close to an **important generalization, they slide in a nasty comment that** wrecks the entire mood. I have ignored them as we are supposed to and frankly, I'd like to take them on and tell them where to get off.

S: I understand. This has been going on every day for a week and at this point you wish you could tell them off instead of ignoring them. I also get the feeling you feel that you have been directed to use one strategy for this situation—ignore the behavior. You resent this directive.

T: That's the real issue as far as I'm concerned, since that new principal came in this fall and told us that he was instituting a new kind of discipline, and that from now on we would use behavior modification instead of what has always worked for me. He gives me no support and the kids are beginning to feel they can get away with anything. There's no respect for authority anymore. If I sent one of them out of the class, I would be in trouble, not the kid.

S: Now I hear another problem and, frankly, to me this feels like the more real one. You started out talking about two students you saw as making fun of others who were trying to learn, now you are expressing your resentment of the new principal and his attempt to bring in a new set of rules.

T: I . . . guess . . . well, that is exactly what I've said. I guess I really know how to deal with those students. I can talk to them after class and help them see what they are doing, but what I was trying to do was prove to you, who'd listen, that this new principal is kind of a dummy.

Here we were trying to demonstrate the supervisor reflecting the expressions of the teacher. In doing so he used paraphrasing, and he made some intuitive inferences of how the teacher seemed to be feeling about what he was saying. All of our supervisor's inferences seemed to be correct according to the reaction of the teacher; and, of course, everything just seemed to work out perfectly and quickly. Most of us are neither as skilled nor as lucky as this supervisor. Often we do not have a teacher as open to his own experience as this one was. Thus, the reflecting may lead to blind alleys or to dead ends. Sometimes, however, things really do work out and the teacher goes away better able to solve his own problems by having this kind of outside mirror available.

The most common problems we as supervisors may have with this technique are the following:

1. We stop listening carefully and begin to anticipate what the client is going to say. We then respond to what we anticipate rather than what was said.

2. We start to reflect only on selected parts of what is stated and begin to try to manipulate the client in a direction we have selected.

3. Our "inferences" become subtle cues we hope the client will pick up as solutions. They are really not inferences at all except in our hope that we can make them come true by verbalizing them

It is very difficult for most of us to suspend our urge to direct and control others, and we ever so subtly reintroduce our attempts through this kind of technique.

O.K., try it! But first do it with an understanding, critical friend. Have him tell you how well or badly he sees you using this technique. Then try to express to this person how satisfying use of this verbal technique feels to you. Its systematic use requires a whole value reorientation for most of us in this culture since we are voluntarily giving up control and direction of what happens.

Value Clarification Techniques

These are popular words nowadays. They have so many meanings that within a few years they will probably have joined the rest of the educational compost pile of promising ideas, jargonized into unrecognizable but richly smelling refuse. As used here, values clarification techniques mean asking questions of a client to help the client clarify and verbalize his affective and cognitive beliefs about education, teaching and instruction. The resulting self-knowledge may be important in helping some teachers gain perspective.

Additional support for values clarification comes from the work of Mosher (1972).[1] Teachers who became more able to clarify their roles, values and intentions, and to think through the kinds of compromises they wished to make to others' conflicting values and expectations, were perceived as improved teachers by others who were rating them. These results were obtained without the supervisor, who conducted the interviews, overseeing the teaching of this group of teachers.

[1]Mosher's chapter on ego counseling presents data showing change in teacher behavior as a result of a sequence of interviews which used what could now be called values clarification questions.

It is important to realize that values do not necessarily derive from research. They are generalizations a person uses as working assumptions on which to base decisions. The supervisor's concern is not really to derive the source of these values, but to help the client bring his hidden beliefs to a conscious level. While these values may be the basis for a client's decision making, they are not facts, and may not even be believed by others. Finally, the purpose of values clarification techniques in supervision is to help both supervisor and supervisee make connections between the ways they perceive things, i.e., their values and the way they behave and perceive others' behavior.

The following specific categories of values clarification questions we wish to teach in this section are derived, in part, from Raths and Simons (1966).[1]

1. Questions which ask a client to clarify the assumptions or values behind a statement she may have made.

   Client: Students need to be told how they should act. They are more comfortable if they know what is right.

   *Supervisor: What assumptions are you making about people if you believe this is the way students operate best.

At this point there are many possible directions the supervisor can go with the client. The supervisor can drop the issue entirely after showing his understanding of the clients' values. The client can be asked to explore the implications, both immediate and long-range, of her assumptions. The client can be helped to plan ways to achieve the kind of values and clarity she believes are desirable in her instructional setting. The client can be sensitized to her use of certain language, such as the possessive pronoun used when describing the students or the classroom. The client can be asked to resolve apparent conficts between this value position and other statements of value positions made earlier; e.g., the value that students should learn responsibility and practice democratic ideals. Finally, the client can be asked how she thinks someone else in her position might react to her statements of beliefs. These categories of supervisory response are the only ones we wish to teach here.

Values clarification episodes in supervision are usually short, focused sessions that leave things hanging in the client's mind. The packages are not wrapped and tied with bows to look neat and finished. They just trail off as supervisor and client move on to something else.

---

[1]This book published in 1966 really started this vocabulary and suggested many of the strategies used in the field. The second book in the field, with Simons as the senior author, *Values Clarification*, further develops the ideas. Their applications are generally directed to teaching situations with groups of students, but they seem immediately applicable to supervision, both as supervisory techniques and self-examination questions for supervisors. We see Mosher's work, done earlier, as fitting directly into this same area.

We highly recommend that you read either of the Raths-Simons books as background for these techniques. There are more than 30 different specific categories of clarifying responses suggested in these books.

*Represents the specific category of values clarification response we are exemplifying.

What we'd like to do now is to take our original dialogue with the client, identify a category of values clarification and invent possible dialogue in which the supervisor uses a techique in the category.

2. The client can be led to explore the implications, both immediate and long-range, of her assumptions.

Client: Students need to be told how they should act. They are more comforatable if they know what is right.

*Supervisor: What are the implications of that statement for you?

Client: Well, it means that I've got to give each of my students clear directions and tell them when they are behaving the way I want them to.

*Supervisor: Then you will set up clear expectations and criteria of mastery for the students?

Client: Yes.

This conversation can be extended to greater depths and specifics or it can be ended here. One way to end the values clarification section of this conference could be to move into specific planning of the rules under which the students will be expected to operate. (See Category 3)

3. The client can be helped to plan ways to achieve the kind of values and clarity he believes are desirable in his instructional setting.

(Here we will simply pick up the dialogue where we left it in example 2.)

*Supervisor: Then with this value let's see what specific expectations you plan to set up with this group of students.

Client: Well, I want it to be quiet, except when I call upon my students to speak.

*Supervisor: How will you share that value with your students?

4. The client can be sensitized to her use of certain language, such as the possessive pronoun when describing the students or the classroom.

*Supervisor: What are the implications of that statement for you?

Client: Well, it means that I've got to give each of my students clear directions and tell them when they are behaving the way I want them to.

*Supervisor: How will you feel if all this happens?

Client: Well, I'll feel that I've got pretty good control of my instructional area, and that I'm in a position to really begin to teach my students what they should do and how they should act.

*Supervisor: Before we go on, I'd like your permission to go back for just a second and ask you about your choice of words in the last few minutes.

Client: O.K., I guess.

*Supervisor: There is a language pattern I'd like to call to your attention—just to ask you to think about. You use the words "I want them to," and "what they should do," which sound like controlling directive words. If you want to discuss these, we can; or you can just think about what these mean to you.

Client: Well, I'd like to discuss these. Are they wrong?

*Supervisor: I hope I'm not sending that message. We need to avoid making any judgments of rightness and wrongness and discuss instead hidden values we hold and their effects on us and our students. When I mentioned that I only wanted you to be aware of something I noticed, we can either explore it or drop it, whatever you decide.

5. The client can be asked to explore apparent conflicts between this value position and other statements of values or value positions made earlier.

*Supervisor: Then you will set up clear criteria of expectations and of mastery for the students?

Client: Yes.

*Supervisor: O.K., from the students' point of view, what are they learning about whose decisions are important in the instructional setting?

Client: Well, my decisions are important. That's what all my training and experience give me the responsibility for.

*Supervisor: Last week, however, you said this: "One of my biggest roles as a teacher is to teach democratic ideas and to give students a chance to practice those ideas within my class." Do you see any conflict between those two sets of statements, last week's and today's?

Client: Only one big enough to park a battleship in. Let me decide which of these, or some combination of them, I really believe. I wonder if my students get as confused as I do?

6. The client is asked to consider how others might respond to similar situations.

Client:	Students need to be told how they should act. They are more comfortable if they know what is right.
*Supervisor:	That statement involves some assumptions you are making about people.
Client:	Well, yes, that's true; but that's the way people are.
*Supervisor:	How do you think Ms. Sommers down the hall would react to those statements?
Client:	I know she'd disagree with me, with that open classroom she runs.
*Supervisor:	How do you think your principal would state the same ideas?
Client:	About the same way I do. I guess that's why she and I get along so well.
*Supervisor:	Let's take two of your students. How do you think John would react to that original statement? Then, how do you think Jena would react to it?
Client:	Well, those are two very different kettles of fish. John is an absolute free thinker; just give him an idea and he wants to go off in a corner and do something with it. Jena, on the other hand, really needs an individual tutor. She just stops when she has reached the end of the specific step explained to her.
	O.K., let me decide what it was I really meant. Why don't you let me live in my naive, simple world and be happy there?

Raths, et al. (1966, pp.53-54) list ten criteria for effective clarifying responses. We summarize and interpret them here for you, but at the same time we recommend that you read *Values and Teaching* for yourself. We are too biased in favor of these techniques to be completely trusted.

1. This response does not moralize, criticize or suggest the right answer.

2. It leaves the responsibility with the client for deciding what, if anything, he wishes to do about the value.

3. It leaves the client the right *not* to do anything with the question.

4. It does not attempt to cause giant changes. It seeks continued introspection or small increments of action.

5. This clarifying question is not an interrogation. The only client answer may be a quiet withdrawal.

6. Most values clarifications episodes are short.

7. Usually values clarification episodes are individual, not group in nature.

8. The techniques of values clarification are not used in every situation. They are used selectively.

9. There are no right answers to values clarification questions.

10. There is no strict fomula for this technique. As with other techniques, it must be used with thought and care.

Using any of these values clarifying responses is difficult, and using all with any real facility is very difficult. One reason is that the available cues indicating which technique to use are few and not explicit. It becomes a matter of intuitive judgment to decide how far to push.

A second reason this is a difficult task is that practice has to be deliberately staged so the clarifying response is appropriate. That means you have to seek out a friend who can utter judgmental statements you can recognize and then clarify. You will probably have to teach this friend the whole conceptual system of values clarification so he doesn't become hostile and tell you to go away.

A third reason for difficulty in learning this mode of supervision is that our culture does not support it. We are taught to argue, to convince, or to try to convert. We are not reinforced for acceptance of difference or for clarification of this difference.

"Our group believes" or "Don't you agree" are much more commonly heard than "Then you really value . . ." For us to actually use this language and then leave that value alone is very rare. Probably we have bought into the value that our role is indeed to convince, convert, or seduce.

If you want to explore these ideas further, read any of the Raths-Simons books.

Last-Resort Honesty

The last specific technique we wish to teach in this unit is last-resort honesty. We mean one very explicit thing by last-resort honesty. If your client appears to be verbally or non-verbally lying to you or is hostile, uncooperative, or avoiding an issue, then you need to productively raise the issue of that behavior with your client.

There may be many reasons why a client chooses not to level with you, some related to your status or behavior. If you have a reputation for using what you learn about a person against him at some later time, you have generated reasons for deceit or avoidance behavior. That is not to say that you are always responsible when the supervisee is not being honest with himself or you. It may be the supervisee's characteristic mode of acting, or may be a defense he developed during past unfortunate experiences with supervisors.

When you believe you and your client are not communicating honestly, for whatever reason, you call a time out and say, but more tactfully, "Hey, client, we are not really leveling with each other. What is the trouble? Neither of us is going to be of much help to the other until we can trust each other with the truth. Now what is it that is not quite out on the table but is getting in the way?"

Note: It really took us a long time to come to use this kind of honesty with ourselves and then with others. We have finally gotten to this place because we only want to do real things. Discussing unreal things with unreal people isn't one of the ways we want to use our time.

The basic strategy here is not to push anyone into a corner or make any accusations. This strategy assumes you really want to strip away several layers of pretense and get down to sharing where you really are at. If you enjoy this kind of interaction, look forward to it, and invent reasons to initiate this strategy, you may wish to investigate reasons why you are in this field. Whose needs are being met in your supervisory interaction? Your purpose here should be to give a person relatively straightforward opportunities to level. Usually the best approach is to come out of yourself and report your impressions and feelings as tentative inferences you have made about interactions with your client.

Several examples of this strategy follow. Some discussion of the conditions when this strategy seems appropriate follow the examples.

1. Confrontations of client evading responsibility for behaviors and results.

Supervisor: Then we are agreed that neither of us is satisfied with the achievement of most of the students in this area of instruction?

Client: You are absolutely right. From day one, that group just came in with a bad attitude. They just wanted an easy time of it, and they decided to bug me until I gave it to them.

Supervisor: Is there any other possible reason for their slow rate of growth.

Client: The personnel director in this building refuses to transfer the loafers out of my section to somewhere else. He says I've just got to deal with them. Now some of those students are lazy; they come from bad backgrounds and . . .

Supervisor: What special kinds of planning have you done for this group? I've just received the records, and they seem on the average to be ahead of every other group in reading comprehension and math skill.

Client: I never did trust standardized tests anyway, and this example just goes to prove it. And another thing, I've put in five requisitions for special materials in the last two weeks for this kind of learner. You can't do anything without lots of high interest materials.

Supervisor: Client, I am feeling very frustrated right now. We are both agreed that neither of us is satisfied with the students' progress; and now, after successfully blaming the students, the personnel director, the testing and the materials, we still haven't begun to talk to the real problem. What can we do in this meeting with these students with these materials to begin to get better progress in the skills we are trying to teach?

Client: Well, all those things are problems. I can't fight city hall. What do you think I should do? I'll try anything you suggest.

Supervisor: I'd like to report what went through my mind as you were talking. I was thinking, "Oh, no. I'm not going to suggest something so that tomorrow he can add me to the list of causes for failure in this setting."

Client: It's funny. That strategy always worked before with my other supervisors. It got people off my back. O.K., so you want to really get down to cases. You are sure you want to take the time? I'm tired of being blamed. I'd like some success this year.

Supervisor: I've got the next two hours today, and some time tomorrow. What do you want help with?

Client: Well, the real problem in this group is the wide range of skills the students have. I just don't know how to plan, organize or manage an individual approach that will reach most of the students where they are. I seem to have to be everywhere at once.

Supervisor: Now that is something I can be helpful with. It will take a lot of work to get it organized, but after that you can manage it by yourself with about the same amount of planning time a teacher normally spends for a group this size.

Summary of Issues and Strategies

This teacher could have extended the list of avoidance behaviors for as long as the supervisor had time to listen. All of these reasons had

some validity so it is harder to turn them off or to get at the real problem. The dialogue reported here sounds as if the supervisor was trying
to cut through these other issues and get the client to deal with the
reality of the situation and then take responsibility for trying some
action. The supervisor tried to report his feelings of frustration at their
lack of progress in the conference as a way to get the client to change
his strategy. In our dialogue, the teacher capitulated easily. Sometimes
this happens, sometimes not. Certainly nothing was being accomplished
with the other strategies being used. As a final resort, had this strategy
not worked, the supervisor might have stated: "Even if these things are
all major contributing factors to the setting, we've got to get down to
doing something. Now let's recognize the situation and begin to plan for
tomorrow with the materials we have. What would you like to begin to
work on tomorrow?" This last strategy is less likely to be successful in
the beginning since it seems more threatening to the teacher; but it is
preferable to a continued exchange of inanities followed by terminal
platitudes.

2. Last-resort honesty with a client who is hostile or uncooperative.

    Supervisor: I'll be in your area next week on Monday, Tuesday and
                  Wednesday. When would be a good time for me to see
                  you and then to plan an observation and a follow-up
                  conference? You remember you were testing all the last
                  time I was in your area?

    Client: Well, you just happened to run into another special
                  time. We are doing some special small group commit-
                  tee work where you wouldn't be able to see anything of
                  interest.

    Supervisor: That sounds very interesting. I'd like to see that unit.
                  Perhaps I could be of help.

    Client: No, I think you'd just be in the way and upset the
                  students.

    Supervisor: Well then, you name a day and I'll make a special trip.

    Client: Well frankly, I'm not sure that at this time I need any
                  help. Things are just going along fine. I'll call you if I
                  need anything. Why don't you concentrate on those
                  teachers who really need help; I don't.

    Supervisor: Wait, wait, wait a minute! Two months ago you told
                  me you had some problems you wanted help with.
                  Since then, you've made and broken six conference
                  appointments, and now you tell me you don't want any
                  supervisory help. I frankly feel you are avoiding facing
                  your problems and right now you are preparing to get
                  angry and hostile at me as a way of driving me away so

you won't have to risk anyone knowing that you want
help. Now which of the three days of next week shall
we plan an observation and a post conference? Do you
want to pick the day or should I?

Certainly you should only use this sort of strategy when you are
almost certain that no other will work. You have taken responsibility
for the course of action in the face of objections from your client. Temporarily you are denying condition number two of Argyris' three criteria
for successful intervention, the autonomy of the client. You have made
a deliberate choice that real data on the teaching is necessary before you
can establish any kind of honest helping relationship. You may have
alienated this teacher for some time. That is why this is "last-resort"
honesty, to be used only when there is no other mode.

But when the supervisee persists, avoidance of him because his behavior is an effective protective wall certainly does not demonstrate a caring
concern for him. Nor is it a real commitment to the students who are
under the care of this supervisee.

Simulate with an understanding friend the use of the particular skills
described here.

Then move on to other units.

Unit 8

Giving and Receiving Feedback

Content Overview and Rationale for this Unit

The skills of an effective Theory Y supervisor—encouraging autonomy in the supervisee, knowing when the supervisee is or is not ready to try a new method, running a productive conference, facilitating groups—are all learned. An effective supervisor, in other words, is made not born. Social skills that facilitate others' trust can be learned if we want to learn them and if we try hard enough.

Behaviors are learned through various means, all of which require feedback concerning the relative success of each attempt. The skills of throwing a dart or firing a rifle are learned by the most direct form of feedback: observing the results in the target. Unfortunately, in interpersonal communication a behavior may not result in clear, honest feedback, so the appropriateness of the behavior cannot be measured directly. A supervisee may smile and agree, while inwardly his stomach grinds with anger or frustration.

Without accurate feedback concerning the effect your behavior has on supervisees, you will have difficulty learning new, more effective behavior. The same is true for feedback you give teachers or any other supervisees. If you are not able to give accurate, useful feedback, the teacher will have little more information on which to evaluate his new behavior than he had without your presence. That's not good enough.

Feedback is also important to help us gain the self-knowledge prerequisite to accurate knowledge of others. Jourard (1963, 1980) discusses the "selves" each of us has lurking in our minds. The "real" self is what we actually are, but no one can describe it. The social self, on the other hand, is what we believe others see when they look at us. Jourard points out that the social self has a different personality and appearance from the real self and that to act according to the social self often puts us at a disadvantage. For instance: if a woman believes that men over forty view her as inept or immature, she will interpret their actions as confirming that belief (self-fulfilling prophecy) and will act accordingly (by becoming defensive if a man over forty criticizes her or by trying too hard to prove she is capable and mature).

To some extent, we all have inaccurate conceptions of how others view us. Only through feedback from others can each of us gain an understanding of how they actually view us.

Feedback is important also because your supervision will be effective only if you have a satisfactory affective relationship with the supervisee. As you know, Maslow, McGregor, and Argyris emphasize the need to consider the client's affect and commitment. That affect may be hidden. For instance, you may feel that you need to be especially tactful and cautious, but the supervisee might really want frankness and be put-off, frustrated, or insulted by your "beating around the bush". On the other hand, another supervisee may appear bold and brassy so you come on bold and brassy, not realizing that the boldness was to cover-up deep-seated feelings of inadequacy, which require tact. You will have to learn to elicit and accept feedback about your behavior to see whether you are maintaining the supervisee's self-esteem. Of course, you will also have to learn to look for and infer from non-verbal behavior.

Competencies

Before you go on to the next unit you should:
1. List several reasons why accurate feedback is an important element of effective supervision.
2. Describe accurately how you give feedback to supervisees.
3. Identify specific methods of giving feedback you wish to change or reemphasize in supervision.
4. Describe your progress in changing your use of feedback.

We hope you will value the giving and receiving of accurate feedback enough to try to give it and to ask for it regularly.

Activity to Demonstrate the Need

This activity emphasizes the fact that all of us need feedback from others because our views of the ways others view us (our social selves) are often not entirely accurate. Since that is true, the supervisory behavior we exhibit may not have the favorable effect we believe it does. Here come the data; you are going to collect them yourselves.

The following survey (Survey I) may be answered by you about you. You should "guess" how a group of supervisees would answer this survey about you.

If you wish to go beyond your secret hunches about now others perceive you, it would be really great if you could get a small group of people who know you to answer these questions. You might consider work colleagues, fellow students in a class, friends, family. Ask any group you use to pretend they are supervisees of yours. Each person will predict from his knowledge of you how you would behave in a real supervisory situation. If you actually have supervisees, then ask them to express an accurate view of how they view your supervision. (Five to eight people should be enough for this sampling).

SURVEY I

Circle the number that indicates most closely how you view the supervision I have given in the past.

This supervisor:

1. encourages creativity
   1 2 3 4 5 6 7 8
   very much   very little

2. is domineering
   1 2 3 4 5 6 7 8
   usually   never

3. stimulates me to teach better
   1 2 3 4 5 6 7 8
   very much   very little

4. considers feelings and concerns
   1 2 3 4 5 6 7 8
   usually   never

5. gives me honest feedback
   1 2 3 4 5 6 7 8
   usually   never

6. stimulates me to try new methods
   1 2 3 4 5 6 7 8
   usually   never

7. knows when to say the right thing
   1 2 3 4 5 6 7 8
   usually   never

8. reacts well to criticism
   1 2 3 4 5 6 7 8
   usually   never

9. becomes involved in my concerns
   1 2 3 4 5 6 7 8
   usually   never

10. shows trust
    1 2 3 4 5 6 7 8
    usually   never

11. shows acceptance
    1 2 3 4 5 6 7 8
    usually   never

12. presents data to support conclusions
    1 2 3 4 5 6 7 8
    usually   never

13. allows me to make choices
    1 2 3 4 5 6 7 8
    usually   never

14. gets me to feel responsible for choices
    1 2 3 4 5 6 7 8
    usually   never

15. develops several alternatives with me before we decide
    1 2 3 4 5 6 7 8
    usually   never

DISCUSSION

You will probably discover that your view of yourself was somewhat different from others' views of you, and that they differed also among themselves. Only through gaining feedback from them as individuals can you discover how your behavior has been affecting them and alter it to have the effect you desire. Seeking feedback should be a regular part of your supervision so you can regularly discover and improve your effectiveness.

Do you now value the need for feedback?

1. I feel that feedback given to me on my behavior and values is important and wish to learn how to elicit it from others.

    yes_____ no_____

2. I feel my feedback to my supervisees is important and wish to learn how to give it more effectively.

    yes_____ no_____

3. I'm not sure I see the need for feedback, but I'm willing to continue because it seems that I should be able to see the need.

    yes_____ no_____

4. I don't see the need for feedback for myself or my supervisees.

    yes_____ no_____

If you agreed with 1, 2 or 3, continue with this unit. If you agreed with only 4, and especially if you also were very high at the Theory X end of the scale in Unit 1, you may have to resign yourself for now to being a telling-structuring supervisor and accept all of the interpersonal problems and poor communication that go along with this role.

However, reading this unit may be useful; it may give you more perspective on feedback and it will offer some limited supervisory behaviors you might feel comfortable using.

The Supervisor as the Researcher

We, along with Cogan and Argyris, have proposed that in order to be effective supervisors of people we need to use a data-based approach with less of the assumption, superstition, and ignorance that have caused problems and ill-feelings between supervisees and supervisors in the past.[1] The use of verifiable fact is most important in the feedback given and received. We are asking that your orientation to this unit be that of researcher, for every act of supervision should, in reality , be a research investigation.

You and the persons you supervise set up conditions or, at least become aware of the conditions which exist. Then you can manipulate independent variables (or you enumerate the variables operating without your direct manipulation) and discover the effects.

The effect, in order to be meaningful, must be reported factually. For example, a teacher wishes to teach students to do X in a new way; she explains the new way to you; the two of you decide on a method of gathering data to see whether the new method is more effective than the old. You gather the data and discuss the facts. It would not be useful to discuss assumptions and superstitions drawing such conclusions as, "Even though the new method didn't teach as well as the old, I have the

---

[1] The title of Arthus Blumberg's book *Supervisors vs. Teachers: The Private Cold War* (McCutchan, 1974) suggests some of the results of this pattern.

feeling (intuition) that it made a favorable impression on the students (not measured), so I'm going to continue using it." If we allow ourselves to rely on intuition, we will probably do little to improve instruction.

Facts are not conclusions. The reason for using facts instead of conclusions in feedback is that all people tend to base their conclusions on subjective values, feelings and intuitions, so that the conclusions come out biased and distorted. That is only human. The supervisee's biases may differ from the supervisor's; worse, both may agree on biased conclusions for which there is no factual justification. For example "I don't like lecturing, and neither does the teacher, even though she lectures well. So we agreed that she would cut out the lectures and use small group discussion instead." Why? Only biased conclusions.

Feeding back conclusions may aggravate the feelings of insecurity the supervisee inevitably has already. Because the supervisor is a superior, and because the supervisee has come to the supervisor for help, the supervisee may think "You're OK, but I'm a klutz." If that diminished self-esteem is reinforced by the supervisor's biased and negative conclusions ("That was a bad class; you need improvement."), defensiveness, withdrawal, and unhappiness may result. The teacher may also accept the conclusions, without the data, and use them inappropriately. If that occurs, effective supervision cannot result. On the other hand, if the feedback consists of biased and positive conclusions ("That was a good class; you really don't need improvement."), unrealistic opinions result and inappropriate behavior may be reinforced.

To avoid these biased conclusions, to encourage the supervisee to take as active a role as possible in the supervision, and to move the supervision beyond the witch-doctor stage of superstition, report facts when giving feedback. Then, together with the supervisee, begin cautiously to draw inferences from the facts.

FACTS AND BEHAVIOR

The facts you report about human interaction will usually be behaviors. Behaviors are facts because they are overt, verifiable actions. They can be observed. As you are aware from Unit II, "Joan furrowed her brow, stamped her foot, then slammed the door as she left" and "Joan stated that she was angry" are facts—overt behaviors. On the other hand, the statement "Joan was angry" is an inference based on facts.

Because of the need for facts, certain conditions must be met in the feedback. First, there must be some agreed-upon purpose for gathering the data: for example,

   a. to discover whether method X has a favorable effect on students,
or
   b. to discover how much positive reinforcement a teacher gives in 10 minutes,
or
   c. to discover whether or not the supervisor dominates the supervisor-supervisee conference.

Then, the type of feedback needed can be determined:

a. objective tests,

or

b. affective surveys,

or

c. counting the number of positively reinforcing statements the teacher makes,

or

d. counting the number of times the teacher is interrupted by the supervisor.

Finally, a method of collecting the data can be determined:

a. administering a test to students,

or

b. administering a survey to students,

or

c. taping a class and listening to the tape,

or

d. taping a conference and typing a script from the tape.

The feedback should be factual and serve only the agreed-upon purpose.

Once the data have been reviewed, both teacher and supervisor together can make inferences, with the realization that inferences are tentative and subjective. If the inferences are only "possible" rather than "probable," the supervisor and supervisee can discuss methods of gathering more data to make more reliable inferences.

PERSONAL FEELINGS

Personal feelings are factual data if stated explicitly: "I had the feeling that . . . ," "It hit me as . . . ," etc. When using such subjective data, follow the statement with a description of behaviors that caused you to have the feeling. The personal feeling reported this way differ from judgments described in Unit II. Since judgments reflect much subjectivity and bias and little fact, you will want to avoid them in giving feedback. They tend only to obstruct growth and irritate. Instead of saying, "You were wrong to reprimand that student," describe the effects of the reprimand on the student (After reprimanding that student, the student did not raise his hand any more during class); or, if those data are not available, be honest and state, subjectively, "It concerned me that the student might have had a negative feeling about your reprimand, but I didn't notice any reaction from him. Did you get that feeling also? What ways can we check out our inferences?"

SAFE ENVIRONMENT

In giving feedback, we have often heard those with whom we work ask, "well, how can I give negative feedback and still maintain the

supervisee's feelings of self-worth and self-esteem?" If by negative feedback you mean judgments of the worth of the supervisee's performance
embodied in words such as "wrong, terrible, not adequte, unsatisfactory," the best way to maintain the supervisee's feelings of self-worth
and self-esteem is don't use the words—they are judgments. If, on the
other hand, you mean by negative feedback facts which might indicate
that some effect the supervisee hoped would occur, did not or an effect
the supervisee hoped would not occur, did, then present the facts as
both of you decided beforehand you would, without inference or judgment. Both of you together make inferences on the basis of the facts you
have collected. Even if the supervisee asks for your judgments, don't
give them. Explain that your business is collecting data so both of you
can make inferences together and then decide on ways to check them
out.

Those "negative" facts will be accepted by the supervisee and dealt
with maturely and constructively if the supervisee does not feel that they
are given as an attack on his/her proficiency or self-worth. That feeling
will continue if the supervisee and supervisor have had a past relationship in which the supervisor has been accepting of the supervisee, supportive in instances where negative data is given, and *not judgmental*
based on the supervisor's own biases. It is important to remember that
feedback is useful only for growth. Less growth will occur if there is
defensiveness, anxiety, and lowered feelings of self-esteem. Deciding
between you on the type of feedback, giving only facts, together making inferences, and positively reinforcing behavior you have together
decided is desirable will promote growth. If there is other feedback you
wish to give, don't. Even if the supervisee says to go ahead, you are
violating an implicit contract you made to stick to certain areas. This
violation makes it more difficult for the supervisee to trust you in the
next round.

AFFECTIVE FEEDBACK

One way of gaining knowledge of supervisees' feelings toward the
supervision and you is to ask for them. It will be useful to end conferences by attempting to gain factual feedback about the supervisee's perceptions of the conference. After asking a general, "How did you feel
about the conference", you might ask more specific questions: "Did it
bother you that I mentioned_____twice," "I was trying to interrupt you less. How often did that behavior occur?" In that way you will
gain more factual data about the supervisee's view of you, and improve
your self-knowledge.

IMPLICATIONS OF COMMON PATTERNS
IN SUPERVISOR BEHAVIOR

We cite here some common patterns in supervisor behavior with
supervisees. We then identify possible messages received by the supervisee as a result of the pattern. Our purpose in presenting these patterns is

to give you a knd of feedback. Be aware, as we are, that any of these possible effects can be enhanced, cancelled out or blunted by a non-verbal message sent at the same time. People often believe the non-verbal message more readily than the verbal one. You may wish to think about your behavior to see if it commonly contains these patterns.

The Patterns

1. The supervisor uses "I" (e.g. "I saw this" or " I like this").

If this is a common behavior pattern it may suggest an owning of what the supervisor is saying or it may be perceived by supervisees as the supervisor establishing a superiority in the relationship. "I" can convey a veiled command or a disinterest in the other's point of view. If you have this pattern in your relationships, what do you think it conveys? Does a strong "I" pattern as you use it help create a safe environment?

2. The supervisor uses "you" (e.g. "*You* did this" or "When *you* walked toward John . . .". This pattern can mean any of the following:
   a. A constant awareness that the supervisee is responsible for what happens,
   b. A kind of separation, a disowning of responsibility on the part of the supervisor,
   c. An accusation or laying of blame by the supervisor,
   d. A recognition by both parties that the supervisee is in charge and will make the final decisions in the situation.

Do any of these implications fit your situation? Does your "you" pattern create a safe environment for the supervisee?

3. The supervisor uses positive reinforcers (e.g. "I like that" or "What a great idea").

4. The supervisor uses negative statements (e.g. "I do not like that" or "That was a lousy idea").

5. The supervisor makes judgments (e.g. "I do not like that" or "That was bad").

Carl Rogers suggests that any judgmental feedback, whether positive or negative, is ultimately threatening to the client (supervisee). He reasons that if we allow ourselves to praise, and our supervisees accept or even honor the praising judgment, then we are also in a position to punish, and they are helpless against it. We may be creating anxiety or tension when we least mean to by giving praise meant to dispel it. He suggests that we restrict ourselves at all times to non-judgmental feedback. We are almost as untrained at giving this kind of feedback, as our supervisees are untrained at hearing it. They want to hear us valuing their behavior. Can we afford the luxury of providing judgmental feedback when we know its effects?

This job of supervising gets harder and harder doesn't it? Does your judgmental feedback help your supervisee feel comfortable and safe?

6. The supervisor uses paraphrasing (e.g. "What you are saying is" or "The idea I hear you expressing is").

Paraphrasing is a way of checking to see if you have correctly received the message being communicated. It is a non-judgmental tool which, if used carefully, often elicits supervisees' initiation, self-evaluation problem solving, or values clarification. Used badly, it often has supervisees perceiving you as a phony with nothing to offer. Do you use this technique? How does it seem to come across? What do supervisees do after your paraphrasing? Does their behavior suggest a safe feeling on their part?

7. The supervisor builds on the supervisee's comments (e.g. "If what you say is true, then what follows is" or "The implications of your statement are . . .").

Building on supervisees' comments suggests extending and drawing implications about what the supervisee has said. It also suggests that you have heard, understood and valued what the supervisee is saying. This pattern should suggest a more equal relationship and should promote a feeling of caring and safety on the part of supervisees. Does it work this way in your conferences? How do you know?

8. The supervisor expresses feelings (e.g. "I really felt good when" or "I've always felt badly when I felt I had to discipline . . .").

Expressing your feelings can be a very threatening experience to your supervisees. They may feel intimidated and fail to disagree out loud, or they may feel safe and feel that your expression of feelings allows them to do likewise. Again, this can be a very threatening experience or a very rewarding one depending on the non-verbal messages accompanying the expression. The reaction also depends on the relationship—its strength, its honesty, and its norms. The behavior of supervisees after your expression of feelings is the only indication we have of their reaction. What behaviors usually follow from your expression of feelings? What inferences seem probable from these behaviors?

9. The supervisor ellicits feelings (e.g. 'How did you feel when" or "Were you feeling happy when . . .").

This pattern may produce very useful data if the supervisee is willing to honestly communicate feelings. It might be valuable for you to know how a supervisee feels when he is doing or saying certain things. However, giving this information may be threatening for the supervisee. He may view it as displaying a part of him you don't need to see, for purposes of which he is not sure. He may decide how he is "supposed" to feel, and tell you he feels that way. Particularly if the supervisee feels vulnerable and fears that he may lose self-esteem or that you will judge him as weak or unstable will he be reluctant or dishonest. The supervisee will feel that way if a trusting, safe environment has not been established. Do you believe you set up a safe enough atmosphere to get his information easily and confidently? How do you plan to use it once you get it?

10. The supervisor gives directions or orders (e.g. "When asked that kind of question by a student, you should say . . ." or "In my classrooms you may not use_____method of instruction").

11. The supervisor corrects the supervisee (e.g. "You were wrong

when you said . . ." or "That's not right, what I said was . . .").

Both of these patterns will probably have some bearing on the feelings of the supervisees about the relationship. They may begin to watch their words very carefully, to be very careful of what they do when you are watching. These patterns rarely lead to an open, trusting, safe relationship. You may feel that at times it is necessary for you to behave this way. That may sometimes be true, but realize, also, the likely results.

12. The supervisor ellicits criticism of her own supervision (e.g. "I have been very directive. How else may I work with you to be more effective?" or "Tell me some of your reactions and criticisms to my supervision.").

It may be very hard for supervisees to respond to questions or statements like these. They must trust you highly enough that they will risk telling you what you are asking to hear. Your response to their criticism is a key factor in maintaining a safe environment. If you become defensive or hostile then you have probably destroyed your chances of gaining future honest feedback. You will be perceived as an authority figure with power. You must, therefore, be careful of using that power if you are trying to establish a safe environment.

13. The supervisor rejects ideas or suggestions (e.g. "No that is not an acceptable way of solving that problem." or "I don't think we should consider that suggestion.").

Much of the previous discussion applies here. If you wish your supervision to be an equal sharing of colleagues, then these patterns of behavior are very likely to interfere with that relationship.

14. The supervisor ignores the supervisees' statements.

15. The supervisor criticizes the supervisees as persons.

16. The supervisor interrupts the supervisees' statements (no examples seem necessary here).

These last three patterns seem rude and thoughtless for the power figure in a relationship. None is really available to the supervisee as response. The supervisor is simply teaching the supervisee which person is powerful and which is powerless in the relationship. Is that the message you choose to send? Who gave a supervisor that right? More importantly, why would a supervisor engage in behaviors of such low productivity?

Some Supervisee Patterns of Behavior and Possible Inferences from Them

1. The supervisee initiates ideas.
2. The supervisee asks for help.
3. The supervisee asks questions.
4. The supervisee volunteers data.
5. The supervisee volunteers feelings.
6. The supervisee accepts supervisors' data with little defensive behavior.
7. The supervisee initiates self-evaluation (both positive and negative).

8. The supervisee interrupts supervisor to add own ideas.

All of these behavior patterns were carefully chosen to exemplify some pretty clear signals that the supervisee feels safe in the setting. The opposite of these patterns is usually indicative of supervisee's feelings of lack of safety in the atmosphere you have established. We have tried, in this unit, to explain, briefly and concisely, some methods of giving and interpreting feedback. Hopefully, you will be able to use the information to learn and to teach.

Unit 9

Supervisory Relationships

Content

This unit is an integrating one. It seeks to draw together the interpersonal skills and valuing systems you have been learning about into a system of behaviors which are characterized as "helping" or as the "helping relationship."

Using the Unit

This unit asks you to think out applications of its ideas by relating them to the conceptual schemes of unit 1 and consultant supervision.

Entry Skills

It is expected that you will be able to appropriately use the vocabulary of the previous seven units. You should have developed many of the skills you worked at in the previous units.

Competencies

When you finish this unit you should be able to demonstrate your ability to:

1. explain the characteristics of a "helper."
2. point out "helping behaviors" and "nonhelping behaviors" you and others use.
3. design a plan to adopt new behaviors you wish to use after recognizing the helping behaviors you now use.

Explanation and Rationale for these Competencies

The only way your supervisory practice will make sense to your supervisees is for them to recognize some consistent patterns in that practice.

We see many schools and people in them not functioning well because they don't have consistent leaders operating from clear values and techniques. Their leaders' verbalized values clash with unverbalized values they express with other behaviors.

Here we ask you to examine your helping behaviors to see if they form a pattern evident to you and to others, consistent with all your other value positions.

Helping Behaviors

ACTIVITY I

1. List below the names of two persons to whom you would go for help in solving a problem.

a. _____

b. _____

2. List below the important characteristics these persons seem to have that make you feel comfortable going to them.

a. _____

b. _____

c. _____

d. _____

e. _____

f. _____

g. _____

h. _____

3. Explain below how these attributes demonstrate skills of supervision similar to those you have learned thus far in this book. How do those helping persons, in their own way, follow suggestions of Maslow, Argyris, and McGregor?

_____

_____

_____

_____

_____

_____

_____

Our purpose in beginning with this activity is to focus your attention on those behaviors that help you work on issues important to you. We are also trying to relate the skills we have been teaching to these same helping behaviors.

ACTIVITY II

Below we present ten characteristics of the "helping relationship" described by Carl R. Rogers (Jourard, 1963, p. 43). In the space below each of these characteristics write how you see it relating to the ideas and techniques of Maslow, McGregor, and Argyris.

An effective helper has the following characteristics:

1. *Trustworthiness.* He is of good will and he can be depended on to keep his word.

_____

_____

_____

2. *Openness.* He communicates his feelings and reactions fully to the other person.

_____

_____

_____

3. *Not afraid to like.* He permits himself to experience and express positive feelings for the other person.

_____

_____

_____

4. *Respect for differences.* He shows the courage to respect the different opinions and attitudes other persons hold.

_____

_____

_____

5. *"Letting be."* He shows willingness to permit the other person to be himself.

_____

_____

_____

6. *Empathy.* He has the ability and willingness to see the world from the other person's point of view.

_____

_____

_____

7. *Positive regard.* He displays honest acceptance of the other person, in all his difference.

_____

_____

_____

8. *Tact.* He has enough sensitivity to avoid threatening the other person.

_____

_____

_____

9. *Permissiveness*. He avoids judging or evaluating the conduct or experience of the other person.

_____

_____

_____

10. *Faith in man's potentials*. He is profoundly committed to the belief that people can change and grow.

_____

_____

_____

Not surprisingly, some psychologists indicate that a "healthy personality" includes many attributes of an effective helper. Alfred Adler, a psychoanalyst, describes the goal of personal growth and of therapy as the attainment of *gemeinschaftgeful*, or "social interest—social feeling" (Jourard, 1963, p. 7-8). Jourard describes this goal as a "feeling of oneness, a brotherly feeling towards one's fellow man." He writes that, "people who have achieved *gemeinschaftgeful* no longer compete irrationally with others, nor do they strive to be *one-up* on them. They see their fellow men as worthy beings to be regarded as ends in themselves, not as threats or as mere tools to be used for self-advancement."

Both as people and as middle manager-supervisors, we see ourselves and you as achieving greater mental health and effectiveness when we increase our abilities and inclinations to empathize with others, to establish helping relationships.

A "safe environment" is partly the result of the presence of a helper who has those helping attributes. The supervisee is able to feel comfortable, i.e. safe, with a supervisor who is comfortable with himself, who is nonjudgmental and accepting. There must also be other conditions present, such as physical safety, a sense of group belongingness, and so forth, but this helping person seems essential.

AUTONOMY

We have, in Unit I (*A Framework of Theory and Concepts*) written about Argyris' three tasks for an effective interventionist. The third of these tasks is the development of internal commitment. The whole focus of Argyris' argument for internal commitment is based on the necessity for increasing clients' sense of autonomy, of lowering their dependence on outside others. We, as supervisors, should be actively trying to work ourselves out of each helping role we take on. We may go back to other helping roles with the same persons, but if we are needed in the same roles we are fostering dependence and not autonomy by our methods of helping.

You can encourage autonomy and independence, while helping, by encouraging the supervisee to make his choices and by encouraging him to set his own directions and criteria of evaluation. You will grow in the skill of doing this if you are conscious of the need. The continuum on the next page illustrates the varying degrees of responsibility the supervisee might assume as she becomes more autonomous.

THE COLLEGIAL RELATIONSHIP

One goal of supervision is to establish an environment in which supervisees become more independent, more competent and more autonomous. Developing and extending this environment are never-ending tasks which, like the preservation of liberty, require eternal vigilance. If supervisees are to become more in the ways listed above then the role of the supervisor must be constantly changing to allow this growth and development. The final goal of supervision is not, and should not be, the development of supervisees who never come to supervisors. It is the development of autonomous professionals who seek out and manage the supervisors' special skills as they engage themselves in the development of their craft of teaching. Autonomy which results in avoidance of external help for growing and evaluating is not real autonomy at all. It fails the final test of being able to use the special, divergent views of others, including supervisors, in examining beliefs and shaping behaviors. Not involving others in growing may result in mental incest, inbreeding distorted, disfigured views of reality and behavior.

It is clearly better to hire an architect to design our house than it is to learn the architect's skills, then design our own. We tell the architect our values, needs and resources. He tells us the options and then helps us make a final design reflecting our preferences. It is not efficient nor really desirable for supervisees to become the masters of the special skills of the supervisors: data collection, observation, knowledge of alternate teaching and learning strategies, values clarification, etc. The end of the continuum of "helping relationships" is the last stage, the collegial relationship, where the supervisee manages the supervisor to meet the supervisee's development goals. This collegial relationship is the same as a consultant-client relationship: the purpose of the coming together is the discussion of the end product (in this case more effective learning for students through the self-growth and initiative of the supervisee) with the supervisee choosing and managing the special skills of the supervisor as a consultant in this task.

The Supervisory Model
Continuum of Stages of Directiveness
The Interventionist's Role

Directive

Stages	The Interventionist Role	Example
1.	Interventionist initiates; Interventionist chooses.	The interventionist proposes all of the alternatives and then chooses one.
2.	Interventionist initiates; Interventionist and client choose.	The interventionist proposes all of the alternative strategies: they jointly choose one.
3.	Interventionist initiates; Client chooses.	The interventionist proposes all the alternative strategies. The client chooses one.
4.	Interventionist and client both initiate; interventionist and client choose	Both interventionist and client propose strategies. Both make a choice.
5.	Interventionist and client both initiate; client chooses	Both interventionist and client propose strategies and the client chooses one.
6.	Client initiates; interventionist and client choose	The client proposes alternatives, both the interventionist and client choose one.
7.	Client initiates; interventionist questions, client chooses.	The client proposes alternatives, the interventionist asks clarifying question, the client chooses.
8.	Client initiates; client chooses	The client proposes alternatives, the client chooses, the interventionist listens.
9.	Client initiates; client defines role of interventionist; client chooses.	The client proposes the alternatives, defines a role for the interventionist, and makes the choice.

We hope you are at a readiness level which will allow you to consider a more fully collegial relationship or are actually practicing some of the behaviors required. It will take time for supervisees to believe that you value them as colleagues. The relationship grows through your statements and actions, which may often fly in the face of their previous experience with supervisors. You may have to discuss these differences openly with your supervisees.

Also inherent in the collegial relationship is encouraging the supervisee to understand and participate in the supervisory process. The relationship is collegial—i.e., professional. Therefore, each person bears equal responsibility for ensuring that the relationship is satisfying and productive. The relationship should be openly discussed, and the supervisee should be giving suggestions to improve its effectiveness for him.

All of this may be too much for you at your present stage of mastery of your supervisory role. You may wish to leave this unit and come back to it at some time in the future when you are more nearly ready.

BARRIERS TO A COLLEGIAL RELATIONSHIP

There are many.

Our culture is authority oriented. We look for the boss with questions like:

Who is in charge here?

Who is responsible?

What are the rules?

Almost all our organizations are organized hierarchically to reflect this orientation. Bosses and subordinates expect leaders to be in charge. The belief is that if leaders don't give orders, perhaps they aren't necessary or are ineffective. That is one barrier to the establishment of collegial relationships in most educational organizations.

The norm in most organizations is that supervisory-managerial personnel are experts who give advice, solve problems, have answers, and render value judgments. Not only do supervisors behave this way, but most supervisees expect them to and then reinforce them for it. If, in addition, the advice is helpful and given with a smile, it is hard for both parties not to be seducing each other into continuing this dependent, unequal role. This set of expectations may be the most powerful barrier of all to the establishment of collegial relationships.

With increasing demands for accountability, declining enrollments, cutting of staff, and fewer resources, many middle managers and many teachers are feeling threatened and are less willing to risk openness, honesty or the establishment of new relationships without perceived power figures. This is a second major barrier to the establishment of collegial relationships between supervisor and supervisee.

There are certain legal or formal duties imposed on the middle manager-supervisors which make them responsible for keeping track of sick leave and personal days, assigning extra-class duties, making class schedules, evaluating performance and others. These formal duties create one more set of hierarchical expectations which are often imposed on the supervisory relationship. Many managers and supervisees have great difficulty separating this structuring ordering part of the relationship from those parts in which they can work with teachers as colleagues. Barrier number three.

EXISTING SUPPORT FOR THE ESTABLISHMENT OF COLLEGIAL RELATIONSHIPS

We were tempted to leave this page blank as a way to suggest that there are few or no supports for this kind of relationship in our various educational organizations today. And the forces working against this relationship are strong. It will take a resolved, clear leader to beat them down.

Perhaps the strongest forces working for the establishment of this relationship are the facts that the behaviors which support this collegial relationship have been identified, are manageable by ordinary folk, and the role can be learned. Trained role models who exemplify this role are appearing, even though slowly, as managers more clearly understand it.

A second force which will work toward this working together of colleagues is the increasing professionalism of teachers. Whatever the temporary effects of unionization in splitting educational institutions into us-and-them camps, the long view possibilities of having strong, secure teachers suggest that these will be equals in schools.

Another reason the collegial relationship is necessary is that no supervisor-manager in educational institutions can convincingly pretend expertise in all the areas of teachers' competencies. To do so is destructive to any supervisory productivity. If the supervisor truly develops competency in the observation of learning settings, in recording and presenting data, in clarification techniques, and so forth, and the teacher has greater competence in content knowledge, diagnostic teaching skills, relationship building, and other teaching skills, then there exists a real basis for the coming together of equals. Both parties have skills the other needs. Both can learn to recognize their need for each other.

ACTIVITY IV

A. 1. Do you believe in this collegial supervisory relationship?

_____Yes   _____No

2. Do you believe you know the implications of this relationship?

_____Yes   _____No

3. Do you believe your values, personality and behaviors are compatible within this role?

_____Yes   _____No

B. 1. If you checked one or more answers to these questions "No" then respond to the situations in C.

2. If you checked all three yes answers then skip down to   p. 170.

C. Specifically how would *you* respond to the following situations if you want to build or maintain a collegial relationship? Commit yourself to a direction before reading our discussions on the next pages. We have left some space if you want to write these responses so you can't edit them in your head to make them match ours.

1. An experienced teacher who in the past has been a strong member of the staff comes to you and says he feels inadequate in class this year. He says that things just don't seem to settle down. What is your response if you are trying to create a collegial relationship? _____

_____

_____

_____

_____

2. You see a teacher backing a student up against the wall, yelling at that student that his behavior in class is unacceptable. What is your response if you are trying to maintain a collegial relationship?_____

_____

_____

_____

_____

3. You observe a really outstanding lesson a teacher has with her class. What is your response if you are trying to develop a collegial relationship? _____

_____

_____

_____

_____

4. A teacher has developed a new pattern of being a few minutes late for a number of mornings in a row. Her students are being left unsupervised in the attendance homeroom? What do you do? _____

_____

_____

Discussion of These Four Situations

A successful working collegial relationship is built with the bricks of many separate acts. Even a few ill-considered moves on your part can deny or destroy that atmosphere you are trying to establish. It may really be that it is impossible to create a truly collegial relationship when one person has formal, hierarchical authority over the "colleague." This superior-subordinate reality can be managed, but it will not often disappear, no matter how hard we try.

In Situation I, attempts by the supervisor to solve the perceived problems *for* the teacher destroy the possibility of an equal relationship. Both giving too much support and taking the responsibility away from the teacher damage the supervisee's autonomy.

Situation 2: Here you are often in a bind; you have a formal, official responsibility to be sure that kids aren't hurt by teachers' actions. You have to be careful not to destroy the collegial relationship you desire while making clear your stand on the appropriateness of the behavior as you see (value) it.

Our recommended strategy is to privately ask for a conference with the teacher. Be sure he is cooled off before the conference is held. If he is emotionally upset he won't be able to generate alternatives: he will still be in the flight/fight defensive posture. Start the conference by asking for the data which describe what lead up to the incidents you watched. Listen to the teacher's inferences and feelings, but get clear descriptions of the actual behaviors of each participant in the incident. If possible, ask the teacher's permission and get a separate description from the student prior to the conference with the teacher. Convey to the teacher the students' perception of the incident. Then, without looking to fix blame, move immediately to generating and exploring the implications of several alternative ways to handle this incident or similar incidents in the future. Finally, have the teacher choose one of the alternatives and own responsibility for it. No blame has been assigned, the incident has been used as a means to develop and explore more creative ways to proceed in the future. Argyris' tasks provide a direction for proceeding within the framework of a collegial relationship. You may not have had the emotional release of yelling at the teacher or enforcing your authority over him, but you have modeled another way of reacting to stressful situations. You have also preserved the teacher's sense of responsible control of his own professional behaviors.

Situation 3: Here we run the risk of establishing ourselves as the persons who determine what is or is not a *good* teaching lesson. If we as supervisors determine what is good, we also are accepting the role of determining what is *not* good. That role endangers the teacher's responsibility for being self-evaluating, eroding the quality of evaluating together.

One way around this trap is for you and the teacher together to go through a three step procedure as part of your supervisory processes:

a. Have a short pre-conference before an observation whose purpose is to establish the data which will determine the success of the lesson;

b. Observe the teaching and collect the data; and

c. Share the data with the teacher and together determine the success of the lesson.

Did your plans recognize this issue? Did you solve it in another way? Was your solution useful to the teacher, and did it promote a collegial relationship?

Would you now change any of your initial answers to the three questions in Section A of this activity? If you still don't see yourself being positive about the responses to all three questions now, then perhaps you should leave the issue for now, coming back to it after a period of time has made you want to think about the issue again.

Note: One of us was once the doctoral advisor of the other. Under most circumstances, doctoral advisors tower over the student or ex-student with the might of a graduate institution in their hands, over-powering, and smothering the student with the force of genius emanating from legendary rooms inhabited by powerful, prophetic full professors. With the edge of this power, the advisor's admonitions and praise alternately bludgeon and salve, often mysteriously, sometimes senselessly. After months and years of struggle against self-doubt, financial burdens, and uncaring or unreachable professors, the student stands before the bench awaiting a verdict. Without a favorable vote, the dissertation is delayed or thwarted and the student openly, swiftly sees his effort and self-worth disintegrate.

How, when the advisor traditionally wields such power could we manage to have anything like a collegial relationship?

But we did. Primarily because of the initiative of the advisor, who encouraged the breakdown of the superior-subordinate relationship by concentrating the efforts of both on the dissertation product by accepting the advisee as the sole and final expert on the content and substance of the dissertation, and by encouraging him to use the advisor's expertise to bring it to an end that would be acceptable to the committee. The process began months before, however, and reached fruition in the dissertation.

The advisee allowed the advisor to make certain editing decisions— style, format, transitions—meeting the University standard for quality, while the advisee reserved certain functions for himself: overall organization, shape of the intellectual arguments, amount of evidence used to support each contention, choice of procedure when we had several options, the rate of progress, and finally the right to say when the dissertation was completed. No formal contract of these divisions was made, although a formal contract with such conditions is an excellent idea. The roles evolved as the advisor criticized, commented upon, queried, and explained, receiving reactions from the advisee. When the advisor's comments were accepted and encouraged, he continued in that area. Where they were rejected in favor of the advisee's he backed off, at all times explaining problems the advisee might encounter with the committe, but permitting the advisee to make final choices. The advisee felt responsible for *his* product and the advisor had certain advisory powers delegated to him. Both remained equal colleages in the process. The advisor could have insisted on his formal legal veto powers and destroyed the collegial relationship. Both advisor and advisee knew the advisor had the right to do so. Both also knew that the product would be inferior, the relationship sterile and unrewarding and the potential for growth and learning by both parties, destroyed. It took the advisee a long time to trust that these rules would survive stress—that the collegial relationship was real. Every interaction in the beginning was an unconcious test of the advisor's motives. In those early days one slip or failure could have been tolerated, but two, three, more, would have destroyed the collegial interactions that had been the finely woven fabric of the relationship. It took the advisor years to learn how to be that way and still be honestly critical and honestly meet his obligations to represent the university community. It seems to us that the middle manager in schools is in exactly analogous situations to the university advisor and can gain that posture if he desires it.

Unit 10

Intervention Style

Content

The spiderweb spun in the shape of a wagon wheel is an intricate communication system whose strands lead to the spider's lair. Any motion, even at the outermost perimeters is telegraphed to all the strands throughout the web and the spider reacts.

The human organization is a similar, but not as orderly, web of interconnecting strands. When one person or group is set in motion by an interventionist, all other groups and persons receive some effect of that motion. The supervisor or principal, demanding all members of a committee accept her proposal, sends waves of communication through the total organization web—affecting changes in behavior.

Unlike the spider web, the interventionist's effects persist after the initial disturbance has subsided. Also unlike the spider web, the interventionist's effects are not always those predicted. Human organizations have memories. Your style and your intent affect other members of the organization's behavior, thoughts and actions. You are affecting norms, activities, interactions and sentiments. You thus change the organization as well as cause immediate effects.

We raise these issues not to paralyze you from taking any action in the spider web of your organization, but to help you be more conscious of the possible effects of your intervention style. We hope, through this consciousness, that you may plan and catalyze the effects you desire. You may explore for yourself the implications of your intervention style. For a style you do have, and effects you do cause.

Objectives

By the time you finish this unit you should be able to explain your characteristic intervention style. This explanation should be related to both Jung's and Maslow's ideas. You should also be able to explain what parts of that style are successful and unsuccessful with which kinds of people. You should be making decisions about any changes you plan in your intervention style as a consultant supervisor.

Entry Skills
You should have read all the affective units. The ideas in the Jungian typology unit should be especially current. Unit IV which explains the power task, affiliation vocabulary is also referred to here. You need to check that out again.

Activity I
We begin with an activity instead of logical arguments. This is a very complicated activity. Take time to puzzle it out before you begin.

Nine situations are described below. You are asked to make decisions on how you would act in response to each situation if you were actually facing it. To make this easier for you, we have listed pages of possible actions in each of seven categories. The lists of possible action occur on pages 172-174. You select those actions closest to the way you believe you would act if you were in this situation.

A. First *read* each situation.

B. Then *choose* from among the seven categories of possible actions the specific actions you would take in that situation.

C. After each situation, *list* the numbers of the actions you would take.

D. When you have finished this whole activity we have directions for your analysis of your patterns. These directions begin on page 174.

Nine Situations
Situation 1
You have heard the rumor that one of your untenured teachers, concerned that his position in the school is in jeopardy, has begun to complain to students that he may not be rehired next year. He is rumored to be less conscientious in the classroom. What would you do?

I would take the following numbered actions: *

Situation 2
A parent group wishes to meet with you to discuss ways of economizing in the school. The superintendent has agreed to such a meeting if the parent-group can find someone willing to talk to them. What do you do?

I would take the following numbered actions:*

Situation 3
An opportunity for inter-departmental cooperation has arisen that could benefit the school. It seems the responsibility for getting it underway has fallen on you. What do you do?

I would take the following numbered actions:*

---

* Use as many numbers as you wish, but only those you really believe you would do in the actual situation. Consider all seven categories of actions on pages 172-174.

Situation 4

A student who has asked to speak to you tearfully explains that her teacher yells at her. What do you do?

I would take the following numbered actions:

Situation 5

Three teachers who must share a room during the day have a conflict over putting up displays on the walls. They ask you to mediate a discussion. What do you do?

I would take the following numbered actions:

Situation 6

You have heard that a higher administrator dislikes you. What do you do?

I would take the following numbered actions:

Situation 7

In a supervisory conference the teacher becomes sullen and quiet. The conference time is over before you can work out whatever the problem is. What do you do later?

I would take the following numbered actions:

Situation 8

A new teacher joins a team. The teacher has been hired because she is innovative and creative. "The other team members," she explains after four weeks, "seem to be ostracizing me." What do you do?

I would take the following numbered actions:

Situation 9

During a committee meeting it becomes obvious that two teachers regard your proposal and you as hairbrained. What do you do?

I would take the following numbered actions:

List of Seven Categories of Possible Actions You Might Take:

A. You would immediately:
   1. Say what you think then
   2. Write a firm note to the persons involved
   3. Defend your prestige and position immediately
   4. Suggest that the problem is interfering with getting the job done and that it should be dropped
   5. Wait to see what else develops
   6. Work on the emotional forces acting right now
B. Then, to get the problem straight you would:
   7. Send out notes or surveys asking cogent questions
   8. Appoint persons to search out the facts

9. Search out and diagnose the facts myself

10. Examine elements in the system to see what has occurred and how it can be altered in the future

11. Discover the concrete facts that occurred and record them as accurately as possible

12. Gather impressions of what has occurred to make a Gestalt judgment

C. If you intend to *discuss* the facts with people involved, then you would:

13. Listen quietly, mulling over the facts and possibilities as the people involved discuss the problem

14. Participate in brainstorming, communicating my ideas with the others as they come

15. Have an informal chat over coffee

16. Have one or two consultants come in for a question-answer discussion

17. Take pains to insure that the discussion is always on the track

18. Allow some digressions to keep the atmosphere light

19. Have discussants fill out descriptions of the forces acting and collate them to form a majority opinion

20. Limit discussion to facts

21. Permit discussants to make intuitive comments

22. Make sure discussants come to valid conclusions

D. If you intend to have a lecture or presentation to come to a satisfactory solution you would:

23. Have a panel of consultants come in for a presentation

24. Bring in a consultant to discuss the organization and structures that will avoid the problem in the future

25. Bring the faculty together as a body and give what I see to be the problems and the solutions

26. Have an analyst come in to examine the system

27. Use a film, I have found, to present similar problems and their solutions in other districts

E. If you intend to have an individual talk with person(s) involved to reach a satisfactory conclusion, you would:

28. Get together, one at a time, with the people involved and find out what the facts are

29. Ask a superior who can suggest some solutions to give you direction in working with the individuals

30. Discuss how you feel about what is going on

31. Encourage each person to discuss how (s)he feels about what is going on

32. Ask the person involved to explain what is going on and quietly listen

33. Encourage each person to work out the problem in a way (s)he feels would most benefit them and the institution

F. If you intend to approach the entire organization you would:

34. Encourage ways of having people share feelings and have more consensus
35. Try to be more open about my own feelings to the people involved so they would open up
36. Establish mechanisms so that such problems could be minimized or eliminated before people have them
37. Gather together important figures of the organization to brainstorm ways of changing the organization

G. After all of this you intend:

38. When all the facts are in, mulling them over and coming to a judgment by yourself
39. Coming to a conclusion that will please my superiors
40. Coming to a conclusion that will enhance the faculty's attitude towards me
41. Allowing forces and people in the situation to make the decision
42. Setting up a structure whereby the desirable solution will result, even if I have to make it do so
43. Allowing people involved to make the decision, but sway them by subtle guidance to one that seems right to me
44. Suggesting conclusions that concentrate on mending problems in the overall system
45. Coming to a conclusion that intuition, as well as logic, indicates is valid

Each action seems to us more representative of one dimension of the Jungian typology than the others. For that reason, it will now be possible for you to examine your choices to see how much your typology affected them, or whether your typology seems to have any real bearing on your behavior choices. Note: This activity has an unknown reliability or validity.

The letters to the left in the list that follows represent dimensions in the typology. To the right are the numbers of responses that are probably representative of each dimension. Place a small dash under each number for each time you chose it as an action. You probably will have several dashes under some numbers, none under most.

When you have finished, count the total dashes under numbers in each dimension and write the total in the blank to the right of the dimension. The resulting sums indicate whether your responses are heavily influenced by your Jungian Personality typology or are influenced by other factors as well.

Jungian Type Category Letters

Sum

I (1, 9, 13, 28, 32, 38, 43)   I_____
E (14, 24, 26, 29, 33, 37, 39)   E_____

N (10, 12, 13, 24, 42, 45)   N_____
S (7, 8, 11, 20, 27, 28)   S_____
T (7, 16, 17, 19, 23, 25, 26, 27, 36, 38)   T_____
F (6, 12, 15, 18, 21, 30, 31, 34, 35, 45)   F_____
P (5, 29, 26, 24, 33, 37, 39, 41)   P_____
J (1, 2, 4, 17, 22, 24, 43, 44)   J_____

Repeat these procedures for the power-task-affiliation categories listed here.

Power, Task, Affiliation Orientations

Sum

Power (3, 9, 22, 25, 28, 39, 43)   Power _____
Task (4, 10, 14, 17, 19, 22, 27)   Task _____
Affiliation (6, 15, 18, 39, 31, 33, 34, 40, 41)   Affiliation _____

Are there strong preference patterns in your choice of actions? Or, do you tend to use a large number of actions scattered about the eight Jungian categories and the power-task-affiliation categories?

If you have dominant actions, are they congruent with your Jungian typology? _____ Why or why not?_____

Are dominant patterns, if any, congruent with your power-task-affiliation dominance? _____ Why or why not?_____

We believe that each of us and each of you have characteristic intervention styles in situations we face. We also believe that our dominant Jungian attitudes and functions are one of the strongest influences on our usual intervention style. But other factors, especially context factors are also important. What we have the urge to do may not be the wisest choice We then curb our impulses and act in other ways. We must be conscious of our impulses and the problems they might lead us to.

The power-task-affiliation behaviors are based on our attempts to fulfill Maslowian needs as they are important to us in various settings at various times.

We believe these two basic schemes are necessary to explain our intervention styles. You may have to now think aloud with one or more people you trust, to fully understand your own style of intervention and to understand the reasons for this style. This understanding may provide comfort. It should also lead you to clearer decisions about possible implications of your intervention style, for you, and for your organization.

Some may reject our explanation that daily actions are largely ego-centered. We are saying that an important basis for our intervention styles are our attempts to fulfill personal needs. Our resulting actions depend on the ways we perceive the world and make judgments about it.

You can adapt your style, in honest ways, so that some of your needs are being met while some of the other persons needs are being taken care of. That kind of necessary compromise is the only structure which allows us to generally move around without a weapon in our hands all the time. It also allows each of us the maximum amount of freedom and safety possible where more than one person must use the same resources. The most effective intervention style possible is that which meets as many of your needs as possible while encouraging and allowing others to also meet their needs.

With this understanding of your own characteristic mode of intervening, we can now shift to specifics. In the next pages we shall try to answer the following four questions:[1]

1. How do you behave in intervening?
2. What information should you be collecting about the people around you to determine your effects when you intervene?
3. What information do you look for to decide what typology people are and what needs they are acting out of?
4. How do you think you should behave as an intervenor?

1. How do you behave in intervening?

We have tried, through Activity I, to help you identify your intervention style. We have tried to relate this characteristic style to your Jungian typology and to your Maslow needs. It is possible that as you interact in real situations similar to our nine hypothetical ones, you will find your characteristic actions are much more varied than the few you chose in response to our simulation. That is to be expected. You responded to all of these at the same time, in the same place, in the same mood, with the distance an "out there" hypothetical circumstance gives. Your real responses, however, will probably be similar to those you made here.

We would like to suggest that greater self-knowledge of our intervention style does not free us from it; we are still trapped in it. We can try to be adaptable and meet other's needs as well as our own. We can really only view the world from the perceptual decision making framework in which we live.

We can hopefully learn to accept that others have other ways of being that are just as meaningful to them as our way is to us. We may be able to be less critical and judgmental of these other ways. We may be able to adapt our intervention style to allow others to be informal, autonomous, responsible, confident, choosing individuals. That kind of flexibility of approach to intervention is what this unit is about.

2. What information should you be collecting about the people around you to determine your effects when you intervene?
   a. You first want to know if people are understanding you.

[1]You may not wish to finish reading this unit if you reject our logic in it.

   b. Then you want to know if you are convincing them, if they will go along or oppose you.
   c. Finally, you want to know if you have said enough and should now move along.
To find answers to these questions you need other data on both verbal and non-verbal behaviors.

Non-verbal data:

Many researchers (among them Birdwhistell (1970), Hall (1959), Galloway (1968) have written about the non-verbal cues which tell you if you are being understood. Generally, when people are communicating they are moving in some sort of synchronous rhythm. Their heads nod and their bodies move together almost as if they were dancing. Some of those you are talking with will be more obvious than others with these gestures. One of us was once told by a teacher, "If I want to know what the class is thinking, I look at you — you give away your thoughts by your face and gestures." That teacher was fairly alert to non-verbal cues.

Usually the non-verbal cues are more accurate and less controlled messages of internal states than the verbal cues. If you are getting verbal feedback and non-verbal cues both saying the same things to you, you probably can trust the message. If you are getting mixed verbal and non-verbal messages, trust the non-verbal ones and proceed from there. If their words are saying yes and their faces are saying no, or their pupils are contracting, they are probably lying to you — or at least not sharing all their thinking (to us a form of lying).

To summarize, if people's verbal and non-verbal cues are congruent, and if they are moving in some rhythm with you, you are probably being understood and accepted.

One journal we were reading recently (Human Behavior, 1977) suggested that there are specific signals given by speakers who are finishing their verbal piece, such as changing their pitch, speaking phrases like "you know," or pausing. Listeners communicate their understanding or lack of it by nodding, mmhmmming, requesting clarification, restating the message or finishing the speaker's sentence. Listeners trying to communicate their desire to talk turn slightly away from the speaker, inhale audibly and make obvious hand movements. Many speakers invite and use non-verbal cues of acceptance or understanding from listeners without relinquishing the floor. If a listener signals early understanding, it may indicate the speaker can shorten his message and move on.

You may become more receptive of these cues if you begin to look for them. Those of us who are intuitive, internal persons have a great deal of difficulty paying attention to these subtle, specific clues. Inattention to this kind of detail may be one reason IN types are not often good interactive teachers. It may also be a reason people in our society do so little active listening. This kind of full listening simply takes too much energy for us to sustain it. But, we must sustain some level of seeing this feedback if we are to be effective interventionists.

Non-verbal behaviors, then, can indicate to you whether supervisees are really attending, being convinced and being sufficiently informed for you to go on, or are really not attending, are disagreeing and need more explanation and information. These behaviors are more reliable than verbal because, while most people have not learned to deceive with their bodies, all have with their words. Non-verbal behaviors are the innocent, naive child in us blurting out truths that embarrass the sophisticated, sly verbal adult.

Verbal behaviors:

We can, through the verbal techniques discussed in Unit 7 discover whether supervisees are attending to the intervention process, are being convinced, and are being sufficiently informed. Perception checking asks them point-blank about their listening and understanding of messages.

Diagnosis of readiness level through verbal reactions will also give you data indicating commitment or lack of it. Finally, simply asking whether the supervisee understands or needs more explanation will give you data.

3. What information do you look for to decide what typology people are and what needs they are acting out of?

An approximate diagnosis of Jungian typology or Maslow need level of members of your organization is usually better than none at all. Open your information processing to the possibility that your initial guess may be wrong by continuing to collect data after you have made a judgment. Consciously try to be a little P and not so much J, when diagnosing.

"It is so nice to meet you, John. I have heard so much about you. Would you take this personality inventory for me so I can know better how to interact with you? I wish to intervene in your life and I need this data to be as effective as possible."

None of us can survive for long if we act that way, literally or less directly. However, much of our early behavior after meeting a person is a testing, trying behavior. We find after a short period of time, that we "feel comfortable," and "can open up" with some, and "don't like something" about others. They either raise no threats to our safety needs (are safe, and can be trusted) or are kept at arm's length because they may be threats to satisfaction of those needs.

Whether the person's dress is organized, with clear conceptualization of style and current fashion, or whether it is frowsy and uncoordinated may give you a sense of whether the person's primary concern is with external evaluations (extrovert) or internal (introvert).

Does the person give you lots of context and talk out of some conceptualization or does she seem to jump from one specific detail to another? If you ask a conceptual question do you get an answer on the same level or do you get what seems to you to be a mass of specific and relatively unrelated details? Is this person interested in implications of an idea, or in the color of the furniture in the room? Does he want to do long-range planning, or is he interested in what to do right here and now? Would he be interested in the specifics of this unit, or in speculations about applications in his life? These data give you some sense of the intuitive and the sensory dimensions of others' personality types. Hopefully you can then know about ways to relate to their needs.

By what processes does this new person seem to make decisions? Does she reason from data, reach conclusions and then act? Think. Does she use many feeling words in conversation which tend to convince you that her judging function is more feeling than thinking?

4. How do you think you should behave as an intervenor?

Your behavior as an intervenor will always be an attempt to meet your needs in some way. You may be acting out of your needs by trying to behave as you expect your organization expects you to act. If the expected ways are congruent with your personality type, then you may be convincing in the role. If you are expected to come out of what are, for you, inferior functions, you may be perceived as phoney or playing a role.

If you are generally in growth stages then you may be able to be flexible and operate effectively using many styles.

Probably you will be most effective as an intervenor when you have an honest congruence between your style and needs. Often this means that you share your objectives, strategies and thought or feelings more than is usually done in organizations. Some people are put off by this kind of honesty. Usually, after they get over the shock of it, they are able to be more honest and relaxed about themselves with you. This affect increases your effectiveness.

There are situations in which you cannot risk this level of honesty and survive. Don't!

Sometimes, to help other people be more open you have to provide more structure than you really like or need. That kind of adaptation seems an honest one.

We don't wish to write any more here. We think we have raised enough issues for you to think about. Any more and we will become unnecessarily prescriptive.

Individual

Supervisory

Managing

Skills

Unit 11

Clinical Supervision

Content Overview
This unit explains clinical supervision, its organization and the context in which it operates. Clinical supervision is helping teachers before, during, and after teaching. This help is focused around the actual teaching setting—the clinic where the teacher works with students. The unit helps you develop one mode of organizing your work with individual teachers.

Using The Unit
After the explanation, derived from Cogan's work of Clinical Supervision, you are asked to relate this conceptualization to that of Maslow, Argyris and others which was presented earlier in this text. Be prepared to review earlier units.

Entry Skills Necessary
Our assumption is that you have worked through the competencies in the two relationship units, that you know the conceptual organizers in Unit 1 and that you know fact, data and inference differentiations.

Competencies
Before you leave this unit you should be able to:

1. State the ways in which clinical supervision can be used in your work with individual teachers.

2. Describe how you believe this mode of supervision is appropriately used.

3. List the skills you will need to use this mode of supervision.

Explanation and Rationale for These Competencies
You need to have a conceptual organizer for your practice of supervision, Cogan's work provides that framework.

Introduction
Clinical supervision is a pragmatic, rational, logical series of procedures

for working intensively with individual teachers. We believe it is consistent with the humanistic philosophy we have carefully laid out in the conceptual units, and consistent with the intent of the interpersonal skills you have begun to practice in Section B.

The clinical cycle, its basic organizer, begins with the establishment of a professional relationship. The characteristics of this relationship are as much collegial in nature as possible. The teacher is the authority about teaching, about the student with whom he is dealing about the content and process objectives he is trying to reach and about his own motivations. The supervisor is the authority about teaching, about data collection in the classroom, about analysis of patterns of teaching-learning behaviors, about carrying out focused conferences discussing teaching and about assisting in planning behavior changes and evaluation of learning. The supervisor can use these special competencies within a safe, low anxiety setting (Maslow levels 1, 2, 3, 4) which he helps to establish and maintain. Another necessary parameter of this professional relationship of co-equals is that the procedures, limits and objectives of the supervision are explicitly discussed and agreed on (Maslow level 2).

Step 2 of the clinical supervision cycle begins after this relationship is initiated. Here you identify with the individual teacher some issues or problems about which the teacher wishes some feedback, or which the teacher wishes to explore. You may have to suggest areas of interest and/or observe the teaching first. Whatever the issue, the next step is to identify with the teacher some ways you and the teacher can collect some data relevant to that issue. This data may be written lesson plans, teacher made tests, test results, curriculum materials, interviews with students, or recorded data of the actual teaching. The teacher and you agree that after the data is gathered, that data will be shared, analyzed and interpreted with the teacher.

The next phase of this clinical supervision cycle is the specific selection of the issues to be worked on. General areas were selected before the data were gathered. Now it is possible to be more focused. Obviously the teacher should have some input in this selection process. If the supervisor and teacher are colleagues rather than master and slave then they both participate in these decisions. The degree to which the teacher makes this decision about focus depends on factors such as the level of trust between you, the maturity and experience of the teacher, your personal comfort and security, the severity of the problems, previous relationships and successes with this teacher, and the relative success this teacher has had in meeting minimum expectations of the system in which you both work.

Having made the decisions about focus, you and the teacher can turn to planning improvements or changes. The clinical nature of the process becomes evident as you turn to evaluation of the process and replanning what data are to be gathered when the teacher begins implementing the plans agreed on. Then with implementation you continue with your data gathering, planning and revaluation roles.

The cycles continue to the limits of teacher's and manager's time and competence or until you together as a team reach the goals agreed on for that supervision.

We have tried to explain in three pages what Cogan explains in 221 pages of text. Obviously we have left out much of the essence of his arguments and procedures. You should probably mistrust our condensation enough to read his unexpurgated version.

In summary, we list the steps of our clinical supervision cycle:

1. Define and begin a relationship — explain supervision's processes.

2. Evaluate results and identify issues with the teacher.

3. Collect data and observe teaching.

4. Share, analyze and interpret data with the teacher.

5. Plan actions.

6. Implement plans.

7. Begin again.

Let us identify a few assumptions on which our suggestions for your use of clinical supervisory techniques are based:

1. You will not really be productive in your supervision if, on a regular basis, you tried to hold more than two or three of these supervisory cycles (pre-data-gathering conferences, data gathering and observations of teaching analysis, conference and planning) per working day. They are too demanding of your time and energy. Few people can be focused that long and be open and productive. As is said about many demanding activities, "your concentration goes."

2. In a real educational setting probably about 50% of your time will be eaten up with system management, personnel problems, and administrivia. We do not denigrate these uses of your time; they are as necessary for supervision to occur as your possession of the skills to do the actual development supervision. You must also spend a significant portion of your time in group supervision and long-range planning. If you do not carry out these aspects of your job your system descends to maintenance and does not grow. In our "Use of Time" unit, we shall consider these issues in more detail.

Some middle managers set up formal systems for using clinical supervision techniques with all non-tenured teachers and with one-half or one-third of the tenured faculty each year.

Others allocate most of their clinical time to teachers asking for help. Still others spend their time with teachers having problems. They use other, less time consuming supervisory techniques with the remainder of their staff. We are suggesting that as you learn the special skills needed to implement clinical supervision, you make conscious choices about how and with whom you use it.

In Unit I, we presented you with ideas from Maslow, McGregor, and Argyris. Here we ask you to use those ideas to establish a rationale for using clinical supervision. We suggest that you write out your explanations of how that conceptual base relates to these new concepts because in that way you may make connections in your mind that will last. If you only "think" the connections, they may be quite flimsy and transitory. You will not be able to apply the connections in your thinking or explain them clearly to others.

For your convenience if you cannot get a copy of Cogan's (1974) book, we have summarized some of his suggestions and explanations from that book. We really do recommend your reading it, however.

A. Cogan suggests that part of the relationship established should be an understanding of the cycle of clinical supervision and the roles of the teacher and supervisor. He suggests that the relationship be established before the supervisor enters the classroom to observe the teacher. Some procedures he suggests follow:

1. the involvement of the teacher in a program in which he may gain some of the competencies of clinical supervision;

2. the involvement of the teacher in "safe" observation and analysis by use of:

   a. selected commercial films of teaching performances

   b. microsupervision and simulated supervision

   c. condensed and edited versions of typescripts of teaching, and so forth;

3. the participation of the teacher in decisions about the timing and nature of the processes leading to the supervisor's entrance into the teacher's classroom;

4. the explanation and critical study of the implications of clinical supervision for the professional career of the teacher;

5. the exploration and critical study of the roles, relationships, ethics, rights, and responsibilities of the teacher and the supervisor in clinical supervision (In this area of study and understanding of the relationships among clinical supervisor, teacher, administrators, other teachers, and the Board of Education should be developed);

6. the provision of guarantees to the teacher; assurances of program continuity and duration of supervision;

7. the demonstration that clinical supervision is built around colleague-ship and interaction, not around authoritarian intervention.

B. Cogan suggests that the supervision and planning should include specifications of outcomes, anticipated problems, materials needed, the strategies of teaching, processes of learning and the evaluation or feedback expected.

C. Cogan suggests that the supervisor plan the objectives, processes and technical arrangements for the observation and collection of data at first. As the teacher becomes more familiar with the clinical supervision methods of gathering data, he might become more involved in the process.

D. Finally Cogan lists several strategies for the conference, which might be planned with the teacher during or before the conference. Since some of them flow out of the data to be collected, they may have to be planned during the pre-planning stages of the supervision.

Unit 12

Use of Time

Content
In Unit 12 you will be examining your working time and how you plan to use it.

Using The Unit
We ask for you to be able to put yourself into the situations we pose and react to them as if they were real. How you learn to suspend your reality and react to and learn from our realities is a question we can't answer, but you need this skill if you are to get much from the activities related to this unit.

Competencies
Before you go on to the next unit you should be able to demonstrate:

1. that you are able to identify values which influence your use of time;

2. that you are able to plan a time distribution which reflects your values in supervision. (We hope your plan has been influenced by your work in this program.)

Explanation and Rationale for These Competencies
TIME.
24-hour days (if only there were 2 more hours I could really get into it.)
Daylight savings time.
Standard time, local time.
Clock watcher!
You'll just have to take the time to do it right.
If only I had time to do that.
I'm too busy, no time today—
She always seems to have time to stop and say 'allo.
All I know is, every time I see you, you are rushing somewhere.
We only have twenty minutes time; can we finish by then?
What does she do with her time; she's no help to me.

Two minutes I got, two minutes, I waited all day and two minutes—
Time is money.

We are what we eat, someone has said, but we are perceived as the way
we spend our time. Time is not money. Time cannot be saved nor stored.
We can move back the clock, but time goes only in one direction. Whatever we do strings out behind us, an unchanging, irretrievable fossil, the
dead shell of what we were. However we may change the appearance and
perception of that record, we cannot go back and do it over again. In the
most fundamental way possible, how we spend our time is the truest indicator we and others possess of what we value, what we are trying to
accomplish, what we will continue to do. In our professional lives we owe
it to ourselves to re-examine the way we use this resource at regular intervals. Again and again we have found that most don't know what they do
with each day.

The variation in the ways middle managers use time is very great. This
variation occurs among the separate settings in a given organization as
well as among differing organizations. If we were to draw conclusions
solely from time use of most administrators of school settings we would
have to state rather clearly that supervisory activities whose purpose is
program- or staff-development are of very low priority in almost all settings. That is not what people who head these settings say, but it is what
really occurs if their time use is any indicator.

We maintain that there are two main reasons for this low priority of
developmental supervisory activities:

1. The people who become middle managers are not generally trained
with skills to engage in development supervision.

2. The people who become middle managers react to the real priorities
that upper management values. These priorities do not really value curriculum, program and development supervision.

If you don't agree, let us make at least the bones of a case for what we
assert. Then tell us it isn't so, or follow our reasoning to a new and better
world.

Our Case

In 1969, John M. Nagle (1969) wrote a research monograph which
reported the use of time by a sample of school principals in 82 districts
clustered around Pittsburgh, Pennsylvania. This monograph, based on a
sample of 154 principals corroborates our own qualitative observations.
Dr. Nagle summarizes the data he carefully reports by describing the
composite principal - "Mr. Average" - in his sample. We paraphrase his
summary below (Nagle, 1969, pp. 27-29).

Mr. Average is usually in a suburban junior school or senior high
school. If his faculty numbers 40 or less he serves with no vice-principal. If
there are 60 or more teachers he usually has a vice-principal whose major
duty is to enforce discipline. Almost always, this principal sees improvement of instruction as a primary responsibility. However, chances are only
even that he regards classroom observations as "essential" to his evaluation

of teachers' effectiveness. During a typical week he averages about 2-½ hours observing teachers in their classrooms. Usually observations are a full period, but if he had his choice they would be shorter - 20-25 minutes - which he feels is sufficient time. During each year he averages only about two observations of each teacher - half of which are for state mandated evaluations. Mr. Average usually takes either no notes or a minimum of notes during an observation, but almost always completes a formal evaluation form after each observation. For data for this form he relies on either his memory or those minimum notes. After each observation, Mr. Average principal claims to have some form of feedback conference during which he claims the talk ratio is about 50-50. He claims this ratio despite describing his conference behavior as that of an autocratic or paternalistic expert who knows most of the answers, who can effectively evaluate the teaching and learning acts, and who feels a sincere responsibility to educate his teachers regarding the strengths and weaknesses of their instructional behaviors. Mr. Average principal has greatest confidence in his ability to recognize effective teaching, but the least confidence in his ability to produce changes in teacher behavior.

This average principal has confidence that his supervisory abilities are well developed, but his knowledge of current ideas and techniques related to instruction is a good deal less than strong.

Neither the techniques Mr. Average principal has developed nor the time they devote to development supervisory work appear to justify their claim that the improvement of class room instruction is a primary highly valued responsibility if this sample of principal's self-reported time use is representative.

We maintain that the low portion of time devoted to individual supervision is as much avoidance behavior as it is submission to other duties. The principal finds many other things to do with his time when he realizes his own inadequate skills and his relative ineffectiveness in changing teacher behavior. The time spent in supervision is reduced to the minimum because it is an aversive situation for him as much as for the teachers. It need not be so.

The second part of our explanation for the lack of skill in supervision and emphasis on it comes from an examination of the training programs for these managers. What percent of their program even mentions supervision, instruction or program development skills? How much actual training and practice is there in gathering classroom data, holding teacher conferences, planning teacher in-service, establishing supportive, safe environments for teachers, sharing decision making, assessing teaching methods, developing curriculum or separating data from inference?

Our analysis of the administrative training programs at four universities (two of whom recruit nationally — Harvard and Stanford — and two who mainly serve their regions — Pittsburgh and S.U.N.Y. at Albany) suggests that these specific areas are neglected in each of these programs. In one or two of these universities it was possible to elect a minor in supervision, but even there the courses seemed to focus on global ideas rather than on skills useful to the practicing manager.

Either our emphasis on skill development is misplaced, or these programs and curricular developments are not the "primary responsibilities" of middle managers they are supposed to be.

Our conclusion then, is that little of that most precious of resources, time, is devoted to helping teachers grow in instructional effectiveness, and that even those middle managers who believe they value such supervision do not devote time to it. With that in mind, we are ready to ask you to carefully examine your own use of time.

Finally, as part of this unit we wish to present a brief description of one school district which operated as we are suggesting most districts operate. We report the changes that resulted after their becoming aware of their use of time. (Perhaps, we suggest, the changes were caused by a real emphasis in the district on skills development).

This district in New England (Ward, 1975) (one high school, two middle schools and six elementary schools) had 23 administrative and supervisory personnel (one superintendent, two assistant superintendents, 14 building principals and vice-principals, six special supervisors and reading specialists).

The chart on the following page shows the time use patterns for these administrators before any training in a supervisory skills development program (October, 1974). The second column shows the administrators' time use in May, 1975, after a planned series of training workshops.

An analysis of this chart shows categories 1, 2, 3, and 9, the main supervisory activities of building administrators, increasing from 26% of their time to 54% of their time.

In the two years previous to this training, a sample of seven of these supervisor-managers had reported 58 and 56 conferences with teachers (Ward, 1975, p. 38). During the year of this training, the same sample of supervisor-managers reported 205 conferences with teachers.

In this same period of time (the two previous years) comments on the annual evaluation reports by teachers about the school system showed the following pattern.

Teacher Comments About Supervision

Time Period	No. of Teacher Comments	Comments Generally Positive About Supervision	Comments Generally Negative About Supervision
June 1974 (before training)	218	57	161
June 1975 (after 1 year training)	218	203	15

The total training to teach these skills included only five days of

Results of Time Study for Administrators

(Ward, 1975, p. 41)

Activities	Percent of Time		
	Oct. 1974	May 1975	Difference
1. Individual observation of teacher/classroom	12%	24%	+12%
2. Individual conference with teachers	4%	15%	+11%
3. Planning with groups of teachers	6%	10%	+ 4%
4. Writing memos/reports	15%	8%	- 7%
5. Record Keeping	8%	3%	- 5%
6. Telephone calls	4%	5%	+ 1%
7. Personal planning by myself	2%	2%	0
8. Meeting with district personnel	6%	2%	- 4%
9. Planning in-service	4%	5%	+ 1%
10. Conference with parents	7%	7%	0
11. Conference or meeting with or about students	8%	8%	0
12. General office work	24%	15%	- 9%

The figures in this chart do not quite add to 100%. We assume rounding off errors.

on-site time by two consultants. It did, however, include on-site reinforcement of these skills by the superintendent and two assistant superintendents.

Even cursory analysis of these data suggests that some skill training and reinforcement of use of those skills by the district power figures resulted in dramatic changes in the administrators' time use, and in teachers' perceptions of the supervisory processes used with them. Perhaps, the teachers perceived the values administrators placed on supervision of instruction and responded to these values.

Activity I

1. In the chart below suggest the importance you place on each of the categories of administrative time use by putting an approximation of the percent of time you believe you *ought* to be spending in that category of behavior.
2. In the column next to that indication of intent, list the percent of time you believe that the average supervisor-manager spends in that category of behavior.

Time % Categories for Supervisor-Manager-Administrator

Your Desired Behavior % of Time	Activity	Your Belief About the Average Manager's Use of Time % of Time
%	1. Individual Observation of Teacher/Classroom	%
%	2. Individual Conference with Teachers	%
%	3. Planning with Groups of Teachers	%
%	4. Writing Memos/Reports	%
%	5. Record Keeping	%
%	6. Telephone Calls	%
%	7. Personal Planning by Myself	%
%	8. Meeting with District Personnel	%
%	9. Planning In-service	%
%	10. Conference with Parents	%
%	11. Conference or Meeting with or About Students	%
%	12. General Office Work	%

3. In writing, list the reasons you believe administrators generally differ in their supervisory time spent from the %'s you believe are appropriate for you.

_____

_____

_____

_____

_____

4. Our value is that middle managers ought to spend at least 50% of their actual on-the-job time in supervisory activities of categories 1, 2, 3 and 9. If your desired %'s vary significantly from those we suggest, explain in writing your values which suggest your time use to you.

_____

_____

_____

_____

_____

Unit 13

The Champagne-Morgan
Conference Strategy

Content Overview

This unit's content is a structured format for supervisory conferences which seek to solve problem issues. It is broadly applicable to any problem solving situation. Most of the examples given are teaching ones though we have taught and used it in many settings in business, industry and education. There are some conference situations where problems are being generated or where action solutions are not appropriate. Other techniques are appropriate in those situations.

Using the Unit

You may read this unit. You may generate applicable statements for each step in the format. If, however, you want to use this format effectively you must practice it under conditions where you get detailed feedback from others.

Entry Skills

You should be able to use the skills in the first three units.

Competencies

The single focus of this unit is to insure that, in conferences with individuals or groups, you will be able to use this conference format with sufficient competence that your supervisees express appreciation of your clarity and helpfullness.

Explanation and Rationale for These Competencies

Except in cases where a large rock is falling toward your supervisee's head, establish the relationship slowly and carefully. Negotiate with clarity whatever it is you are about. Expose your possible modes of interaction and let the supervisee participate in the techniques to be used with him.

Don't allow precipitous choices, especially those based only on the supervisee's trust of you, or worse, the supervisee's acceptance of your authority. Be sure the supervisees fully understand the implications of your actions and their own actions. Give reasons for every significant suggestion you make. Ask them for their reasons for each step they wish to make. Most of your reasons and your supervisee's reasons should be referenced to the data base you are building in that setting. Especially at the beginning, make haste slowly.

We recommend that most conferences be planned to take about 20 minutes. You will see how this is possible and why it is desirable after we have explained the conference format we are suggesting. Throughout our explanations of this format, we use the terms interventionist and client to relate this format as strongly as possible to Argyris' work. We wish you to consider general applications of this format beyond teacher-supervisor interactions.

Any communication between the interventionist and the client might be called a conference. We will limit our definition to that sequence of events during which the discussion is intended to make some decisions about the subsequent behavior of either or both of the participants. We eliminate from our definition those communications whose major intent is maintenance of *social* relationships.

This suggested conference model is the summary of the common sense and professional practice of the authors over the past decade. It has not been validated with hard research data. Our practice suggests that most often short conferences (15-20 minutes) are better than long ones. Conferences which focus on one or two issues are better than diffuse ones. Short, focused conferences are more likely to be clear and less likely to be punishing to either person in them. We suggest that you teach your clients this model or at least its general format as soon as you begin to use it. (This is part of helping your client maintain his autonomy by removing mystery from your practices.)

Steps in the Conference Model

Conferences generally follow three sequential phases.

Phase I: Setting of Goals and Commitments to a Goal

Phase II: Generating and Selecting Procedures or Behaviors

Phase III: Specifying Commitments and Criteria of Success

Phase I: Settings of Goals and Commitments to a Goal

Step 1. Objectives of the Conference are specified.

Step 2. All available data relating to the objectives are shared.

Step 3. An agreement is made to focus on "key" objectives within the general objectives specified in Step 1.

Step 4. An agreement is made that some behavior changes are appropriate.

Phase II: Generation and Selection of Procedures or Behavior

Step 5. Positive appropriate behaviors in the setting which are related to the specific objectives are identified and reinforced.

Step 6. Alternative behaviors or re-emphases are identified and examined.

Step 7. An alternative from those proposed is selected.

Step 8. Detailed implementation plans for the alternative selected are completed.

Step 8a. (If appropriate) Plans made are practiced or role-played.

Phase III: Commitments and Criteria of Success are Specified

Step 9. Criteria for successful implementation of the selected behavior are decided and agreed upon.

Step 10. Client gives feedback on purposes, commitments and perceptions of conference.

Step 11. Commitments of interventionist and client are reviewed.

Conference Terminates

We would like to review each of the above steps and establish its purpose in the Conference Model.

Step 1 - Specifying Objectives

The purpose of Step 1 is to make sure that both people in the conference agree on the goals. This sharing is a kind of contract-setting. It establishes an atmosphere of, "Let's get down to business."

Step 2 - Reviewing Data Related to Objectives

Both interventionist and client must have or develop the same perception of what is presently happening in the situation being discussed. Both parties must limit or discipline themselves to describing the *behaviors* that are related to the objectives of the conference.

Step 3 - Selecting a Focus

A focus on one or two issues within the selected objective allows more specific planning and a more rapid change of the client's behavior. It also helps keep the conference short. A short conference is usually more productive than a longer one.

Step 4 - Agreement on Necesssity for Change

The purpose of this step is to seek a commitment to change from the client. This step should be short and done only once. If there is no agreement here, either abort the conference or decide what data needs to be collected to make a commitment to change.

Step 5 - Reinforcement of Aspects of Present Behavior

The purpose of this step is to assure the client that parts of present behavior are appropriate. The task of change becomes an extension of present behaviors rather than a denial of previous behaviors.

Step 6 - Proposing Alternatives

More than one alternative should be considered before a choice is made. Strengthening or extending existing behaviors is one alternative.

Step 7 - Selecting an Alternative

It is difficult to implement several changes at once. If one alternative is selected, the chance for success is better than when more than one alternative is selected.

Step 8 - Specific Planning

Specific Planning includes: the objectives, procedures, and evaluation. It is suggested that the specific planning be written or audio-taped so that both interventionist and client will have a record of their commitments. A record makes both the participants more accountable. It also increases the likelihood of implementation of the changes.

Step 8a - Practicing (If appropriate)

Here we mean simulated tryouts of the new behaviors. The supervisor can role-play students if necessary. This practice is an opportunity for clients to try new behaviors in safe circumstances under conditions where they can get immediate feedback. This practice identifies any insufficiencies in the planning.

Step 9 - Establishing Criteria

This agreement sets a realistic expection for the client. The supervisor should exercise care in seeing that criteria attainable by the client are established.

Step 10 - Giving Feedback on Conference

This step allows the interventionist to find out what the perceptions of the client are about what has been done in the conference. The interventionist should learn how to ask this question to receive an open and honest answer. Interventionists do not defend their behavior here. They simply try to understand the perception of the clients.

Step 11 - Reviewing Commitments

This final check-out and restatement of commitments is necessary. It is a deliberate redundancy preventing major misunderstandings. After the restatement of commitment, the conference should end.

Consulting or Directing

Within this conference format all steps can be made congruent with the establishment and maintenance of client responsibility for, and commitment to, action taken. The entire structure of the conference, while it serves the goal of efficiency in the use of resources, says clearly to the client, "I trust your intelligence, your interest, your professional purpose."

The supervisor insures that the steps in the conference occur, but consciously works to have the supervisee initiate them and follow through. When the supervisor's nudgings, silences and questions about "What come's next?" don't result in supervisee action to initiate the next step, the supervisor must initiate, then stop to see whether the supervisee is ready to take the next step.

The interventionist's role within this conference format can be conceptualized on a continuum from directing to consulting. Any of these roles is legitimate in the context of the agreement between the interventionist and the client. The interventionist in the framework established here should always try to move toward the consulting role and away from the directing role. The continuum of directiveness is on the next page.

The last stage on this continuum is the true test of autonomy, and of honest helping relationships. As clients become more self-directing they can and usually will, manage the interventionist into an active role on a collegial basis. They are then free to seek and use aid, but they determine its application.

Stage 1 is usually self-defeating and is not recommended. There may be times when it is appropriate—depending on the organization in which you work, when certain goals, structures and procedures are not negotiable. Certain directive stages are dictated by these fixed goals, structures and procedures. However, it is never desirable to continue Stage 1 supervision over any extended period of time.

Activity I

PURPOSES

This activity gets you into the conference model. Past students have had some difficulty translating the steps of the model into real words they use. This activity is intended as a transition.

Our first purpose here is to find out if you understand the steps at the application level. Our second purpose is to be sure that you have some vocabulary for moving through the model when you begin to practice using it in the next procedure.

DIRECTIONS

In this activity we are asking you to generate sample statements you might use with each step of the Conference Model we have just described. We list the steps, give you some sample statements that might be appropriate for that step, and ask you to write some of your own statements. Identify with a check those of ours or yours which seem most useful to you *and* which are most congruent with Argyris' tasks. Generate one or two of your own statements that are more consistent with your own vocabulary and are congruent with the step of the conference.

Step I - Objectives of the Conference are specified.

Sample Statements

Ours:1. What is our purpose for getting together?

The Supervisory Model
Continuum of Stages of Directiveness
The Interventionist's Role

Directive

Stages	The Interventionist Role	Example
1.	Interventionist initiates; Interventionist chooses.	The interventionist proposes all of the alternatives and then chooses one.
2.	Interventionist initiates; Interventionist and client choose.	The interventionist proposes all of the alternative strategies: they jointly choose one.
3.	Interventionist initiates; Client chooses.	The interventionist proposes all the alternative strategies. The client chooses one.
4.	Interventionist and client both initiate; interventionist and client choose.	Both interventionist and client propose strategies. Both make a choice.
5.	Interventionist and client both initiate; client chooses.	Both interventionist and client propose strategies and the client chooses one.
6.	Client initiates; interventionist and client choose.	The client proposes alternatives, both the interventionist and client choose one.
7.	Client initiates; interventionist questions, client chooses.	The client proposes alternatives, the interventionist asks clarifying question, the client chooses.
8.	Client initiates; client chooses.	The client proposes alternatives, the client chooses, the interventionist listens.
9.	Client initiates; client defines role of interventionist; client chooses.	The client proposes the alternatives, defines a role for the interventionist, and makes the choice.

Consulting

    2. You asked me to stop in your office this morning. What should we focus on?

    3. I called you in today to discuss the following issues . . .

Yours: 1. _____

    2. _____

Step 2 - All available data relating to the objectives are shared.

Sample Statements

    Ours: 1. Let's look at what is now happening in this situation.

           2. Tell me about what you and the students are now doing.

           3. Let's talk for a few minutes about how you see this and how I see it before we begin to suggest ways to deal with it.

Yours: 1. _____

_____

    2. _____

_____

Step 3 - An agreement to focus on "key" objectives within the general objectives specified in Step 1.

Sample Statements

    Ours: 1. Within this whole issue, which part can we focus on today?

           2. . . . seems to be the key issue that we can begin to work on today.

           3. You have specified several areas. Which one do you want to start with?

Yours: 1. _____

_____

    2. _____

_____

Step 4 - An agreement is made that some behavior changes are appropriate.

Sample Statements

Ours: 1. Am I right that you want to try to do that differently?

2. Are you ready to make a commitment to change this procedure?

3. Then you want me to help you change these results?

Yours: 1. _____

_____

2. _____

_____

Step 5 - Positive appropriate behaviors in the setting which are related to the specific objectives are identified and reinforced.

Sample Statements

Ours: 1. The things I identified that are already going well are the following . . .

2. Let's identify the things you have already mastered that we can build your new procedure on.

3. What was that neat thing you did today; perhaps we can build the new procedure on that?

Yours: 1. _____

_____

2. _____

_____

Step 6 - Alternative behaviors or re-emphases are identified and examined.

Sample Statements

Ours: 1. Before we decide what we are going to do, let us try to think of 3 or 4 different ways to approach this.

2. What ideas would you think might be appropriate in this situation?

3. You propose some solutions, then I will. Then we'll decide which ones to try.

Yours: 1. _____

_____

2. _____

_____

Step 7 - An alternative from those proposed is selected.

Sample Statements

Ours: 1. Can we agree to try just that third proposal right now; the other two may be useful later?

2. Which one of these ideas seems the best one to begin working with?

3. Can we decide together which of these things to select as the direction we want to go?

Yours: 1. _____

_____

2. _____

_____

Step 8 - Detailed implementation plans for the alternative selected are completed.

Sample Statements

Ours: 1. Now that we have selected a way to go, our next step is to plan in detail what that means.

2. If we use this idea, what are the steps in the process?

3. That was a good selection; now these seem to be the steps in implementing that process.

Yours: 1. _____

_____

2. _____

_____

Step 8a - (If appropriate) Plans made are practiced or role-played.

Sample Statements

Ours: 1. Just to be sure that we both understand this process, would you pretend you are beginning to implement this, and start at Step 1 with what you would actually do?

2. O.K., we have finished the plan, let's role-play the first few steps to determine if we are clear on how it will work.

3. Try out Steps 1 and 3 of this process on me here, now. We may need more work on it.

Yours: 1. _____

_____

2. _____

_____

Step 9 - Criteria for successful implementation of the selected behavior are decided and agreed upon.

Sample Statements

Ours: 1. What level of mastery of that process is reasonable in three weeks time?

2. We can't expect complete changes tomorrow but let us agree that by the first of the month 90% of the members will have had this training we have planned.

3. Will you suggest some ways we can measure whether our plans are working?

Yours: 1. _____

_____

2. _____

_____

Step 10 - Client gives feedback on purposes, commitments and perceptions of conference

Sample Statements

Ours: 1. What did we do today, and how do you feel about it?

2. We have worked on . . . today, what do you think we have accomplished?

3. How can I be more effective in working with you?

Yours: 1. _____

_____

2. _____

_____

Step 11 - Commitments of interventionist and client are reviewed.

Sample Statements

Ours: 1. Before we quit, would you review your commitments and I will review mine? We will find out if we both understand what we are to do.

2. O.K., here is what I have promised to do, and here is what I think you have promised to do . . . Do you agree?

3. I'm not sure we are both sure of what is going to happen tomorrow. Let's review where we are.

Yours: 1. _____

_____

2. _____

_____

1. Now go back through all the statements you have written and estimate the degree of directive or consultive behavior you believe each statement is. Place a number corresponding to that place in front of each statement.
2. What pattern do you discover in your suggested statements in this consulting-directing dimension of your behavior? Would you like to change the pattern? Why or why not?

_____

_____

_____

_____

Using This Conference Model

We wrote a little about using this format earlier in this unit. We would like to add a few other suggestions now about when to use it.

When you are having a short pre-conference before an observation of teaching, use this format with minor adaptations. Your purpose in this situation is to focus the observation, make decisions about what data to collect in the observation and to learn the purposes and expectations of the teaching.

When you are having a conference after observing teaching, use this model to establish a focus, share data, develop alternatives and make commitments.

When you are working with groups trying to focus and solve problems, this model for conferencing can be appropriate. Try it.

You will have to practice it, perhaps even have it in front of you as you use it, before you become competent in using this model. Do practice it until you no longer feel confined by it. When your conferences can reach a focus and conclude comfortably in 20 minutes, then you are ready to creatively innovate from this model.

Unit 14

Gathering Data

Content Overview
Consultant supervision must be based on valid, pertinent data gathered with the active agreement, planning and assistance of those being supervised. This unit helps you learn specific data-gathering procedures and means of involving your supervisees in the process.

Using the Unit
This unit asks you to decide on specific data you should collect in various simulated settings. We then give additional guidance to supplement your answers.

Entry Skills
You should be able to separate fact from inference. A quick review of Unit II may be useful here. You should have a conviction that data are important in supervision. See Unit I and II if you need to review this rationale. You should also be able to clarify and focus supervisee's general interests with some behaviors that can be observed in their interactions.

Competencies Taught
Before you go on to the next unit, you should be able to:

1. Assist supervisees in making decisions about the foci of the supervision.

2. Write focused questions leading to data gathering procedures.

3. Decide on the specific data needed to answer the questions, and

4. Design and use specific data collection procedures to collect the data needed.

Explanation and Rationale for the Competencies

One of us is an active research-oriented person who regularly collects and analyzes quantitative data. The other of us can not tolerate actually collecting research data. This person is much more interested in qualitative impressionistic, feeling data (see our Jungian typologies in Unit V if you need an explanation of the preferences). He tries to make that data as reliable as possible by checking it out with various sources. Whatever our commitment to field research, we both share a strong commitment to basing supervision as much on data as possible. Only with valid data can we successfully identify, examine, discuss, alter or evaluate the interactions we observe. We accept Argyris' three tasks for intervention even though we know that no data is valid except in a relative sense. We always and inescapably collect "data." Generating and using as objective data as possible usually reduces the tension and anxiety between supervisees and supervisors. If either supervisors or supervisees rely heavily on their own inferences, without sharing the data on which they are based, the other party in the interaction becomes that much less equal and that much less responsible for decisions made. This unit assists you and your supervisees in deciding what data will contribute meaningfully to your joint solutions of instructional issues you have identified together.

The Objective for Gathering Data

Without being foggy, mysterious, or fancy, we would like to make the following pragmatic assertion:

The specific data to be gathered in any situation flow from the concern being explored.

There are several implications of this asserted axiom. The first is that observation and data collection sessions must be designed with the supervisee's participation. Together you seek to formulate an objective clearly focused enough to help you jointly:

1. decide what data would be meaningful,

2. decide how that data should be collected,

3. decide what that data will mean when they are collected,

4. decide what decisions may be possible from the data.

Q. What constitutes a clear objective?

A. An objective is clear if it embodies something which we can measure or observe.

Q. But how can I observe whether students appreciate literature?

A. You can't. You must state that objective differently. You must decide what "appreciate" and "literature" mean. For instance, does appreciate mean that students ask questions about their assigned readings in class? Or that students read books they like on their own time?

Or that students can tell you the plot, character and major ideas of books you have chosen for them to read in class?

We cannot measure or observe appreciation. We can only measure or observe behavior. If we can help teachers pinpoint the behaviors which indicate the presence of "appreciation," we have already been helpful as supervisors. We can also more successfully assist them in the definition and collection of data to measure the more specific goal.

Recommendation

Help the supervisee define and clarify objectives for the data collection by formulating them as questions to be answered. This is the second step after focusing the objective in some sort of specific student-behavior terms.

Activity I

The purpose of this activity is to help you improve the focus and accuracy of data collection questions.

A. Decide whether each of the questions below is sufficiently focused; if it is, check "focused" and tell why.

B. Write more focused questions for those not sufficiently focused. When terms are unclear, change them.

C. Questions:

1. Do the students in this class like my lectures?   _____Focused

     _____Needs work

(Write your reason or your rewrite on the lines below:)

_____

_____

_____

2. Do students in my classes learn geometry theorems better with the new book or with the old one?

     _____Focused

     _____Needs work

(Write your reason or your rewrite on the lines below:)

_____

_____

_____

3. Is the class going well?   _____Focused

                                               _____Needs work

   (Write your reason or your rewrite on the lines below:)

_____

_____

_____

4. Is the problem of student inattention, stated in the pre-conference, one
   shared by all students or only by a few in the classroom?

                                               _____Focused

                                               _____Needs work

   (Write your reason or your rewrite on the lines below:)

_____

_____

_____

We see questions 1 and 2 as being reasonably focused. They can, of course,
be improved, but specific data can be collected about these two issues. It may
take time to get that data. For instance, number 1 may need a student
questionnaire or some kind of interview of a sample of students.

Number 2 may need a relatively controlled experimental design comparing
student achievement with the two books.

Questions 3 and 4 probably need to be rewritten.

Question 3 needs a behavior definition of the word "well," e.g., quiet
students, responsive question answering, degree of student mastery, before it
can be answered.

Question 4 needs behavioral definitions of "inattention." How much, how
long, what symptoms to be observed, etc. All have to be specified before an
observer can be of much assistance.

Type of Data

Having asked an answerable focused question is necessary, but not sufficient. Deciding the type of data to be collected is an easy point at which to go
astray, as in this example:

Did the students in this class enjoy the simulation they participated in?

The following are four possible data collection methods:

a. Teacher asks a sample of students at the close of the class.
b. Teacher gives a written questionnaire to all students.

c. Teacher has a secret ballot at the close of class.
d. One week after the simulation, the teacher gives an anonymous questionnaire asking students if they would enjoy having a second simulation in class.

We suggest that because students may answer the way they think the teacher desires, the possibility of bias may be too high using the first two techniques. Technique c may be accurate, but may not give you and the teacher enough data to decide whether to have that kind of experience again. Technique d may give the teacher the actual data wanted. If the students like the technique, they will probably want to participate in it again.

Our point here is that people's descriptions of their inner states may not be valid data by themselves. You may have to be very conscious of the conditions under which you collect the data.

Observations of student behaviors may be just as meaningful as the written data you elicit. For instance, do students work at the simulation with few interruptions; do they tend to persevere until the bell rings; do they continue to play their roles after class; do they ask questions related to their roles; are they attempting to extend or enlarge the simulation; do many students groan when there are interruptions in their activities? All of these may be valid data that are also valued by the supervisee and supervisor. Interpreting them may be difficult but data must be meaningful to both parties as well as being valid.

For very important questions, the supervisee and you may have to set up an experimental situation within the setting. This may have to be done with great care to lower the possibility of interfering variables clouding the conditions of your experiment.

Both the supervisor and supervisee can usually agree on the specific data they will find both meaningful and valid. Most time may be spent clarifying the objective and the questions to be asked.

We cannot identify or list all the specific data collection techniques that could be used in educational settings. In one setting where one of us worked, the 20 adminstrators were able to generate over one hundred different data collection devices in a period of a morning workshop. These data collection devices were generated around the questions they were able to list in that short period of time.*

The point is that having asked clear questions, the data collection process ceases to be a stifling difficulty.

We will help you get into the spirit of this kind of activity by asking you to participate in Activity II which follows. After that we will turn you loose as data gatherers.

Activity II

Suggest specific data which might answer the following questions. Then suggest criteria which you would use to make inferences about the data. (We will, of course, comment on possible answers at the close of the activity.)

*There is a 13 volume work published by Research for Better Schools in Philadelphia called *Mirrors for Behavior* which contains hundreds of data collection devices with instructions for their use. Most large university libraries have this publication.

Questions:

1. Did the students in this class enjoy this teacher's lecture on the binomial theorem?

   Possible data to be collected to answer this question:

a. _____

b. _____

c. _____

d. _____

e. _____

2. Is the problem of student inattention, stated in the pre-conference, one shared by all students or by only a few in this classroom?

   Possible data to be collected to answer this question:

a. _____

b. _____

c. _____

d. _____

e. _____

Possible data we see which might be collected for question 1 are:

a. whether student behavior during the lecture is quiet, noisy, note-taking, smiling at jokes, head nodding;

b. unsolicited comments about the lecture after it was over, to teacher, to other students, to parents, to other teachers;

c. responses to questionnaires, verbal solicitation of opinions, request for hand raising, opportunity to choose this mode of instruction over others, interviews of a sample of students;

d. waiting a few days to see reactions to the technique a second time when a choice is given between lecture and other modes. Asking students to rank by preference the instructional modes used in class.

Possible data we see which might be collected for question 2 are:

a. student behaviors during the class period—amount of time spent looking at teacher, looking out the window, with eyes closed, with head down, passing notes, talking to other students, writing notes;

b. who displays attending behavior—their physical location, timing of attending, and non-attending behavior (early, middle, late in class session), "good" students, "bad" students, females, males, good, average, slow classes; type of material being presented when most non-attending behavior occurs; kind of instructional mode being used when various attending behaviors are being observed; early, middle or last attenders (that is, which students drop off first, and which ones hang on longest.)

c. student learning—number of teacher questions asked during class and number of questions answered; number of students who answer; number of right or wrong answers to questions; scores on tests; amount or number of homework assignments completed.

As you notice, each of these data collection techniques sparks a different reaction from you. Each has varying degrees of reliability, and possibilities of producing data rich in implications. The shared perceptions of the supervisee and supervisor about the meaningfulness of the data to them is more important here than the statistical reliability or validity. Although if the supervisor feels that the data being collected have major faults in these areas, he should talk about this feeling with the supervisee. That is especially true if the supervisee has the potential for developing an interest in the use of research data to improve his teaching.

How Must the Data Be Collected?

As much as possible, data must be collected in a relatively permanent objective form that can be shared with the supervisee, such as the permanent records in:

1. marks on paper made by pencil, pen, crayon or other instrument,
2. audio tape,
3. video tape,
4. film - snapshots, polaroids, movies

If the supervisee has a copy of that data, there is a greater likelihood that the relationship can be an honest, nearly equal one. Hidden data or supervisor's memory are not good enough.

Slash marks on a paper are minimally necessary. Ideally, the entire class session should be tape-recorded and the tape listened to again before the slash marks are made. An even more satisfactory design would include the use of a videotape and slash marks pinpointing the specific behaviors being explored. In all of these circumstances there would be permanent records of the phenomena in the interaction.

You will find, however, that it is difficult to make an audible tape of a classroom interaction. A more favorable combination is a tape and a record made by an observer present as the interaction takes place. Once the tape is available, a word-for-word account of what has occurred in the interaction can be written from the tape recording (a tape-script). Of course, non-verbal signals are completely lost, but this is the most accurate method of gathering verbal data. A videotape gathers both verbal and non-verbal data, but does so selectively (the camera cannot be pointed in every direction at once) and magnifies the "presence of the experimenter" effect because of the unusual presence of cameras in the room. The presence of any experimenter or observer distorts the actions of those being observed. They are not completely natural. An interaction may, for instance, be more lively or less lively than usual because of the presence of the observer or any hardware (such as tape recorders, videotape, cameras, etc.)

When such records as tape-scripts or videotapes are not possible, we suggest that you limit the data collected to those things the observer can collect in the specified time and under the necessary conditions. Such data may be quite limited, but a limited amount of valid, objective data is much more valuable than a large amount of incomplete and subjective data. Be realistic in what can be collected by one observer.

Other forms of data gathering are intended to make the data gathering as efficient as possible by employing grids or checklists on which the observer can make tallies to indicate types of interaction occurring at any given time. All grids or checklists, however, raise the level of observer bias and interpretation which make the type-script or limited data collection more desirable in most circumstances. The most famous of these interaction analysis grids is the Flanders' analysis. We rarely use such derivative systems since they tend to push the teacher toward a mold determined by the values inherent in the instrument. We prefer the shared biases of the supervisee and supervisor to someone else's. If, however, any standard data collection instrument seems appropriate, and if both you and the supervisee agree that the device would suit your needs, then use it.

Quite often, in spite of its other strengths, audio, video or film data are either of inadequate quality to be useful, or take so much time to use that they are not useful to the working supervisor.

As you develop more trusting relationships with your supervisees, proving a case becomes less important—that is, the supervisees are better at collecting their own data and require less proof of the existence of the patterns you help identify. You can turn much more quickly to solving the problem because you can both identify the problem more quickly and easily. Thus, mechanized and overly justified data become less necessary.

There always exist some issues which defy easy analysis and which do require some of the more elaborate data collection techniques. You and the supervisee should be able to use these techniques with some facility as necessary.

Unit 15

Data Gathering Instruments

Content Overview

This unit will help you learn a variety of processes for selecting, recording and displaying data about teaching interactions.

Using the Unit

This unit is mostly just a reading exercise. It suggests ideas on data collection instruments.

Entry Skills

We are assuming mastery of Unit II—Fact and Inference. We will not repeat that unit here. We are also assuming that you remember the unit on Jungian personality types. That set of ideas helps you decide what data may be important to you and to those you observe.

Competencies

When you have completed this unit you will be able to:

1. Use several ways of generating observational data about interactions and learning settings where you are in a supervisory role.

2. Choose appropriate dimensions of the teaching interactions for observations.

3. Share with your supervisees the choices of what meaningful data are to be collected during the observation.

4. Consult with your supervisees about the actual data collection forms to be used in the observation.

5. Collect whatever data you both have decided is meaningful.

6. Display and discuss these data with your supervisees during a conference.

Explanation and Rationale for these Competencies

These competencies are an extension of unit XIV. We separated them so that only the general issues would be discussed here. We believe that you should know both the strengths and limitations of all the major categories of data collection systems. Then you and your supervisee must agree on the most meaningful technique after both of you understand its limitations and strengths.

Introduction

There is no such thing as completely valid and reliable data.[1] All data gathering processes are sampling procedures. There are no value free or inference free observations. Our view of the world comes through our perceptual framework and is interpreted through the bias of our previous experience. While we can take steps to increase the fit between what we perceive and what actually occurs, we must come to terms with the reality of our imperfections. We must take safeguards to be as fair as possible in our interpretations.

One safeguard is to teach all clients to gather their own data. A second safeguard is to share and discuss our data and its interpretations with our clients. A third and most difficult safeguard is to know as much about our own value systems and the limitations of our personal perceptual processes as we can.

We recognize the vastness of the field of data collection and interpretations. We shall admit our selective sampling of this field in our attempts to teach you some guidelines for improving your observation techniques. We shall attempt two foci within this unit. First, we shall teach you some techniques most useful in observing situations where one or more persons is in charge of instruction of one or more learners. Second, we shall teach you some techniques useful in observing situations where more than two persons are planning some task related to instruction, but not at that time instructing. So far, it seems, these two situations eliminate little, and include almost everything. To be more precise, we will not teach you any of the standardized observation processes. We see limited usefulness for you with these instruments; you can search these out in standard sources on your own when you identify a need for observation techniques you do not have.

We believe that you ought to generate ad hoc data collection devices with your clients. These will be designed after you have selected the specific focus of the observations. Of course, there are limitations to these self-designed techniques of observations. The important point is that you will be teaching a process to your clients that helps them quickly share in your expertise.

We would like to repeat again the basic and necessary need for you to

[1]We know, as do you, that there are almost no absolute facts or data. Even such a simple statement as "Ted blinked his eye three times" may founder on a definition of blinking, e.g., does the eye close completely during a blink, or is a twitch short enough to count? These differences are *not* trivial when behaviors have such value words as boring, exciting, threatening, and anxious attached to them.

collect data and not inferences when you observe. A content analysis of most supervisory interactions demonstrates massive inference-making with minimal data reporting. You have these two concepts clearly in your head as a result of your completion of Unit II. Care taken in using data to support your inferences will pay you many dividends.

There are more dimensions of any human interaction than anyone can ever pay attention to. Some studies have even taken movies of teaching and then looked at them slowly, frame by frame. Much of what we know about non-verbal communication came from this research technique. Such elaborate work, while useful in the long range, is rarely useful to our attempts to improve ongoing instruction. We lack the time. We learn more than we want to know.

In direct supervision of ongoing instruction we suggest the following paradigm for your behavior:

1. Meet with the instructor or team and decide what dimensions of instruction you are going to observe.

2. Plan and agree on the information you are going to collect.

3. Collect the information as planned. (Except in some very unusual cases, you should stick to your contract with the instructor or team. Occasionally you may encounter some unusual incidents which disrupt your plans. Then you collect whatever information seems appropriate.)

4. Share the information with the instructor or team, develop a shared perception of its meaning and jointly decide what to do as a result of the information.

5. Repeat this cycle as necessary and useful or until the goals are achieved.

Some of the dimensions of information we'd like to mention that you may be concerned with are:

1. Physical movement of teachers and/or students;

2. Interaction patterns of teachers and students (verbal and non-verbal);

3. Learning tasks planned, used, and reactions to them;

4. Student progress in the learning;

5. The feelings of teachers and students in the instructional setting;

6. Degree of structure in the learning setting—how established and maintained;

7. Individual student's behavior in the setting;

8. Question patterns used by teacher;

9. Physical organization of room;

10. Responses to teacher's questions, originators of questions in setting.

You might like to suggest more categories of your own for future reference.

11. _____

12. _____

13. _____

14. _____

15. _____

Data Gathering Techniques

All data collection requires some form of recording on your part. Each form of recording selects some information and eliminates the rest. Part of the bias built into data collection occurs because of this unalterable fact. The choice of data collection technique is determined by the data needed to be collected. While that seems obvious, it is not. Many people try to use the same specific form for all their observations. That is unduly limiting and not making good use of their resources.

General Technique No. I: Verbatim Recording

Definition:

This is an "as spoken" recording of everything said by participants, in either written, audio-tape or video tape form.

Strengths:

This technique gets exact wording with "original" inflections (sometimes). Sequences of interactions often show recurring patterns of behavior on the part of the teacher or students. Recordings often are more convincing to the teacher because actual words are presented, particularly if the teacher is attuned to non-verbal vocal signals. Having this record makes it possible to re-examine and slow down the action for closer examination of the situation. It ignores physical non-verbal behavior temporarily to simplify analysis.

Limitations:

Note-taking:

    a. Fatigue of observer if notes are taken.

    b. Note-taking technique tends to keep observer focused on teacher or on specific incidents because of necessity for limiting data written down.

    c. The words themselves, without the inflection and original emphases, may be poor reflections of the actual situation.

    d. Much is lost in imprecise note-taking.

Audio-tape:

    a. Focusing on what is said automatically eliminates collecting other data which may be necessary for real understanding.

    b. Verbatim recording is difficult especially if teacher is interacting quietly with one or with a small group of students.

   c. Tapes are often difficult to hear, garbled.

Video tape:
   a. The presence of the camera may alter behavior.
   b. The camera can only look at one area at a time.

Even some of the limitations of verbatim note-taking can be overcome if the teacher and observer agree that particular small, specific behaviors only should be recorded. You might limit the recording to:
   a. Record only teacher's statements.
   b. Record only student's statements.
   c. Record only certain categories of teacher or student statements (e.g., questions, responses, direction giving, reinforcement patterns).

   This kind of note-taking recording of teacher's and student's utterances has been used often, especially by Cogan, in clinical supervision. His approach is to, as much as possible, wipe his mind free of advance prejudices or expectations and after being in the class for a few minutes, simply to record everything said that could be heard. Using paper and pen, an observer can record up to 10-12 pages of dialogue for a single class period. Cogan attempted to record student names in case these were important in later analysis. Supervisor and/or teacher would then go back over this mass of data and begin to look for interesting patterns for use in the conference about the teaching.

   This technique requires total concentration on recording, facility at writing and much time for analysis. It sometimes reveals many patterns in the teaching not immediately obvious. Most observers develop a kind of shorthand recording system when they do very much verbatim data recording.

   Using the mechanical aids of audio and video recorders simplifies some of the observer's recording problems, but increases greatly the difficulty of reviewing the specific instance you wish to focus on. It takes much time to search the tape for the incidents you desire. Most classrooms are very "noisy" with lights, fans, air-conditioners, hall noise, and desks moving, so that microphones have a great deal of difficulty recording intelligible sound. Even when the teacher is clear, the students responses are often unclear. Use of several microphones often intrudes unduly into the classroom, and may result in only stereo chaos. But any technique has its limitations: all make selections and each distorts in its own way. The values of verbatim recording, whether done by hand or electrically, outweigh the problems where accurate, effective examination of teaching depends on actual statements of the actors in the setting. Beyond the need for a collegial relationship and satisfaction of Maslowian needs, meeting with the teacher beforehand to limit the type of data and the focus of the observation makes the observer's job more manageable and the more likely to be well done.

General Technique No. 2: The Case Study of all or Part of the Learning Setting

Definition:
The case study is a detailed description of the non-verbal and verbal behavior

of one or more persons in the learning setting. This technique *attempts* to record *all* events that happen in one area, or to a limited number of people in the setting. It tries to describe the behavior of all actions in the area of focus in as complete a way as possible. Usually, a case study includes a minute by minute running account of all behaviors. Frequent times are recorded to get a sense of what was happening elsewhere in the setting. Data recorded may include any or all of the following: perceived stimuli which reach the person being observed; reactions of observee to those stimuli; self-initiated behaviors of the observee; on and off task behavior; and *apparent* depth of involvement of the observee. Later, when teacher and supervisor are going over the "data" recorded, attempts are made to make sense of what was happening that got recorded.

Strengths of this Technique
This microscopic examination of one aspect of the learning setting, and recording all the behaviors in that segment while ignoring the rest of the setting, is often useful for discovering some subtle cause-effect relationships in the teaching and learning. It may be especially useful when certain students appear to be deviating from the intent of the learning but the cause is not clear. It may also be useful when the teacher wants to discover what exactly he/she is doing that is getting student A or B to work while student C sits picking his teeth.

Limitations of Case Study Methods
Some of the same limitations we recorded earlier for verbatim recording of verbal interactions occur with this technique. It is hard work, it is sometimes boring and it is difficult to stay focused on recording behavior and refraining from attribution or value judgments at the time of the recording. This recording of all behaviors is limited by the normal selection of perceptions human beings have. There are always behaviors missed, and they may be important.

Variations Sometimes Useful
   a. Do a time-sampling of recording of your case (e.g., five minutes on, and five minutes of doing something else).
   b. Record only non-verbal case data.
   c. Record only those categories of behavior you have selected in advance of being of interest that day.

   This technique has been used by social workers and helping professionals for many decades. They do their recording of behavior for their permanent records, often putting their inferences by the various events they are recording. These inferences are inserted at a later time.

General Technique No. 3: Sampling or Categorizing System
Definition:
Sampling or categorizing is making an inference about whether a behavior is a member of a class, or whether it was of a certain level or quality. Sometimes we are interested, not in recording the actual events themselves, but only in

recording their rate, intensity, or timing. So, instead of writing down the actual questions a teacher asks, the observer records the number or types of questions asked. What is recorded is not data of the actual behavior, but inferences about what category that behavior exemplifies.

Strengths:

This technique allows recording and classifying behaviors in a large variety of categories in one observation. It also demands less physical work of the observer so general senses of the entire environment are more possible and more likely to be accurate than with either of the two previous techniques. With careful definitions of the category or of the quality which belongs in each subset, high reliability can be achieved. The strengths of this kind of system are the ease of use, high reliability, and large variety of behaviors which can be recorded during a specific observation.

Limitations of the general technique:
   a. The fact that what is recorded is inference and not the specific behavior limits the validity of the data.
   b. The category system may lump together subtly different ideas and obscure them.
   c. The categories may not include measurements of data important or useful to the teacher.
   d. Recording and focusing on categories of behavior eliminates the possibility of recording sequential interactions.
   e. Sometimes the categories chosen occur so infrequently as to waste observation time.

Variations of Category or Sampling Techniques Sometimes Used
   a. Record different categories of behaviors in different segments of the teaching observed.
   b. Intersperse, in regular intervals, sampling and category observations with verbatim or case study observations.

Defining Observation Strategies and Designing Data Collection Forms

Note:

Remember again that in this unit we are concentrating on development supervision, not rating or evaluation. If you are doing the latter of these two different tasks you usually must use either a district or state evaluation form. This form should also be shared with the teacher, but it does not facilitate collegial negotiation process as we describe here.

One important skill related to collecting data is the ability to clearly define terms. For example, if you are two meters tall, you tend to view all other people as being short. However, at about 1.78 meters we tend to view ourselves as average, you at two meters as tall, and people under 1.65 meters as short. It is, as someone said, "a matter of definition."

The issue of definition making is very closely related to the issue of inference making and data collecting. Although a professional vocabulary is useful and necessary, we must have relatively standard definitions of words we use if this vocabulary is to be helpful. You may have been miffed that we used meters instead of the anglo "feet" above. Today you are justified. Ten years from now in the United States you may not be. It is "a matter of definition," agreeing on a set of terms acceptable and meaningful to those involved.

Many hide behind definitions as ways of cloaking behavior in the authority of secret knowledge. If you doubt our words, ask five professionals in your organization to define humanistic, or open education, or basic education.

The first step in your decision making about what and how to observe is to specify and define the aspects of the teaching setting to be observed—define them using behaviors. These may be student behaviors, teacher behaviors or both. The clearer this definition process, the more probable that the observation will be useful.

Persons who cannot decide where to put a statement or a behavior are not good observers for this set of "data" collection techniques. The relatively non-judgmental verbatim or case study methods are better for them. Even for the judgmental person, careful definitions help keep the focus of the observation clear. The definitions should be made clear in pre-observation discussions and use of the system should be practiced.

Constant categorizing requires concentration. Usually, inexperienced observers should use fewer categories with the definitions immediately in view during the observation. The greater number of categories, or the finer the distinction among them, the greater the difficulty for the observer.

Unit 16

Goal Oriented Supervision

Content Overview
This unit describes one way of organizing your time with individual supervisees to efficiently help them focus on specific elements of their teaching behavior, and then to work on improving these behaviors. The supervisee works toward pre-set behavioral goals he helped establish. This way of working includes a large amount of self-supervisory behavior. You reinforce the behavior on a variable ratio schedule using behavior management principles.

Using This Unit
You don't have to do anything in this unit but read it. We do recommend you try the procedures with one or two supervisees to convince yourself of its usefulness.

Entry Skills
It is assumed that you have a clear focused conference with your supervisees which will result in some commitments to action on both your parts. It is also assumed that you will not be offended by applied positive reinforcement theory. You need as well to be able to write clear behavior statements.

Competencies
When you have finished this unit, you should be able to: design a focused, goal oriented checklist with a supervisee (or with a group of supervisees), set up the system, and operate it so that the supervisee takes it seriously enough to work at it and measure accurately his own performance levels.

Explanation and Rationale for These Competencies
A former high school principal, now a superintendent of schools used this model of supervision in high school. It worked so well we wanted you

220

to be able to see the model and its results for him. We believe it has much potential.

Goal Oriented Supervision

This model of supervision is derived from behaviorist or reinforcement psychology principles involving positive reinforcement toward clear behaviors, reinforcement schedules, and task analyses. To us, these principles suggest at least one very clear set of procedures for supervision. There are, of course, others.[1] Our procedures begin with joint decisions on a very clear set of goals for instruction, then a complete behavioral analysis of the steps leading to those goals. With these you can reinforce instructors as they move to the performance of the steps. Do so by determining appropriate reinforcers for various supervisees. Then, continue to reinforce the instructors as they reach the goals and set up various reinforcement schedules to maintain the behaviors desired at the expected levels.

It is relatively simple to mechanically state these steps. Their performance may require subtle insight and careful planning.

Specifically, in supervision a model using these principles is one we have called goal oriented supervision (Whyte, 1972). What we are trying to do is set up a contingency system using variable ratio reinforcement to establish and maintain performance at agreed levels. Within this model, we adhere to the Argyris criteria for effective intervention by explaining the processes to the supervisee, jointly setting individual goals and behaviors within the context of larger system goals, and negotiating the reinforcement schedule. Meeting Maslow higher level needs provides much of the basis for the reinforcement.

The following sequence of steps explains how the model works:

1. First, explain to the whole instructional staff how the model works. Explain the sequence of steps and each party's responsibilities. Get people who are interested in this model to then sit down with you and work out its implications for them. (You must know and explain subsequent steps in this list.)

2. Next, secure enough data on each instructor's teaching, goals and needs to identify areas of emphasis in the supervision. This data may be secured through any or several of the following supervisor observations, audio or video taping, formal and informal student feedback, an inventory of instructional goals for the system, or a review of personal goals of the instructor or of the instructional team.

3. Following this data collection, you and the instructor analyze it to decide on the specific areas of emphasis fully. Select one or two

[1]One Ph.D. graduate in our program even did his dissertation research by constructing a bank of lights in the back of the classroom. These were operated by secondary reinforcers when the teacher demonstrated the behavior he was trying to master. In addition, he used an ear bug, like a doctor's paging system, as a secondary reinforcer. See Dr. N. David Skrak's dissertation, *The Application of Immediate Secondary Reinforcement to Classroom Observations in Clinical Supervision* c. 1975, unpublished Ph.D. dissertation, University of Pittsburgh.

major goals for work.

4. Now, write the best list of specific *instructor* behaviors which you and the instructor believe will help achieve the goals of this supervisory effort. Write these instructor behaviors in the following format:

1. Today I _____

2. Today I _____

Keep the behavior statements short, unambiguous and unidimensional. Some examples may help here. They follow: Yes

a. Today I began each instructional period on time.   _____

b. Today I had at least two small instructional groups
   operating in every instructional period.   _____

c. Today I gave feedback in some form to each of my students. _____

4. Select the 10-12 behavior statements most closely associated (by mutual agreement) with the areas of emphasis you have established for the supervision. Decide on appropriate levels of performance for each behavior.

5. Now, design a one-page form with the following information on it:
   a. Name, date, major goals of the supervision and a list of the 10-12 behavior statements which are deemed most closely related to these major goals.

   b. Leave a short section at the bottom of the form for comments and suggestions.

6. Now duplicate at least three work weeks' worth of these forms. You are ready to begin with the actual reinforcement sequence toward use of the behaviors at the selected level of performance. (A sample form is enclosed at the end of this section.)

7. Be sure that a column headed "yes" appears after each statement. (See samples.) This column is for supervisees and supervisor checking each time the form is used.

8. Now, explain that the supervisee is to go over this form each day during a quiet time and conscientiously think about whether or not he has met the performance standard set for each statement. On those they believe they have met, they check under the "yes" column. Those not met are left blank. There is *not* a "no" column on this form.

9. The supervisor does two things to reinforce this performance expectation. One, he on a variable ratio schedule (shorter periods of 2-3

times/week at first, perhaps one time in every week or ten day period later), drops in and reinforces verbally the regular keeping of this record. He sits down during this visit and goes over the cumulating records. Besides specifically verbally reinforcing the achievement of those goals achieved, he helps the supervisee identify ways to achieve those goals not yet mastered at the stated levels. Additionally, he helps reaffirm the desirability of meeting all the behavior standards on the lists.

10. The second obligation of the supervisor is to make occasional corroborating observations of the instruction to be sure that the supervisee and supervisor do indeed share the same perceptions of the performance achievement, again on a variable ratio reinforcement schedule.

11. As the goals and performance behaviors all seem regularly achieved, the supervisor and supervisee may wish to begin again and redefine new areas of concentration. Make new goal and behavior lists when they become appropriate.

12. Occasionally, get out the original forms to be sure that behaviors already learned are maintained at desired levels of mastery. Revisiting the old behaviors at irregular intervals should constitute an effective variable ratio reinforcement schedule.

Some supervisors are very much put off by the language and assumptions of behaviorism. If this is your initial reaction to this model of supervision, think about why you have this reaction. If we were laying this model on anyone and requiring them to operate within it, we would have the same concerns you do. We are not, nor do we recommend that you do so. As we have defined this model, the supervisee has control of the issues to be treated since he participates in their selection. There are no secret contingencies hidden from anyone. We do know that behavior modification is an extremely effective technique which can help supervisees to learn more effective behavior.

Some guidelines we have found effective follow:

1. Make your goal statements and instructor behaviors as focused and specific as possible.

2. Try hard to clearly reinforce regular and careful completion of the lists. Don't punish the person for non-achievement; reward for achievement.

3. When certain goals are not achieved or when certain behaviors are not observable, be sure that these are re-established as goals and that you help the supervisee work out specific procedures for achievement at the defined levels.

This model may be appropriate for several categories of people:

 a. those for whom no other system seems to be working,

 b. those who honestly prefer this kind of specific direction,

 c. those who cannot translate goals into specific behaviors, and

 d. those who are already beyond minimum expectations in most skills.

In this system most of your time as supervisor is used in establishing the goals and in reinforcing supervisees when they focus on them and achieve them. A much smaller percentage of your time is spent in extended observations or lengthy conferences. The reinforcement conferences may take 5-10 minutes each. You will probably, for most supervisees, have observations about one out of 3-5 times that you have conferences with supervisees in other models of supervision. Much of the responsibility for the supervision is thus transferred to the supervisee where it ultimately must rest anyway.

Of course, a key to this model's effectiveness, beyond those already stated, is the morale, the attitude, the intent of the supervisor and supervisees using it. Filling out the daily goal list, the reinforcement, the thinking of each party as they meet in short concentrated conferences—all these can become cursory, mindless exercises, or they can become thoughtful times of self-evaluation and self-growth. Since you as supervisor can control your own behavior, it appears that your own careful, clear implementation of this model of supervision is the independent variable in its success. If you value it, your supervisees probably will as well.

We feel that the time saved with this model of supervision should allow you to greatly extend the number of people with whom you can effectively work.

Sample Goal Oriented Checklist

NAME _____ DATE _____

Goal I - It is my goal to make each student feel successful in this class.

Behaviors supporting Goal I: Yes

Today I used each student's name at least once. _____

Today I gave praise to each student about something he/she said or did related to the class objectives. _____

Today I had eye contact with each student in the class at least once. _____

Today almost every student mastered at least one learning task in this class _____

Today some student who was not successful yesterday
made progress toward mastery of a skill or attitude.   _____

Goal II - It is my goal to give each student some actual practice in the
skills and attitudes being learned here.

Today every student had at least five minutes individual
practice working on some skill or attitude.   _____

Today at least 80% of the students got some feedback
from me on their performance of the tasks they were
doing.   _____

Today more than half of the students had some opportunity to assist others in the group in learning some skill
we were working on.   _____

Today some student volunteered a new way to work on
a skill or attitude(s) he/she was learning.   _____

Comments
(These may include: procedures to get more complete mastery of the
checklist; other statements which might be added to the checklist; new
directions you wish to go; or statements of your feelings about the day.)

_____

_____

_____

_____

Short Critique of This Sample Checklist
This checklist is a fairly general one for non-content areas. It is
appropriate to goals in the areas expressed. The checklist could as well be
focused on specific content or processes in the field the instructor teaches.

You may have to generate a checklist by doing a task analysis of the
major skills or processes which the students are working toward. This
same kind of analysis of appropriate instructor behavior for teaching the
skills or attitudes is then generated for the final checklist.

Can this simple system have a real effect on real teachers in a real
setting? That was the question asked by a high school principal who was
also a doctoral student in Supervision (LoPresti, 1976). His major conclusions, after using his system with 13 teachers on his staff for a period
of less than three months, were:

There is a statistically significant change in the student's perceptions of the class and the teacher-student relationship, following the

use of a goal oriented supervisory model which emphasizes joint decisions on a very clear set of goals for instruction, a complete behavioral analysis of the steps leading to those goals, and reinforcement of the instructors as they perform those steps.

Goal oriented supervision changed the teachers' perception of the relationship between the supervisor and the supervisee in this supervisory process. Teachers began to see their importance in establishing an effective supervisory model and became aware of the need for self-supervision which could be accomplished each day with the use of a behavioral checklist. This model provided the opportunity for the teachers to see the supervisor as a colleague rather than as one teacher said, "the boss."

Dr. LoPresti's data (LoPresti, 1976, p. 98 ff) show that the teachers:

1. Were more aware of the importance of setting specific objectives for the class and then designing behaviors to accomplish these objectives.

2. Better understood that the supervisory process was different from most evaluative techniques used to "keep us in line."

3. Recognized the supervisor as a counselor or a guide and not a person with all the power.

4. Developed a deeper sense of self-evaluation with daily responsibilities for their own skill reinforcement.

5. Became more self-confident in determining their own professional directions of growth.

6. Realized how much more objective this procedure was than previous methods of supervision.

7. Received significantly more favorable responses from students in their perceptions of: teachers' organization of tasks, matching of students' objectives to teachers' objectives, the teachers' inclusive behavior, the teachers' procedures for evaluating learning and the teacher's response to student's communication behavior.

Many of the teachers in this study continued to use the goal oriented procedures on their own even after the study was completed. Both experienced and inexperienced teachers seemed to benefit from these procedures. No teacher in the study dropped out or thought the procedures were "silly." This mode of supervision did not seem to be an empty exercise for any teacher.

Most significant to us was the fact that pupil attitude changes were in the areas the teachers were working on, even though the pupils had no direct knowledge that the teacher was attempting behavior changes in these or other areas.

We will conclude here with two stories taken from Dr. LoPresti's research.

Teacher L reports at the close of the study (LoPresti, 1976, p. 89):

Q. How has this type of a supervisory process been effective or ineffective in improving my instruction?

A. This has been effective for me because it made me concentrate on continuity in my class. It has helped me plan my lessons better and have better control over the routine problems in a class.

There were statistically significant gains in positive affect on the questionnaire used to measure students' attitude about the class.

Four students chose to write the following comments:

1. I think we have learned much more lately.
2. Mrs. L seems more considerate of the class.
3. The class seems more interesting. Mrs L is changing for the good.
4. I like her better now.

Similar results can be reported for *each* teacher who participated in the study. Rarely do dissertation researches produce such clear results. This graduate even wondered if he should fake some negative data so the committee would believe the rest.

Bibliography

Alfonso, Robert J., et al. *Instructional Supervision*, Boston: Allyn and Bacon, 1975.

Argyris, Chris. *Intervention Theory and Method: A Behavioral Science View*. Reading, MA: Addison-Wesley Publishing Company, 1970, pp. 15-16 ff.

Argyris, Chris and Schon, Donald. *Organizational Learning*. Reading, MA: Addison-Wesley Publishing Company, 1978.

Aspy, D.N. and Roebuck, F.N.. *Kids Don't Learn from People They Don't Like*. Amherst, MA: Human Resource Development Press, 1977.

Bales, Robert. *Interaction Process Analysis: A Method for the Study of Small Groups*. Reading, MA: Addison-Wesley Publishing Company, 1951.

Berliner, David and Tikunoff, William. "The California Beginning Teacher Evaluation Study," *Journal of Teacher Education*. 27 (1976): 24-30.

Birdwhistell, Ray L. *Kinesics and Context*. Phildelphia: University of Pennsylvania Press, 1970.

Champagne, David W. and Morgan, John L. "The Supervisory Conference." Unpublished paper, University of Pittsburgh, 1971.

Cogan, Morris L. *Clinical Supervision*. Boston: Houghton Mifflin Company, 1974.

Dussault, Gille. *A Theory of Supervision and Teacher Education*. New York: Teachers College Press, 1970.

Gage, N.L. (ed.) *Handbook of Research on Teaching*. Chicago: Rand-McNally and Company, 1963.

Galloway, Charles M. *Non-Verbal Communication in Teaching: Vantage Points for Study,* Ronald T. Hyman (ed.). Philadelphia: J.P. Lippincott Company, 1968.

Glasser, W. *Schools Without Failure,* 1969, and *Reality Therapy*, 1965.

Glickman, Carl. *Instructional Supervision*. ASCD, Alexandria, Virginia, 1980.

Goble, Frank. *The Third Force: The Psychology of Abraham Maslow*. New York: Grossman, 1970.

Hall Edward T. *The Silent Language*. New York: Doubleday and Company, 1959.

Harvey, Hunt & Schroder in Joyce & Weil. *Models of Teaching,* 2nd Edition. Englewood Cliffs, New Jersey: Prentice-Hall Inc., 1980, pp. 434-436.

Homans, George C. *The Human Group.* New York: Harcourt, Brace and Company, 1950.

Human Behavior. "Signals That Speak," April 1977, p.22.

Jacobi, Jolande. *C.G. Jung: Psychological Relections.* New Jersey: Princeton University Press, 1970.

Jourard, Sidney M. *Personal Adjustment: An Approach Through the Study of Healthy Personality.* New York: The MacMillan Company, 1963.

Jourard, Sidney M. and Landsman, Ted. *Healthy Personality.* New York: MacMillan Publishing Company,Inc., 1980.

Joyce, B. & Weil, M. *Models of Teaching*, 2nd Edition. Englewood Cliffs, New Jersey: Prentice-Hall Inc., 1980.

Jung, Carl G. *Psychological Types,* translated by H.G. Baynes. New Jersey: Princeton University Press, 1971.

Keirsey, David and Bates, Marilyn. *Please Understand Me: An Essay on Temperament Styles.* Del Mar, California: Promethean Books, Inc., 1978.

Knapp, Mark L. *Non-Verbal Communication.* New York: Holt, Rinehart and winston, Inc., 1972.

Kolb & Boyatis. "On the Dynamics of the Helping Relationship," *The Journal of Applied Behavioral Science,* Vol. 6, No. 3, Summer 1970, pp. 267 ff.

Lewin, Kurt. "Quasi-Stationary Social Equilibria and the Problem of Permanent Changes" in Benni et al. (ed.) *The Planning of Change.* New York: Holt, Rinehart and Winston, Inc., 1969, pp.235-238. Originally published in 1947 in *Human Relations*, Vol. 1, Numbers 1 and 2 under the title "Frontiers in Human Dynamics."

LoPresti, James A. *A Study Investigating the Effects of Goal Oriented Supervision on the Supervisory Process.* Unpublished Ph.D. dissertation, University of Pittsburgh, Pittsburgh, Pennsylvania, 1976.

Maslow, A. in Smith, Darrell. "Integrating Humanism and Behaviorism: Toward Performance," Personnel and Guidance Journal, Vol. 52, 1974, pp. 513-19.

McGregor, Douglas. *The Human Side of Enterprise.* New York: McGraw-Hill Book Company, 1960.

Miles, M. *Learning to Work in Groups.* New York: Teachers' College Press, 1959.

Mogar, Robert. "Toward a Psychological Theory of Learning," *Journal of Humanistic Psychology,* Vol. IX, Spring 1969, No. 1.

Mosher & Purpel. *Supervision: The Reluctant Profession.* Boston: Houghton Mifflin Company, 1972.

Myers-Briggs. Isabel. Palo Alto, California: Consultanting Psychologists Press, 1960.

Nagle, John M. *The Supervisory Activity of Secondary School Principals in Districts in the Tri-State Area School Study Council.* Tri-State Area School Study Council, University of Pittsburgh, Pittsburgh, Pennsylvania, March 1969.

Neff, Walter S. *Work and Human Behavior.* New York: Atherton Press, 1950.

Owens, Robert C. *Organizational Behavior in Schools.* Englewood Cliffs, New Jersey: Prentice-Hall Inc., 1970, Chapter 5 ff.

Raths, Harmin and Simons. *Values and Teaching.* Columbus, Ohio: Charles E. Merrill Publishing Company, 1966.

Rogers, Carl R. *On Becoming a Person.* Cambridge, Mass.: Houghton Mifflin Company, 1961.

Rogers, Carl. in Day, Willard F. "Radical Behaviorism in Reconciliation with Phenomenology." *Journal of the Experimental Analysis of Behavior.* 12 (1969), pp. 315-328.

Rosenshine, Barak, "Classroom Instruction," in *The Psychology of Teaching Methods: The Seventy Fifth Yearbook of the National Society for the Study of Education,* ed. N.L. Gage. University of Chicago Press, 1976, pp 335-371.

Rosenshine, Barak and Furst, Norma. "Research on Teacher Performance Criteria, in *Research in Teacher Education: A Symposium.* ed., B.O. Smith. Englewood Cliffs: Prentice-Hall, 1971, pp 37-72.

Ryans, D.G. *Characteristics of Teachers, Their Description, Comparison and Appraisal.* Washington D.C.: American Council on Education, 1960.

Sergiovanni, Thomas J. *Supervision: Human Perspectives.* 2nd Edition, McGraw-Hill, 1979.

Squires, David A. *A Phenomenological Study of Supervisors' Perceptions of a Positive Supervisory Experience.* Unpublished Doctoral Dissertation, University of Pittsburgh, Pittsburgh, Pennsylvania, 1978.

Sullivan, Cheryl G. *Clinical Supervision.* ASCD, Alexandria, Virginia, 1980.

Ulschak, F.L. et al. Small Group Problem Solving. Reading, Mass.: Addison Wesley Publishing Company, 1981.

Von Franz, Marie-Louise. *Lectures.* C.G. Jung Institute. Zurich: January, 1961.

Wallen, John L. *Charting the Decision Making Structure of an Organization,* in Appendix V, Vol. III: Appendices M-2 of: *A Competency Based, Field Centered Systems Approach to Elementary Teacher Education,* October, 1968, U.S.D.H.E.W., Final Report Project No. 89022.

Ward, William P. Maxi II Practicum Report, Nova University Ed. D. Program for Educational Leaders. *The Development of a Training Program to Improve the Supervisory Competence of Newington Public School Administrator.* Unpublished mimeographed paper, 1975 (ERIC document, ed. 119-387).

Whyte, William F. "New Tool: Reinforcement for Good Work," *Psychology Today,* May, 1972.